THE LIMITS OF
SOCIAL SCIENCE

SAGE has been part of the global academic community since 1965, supporting high quality research and learning that transforms society and our understanding of individuals, groups, and cultures. SAGE is the independent, innovative, natural home for authors, editors and societies who share our commitment and passion for the social sciences.

Find out more at: **www.sagepublications.com**

Connect, Debate, Engage on Methodspace

Connect with other researchers and discuss your research interests

Keep up with announcements in the field, for example calls for papers and jobs

Discover and review resources

Engage with featured content such as key articles, podcasts and videos

Find out about relevant conferences and events

THE LIMITS OF
SOCIAL SCIENCE

CAUSAL EXPLANATION AND VALUE RELEVANCE

MARTYN
HAMMERSLEY

⑤SAGE

Los Angeles | London | New Delhi
Singapore | Washington DC

⑤SAGE

Los Angeles | London | New Delhi
Singapore | Washington DC

SAGE Publications Ltd
1 Oliver's Yard
55 City Road
London EC1Y 1SP

SAGE Publications Inc.
2455 Teller Road
Thousand Oaks, California 91320

SAGE Publications India Pvt Ltd
B 1/I 1 Mohan Cooperative Industrial Area
Mathura Road
New Delhi 110 044

SAGE Publications Asia-Pacific Pte Ltd
3 Church Street
#10-04 Samsung Hub
Singapore 049483

© Martyn Hammersley 2014

First published 2014

Editor: Katie Metzler
Assistant editor: Lily Mehrbod
Production editor: Ian Antcliff
Copyeditor: Sarah Bury
Proofreader: Derek Markham
Marketing manager: Sally Ransom
Cover design: Shaun Mercier
Typeset by: C&M Digitals (P) Ltd, Chennai, India
Printed in India at Replika Press Pvt Ltd

Library of Congress Control Number: 2013951819

British Library Cataloguing in Publication data

A catalogue record for this book is available from the British Library

ISBN 978-1-4462-8749-1
ISBN 978-1-4462-8750-7 (pbk)

Contents

Acknowledgements

Chapter 1 grew out of an earlier attempt to explore the nature of causality: a paper prepared for the ESRC Research Methods Festival, held at St Catherine's College, Oxford in July 2004. This was later published as Hammersley, M. (2008, January 3). 'Causality as conundrum: the case of qualitative inquiry', *Methodological Innovations Online* [Online], 2(3). Available at: http//:erdt.plymouth.ac.uk/mionline/public_html/viewarticle.php?id=63.

Chapter 3 is a revised version of 'Why critical realism fails to justify critical social research', *Methodological Innovations Online*, 4(2), 2009, pp. 1–11. It incorporates some elements from 'Research as emancipatory: the case of Bhaskar's realism', *Journal of Critical Realism*, 1, 1, 2002, pp. 33–48.

An earlier version of Chapter 5 was presented at a symposium on 'Methodological Issues in Research on Social Class, Education and Social Mobility', at the British Educational Research Association's annual conference in Manchester, September 2009, and at the British Sociological Association's annual conference at the London School of Economics, April 2011.

Chapter 6 is based on a talk given at the conference 'Collisions, Coalitions and Riotous Subjects: The Riots One Year On', at South Bank University, September 2012, and at the British Sociological Association's annual conference at the Grand Connaught Rooms, London, April 2013.

I would like to thank several good friends and colleagues for their help and support, in particular Barry Cooper, Jeff Evans, Judith Glaesser, Roger Gomm, and Anna Traianou. Also, thanks to all those who responded with questions or comments at the talks on which these chapters are based.

Introduction

At the start of his book *Forms of Explanation*, Alan Garfinkel (1990: vii) asks: 'If social science is the answer, what is the question?' This is not an idle quip, his whole book is about the importance of being clear in social inquiry about exactly what questions we are addressing – since this has implications for what would count as adequate answers. However, it should be noted that the format implicit in Garfinkel's question here is perhaps not so much *question–answer* as *problem–solution*: he is asking what problem social science is designed to solve – in short, what the point of it is.[1]

In the spirit of Garfinkel's own book, we might consider whether this question is an appropriate one to ask: is social science the kind of thing that is, or ought to be, designed to solve a problem? Garfinkel's question can be read as implying a very particular view about the character, purpose, and justification of social science – to the effect that it should be designed to provide a service to policymakers, practitioners, and/or relevant publics; and that social scientists ought to be accountable in terms of how well they have done this. While this sort of view is increasingly influential – particularly on the part of funders of research, governments, interest groups, and others who use research findings – it is open to serious question, and certainly should not be accepted at face value; not least because it may have damaging practical consequences (Hammersley 2011a; Holmwood 2011a).

Of course, demands for social science to produce usable knowledge, and to have an impact on policy and practice, do not come solely from outside the research community. Many social scientists also see this as their task, and perhaps even regard their work as only justifiable in these terms. This is true, most obviously, of those approaches to social inquiry that are explicitly tied to particular political

---

[1]There is no evidence that Garfinkel intended this question in any more than a playful sense, but the challenge lurks in the background. This issue is addressed in a more direct and sustained manner, and from a very different philosophical angle, by Hutchinson et al. (2008) in their book *There is No Such Thing as a Social Science*.

and social movements, such as feminism, anti-racism, LGBT (lesbian, gay, bisexual, and transgender) rights, or disability activism. Here, the demand is frequently that research must 'make a difference' in terms of its effects, rather than simply be aimed at producing knowledge. And much the same is true of calls for 'public sociology' (Burawoy 2005), or for public forms of social science more generally (Cannella and Lincoln 2004), as well (even more obviously) as arguments in favour of policy science, action research, participatory inquiry and practitioner research (Lerner and Lasswell 1951; Lasswell 1971; Mies 1983; Carr and Kemmis 1986; Reason and Bradbury 2001). Indeed, this view is now to be found quite widely across social science, albeit usually in largely taken-for-granted forms.

All this should be seen against a history of recurrent questioning of the practical contribution that social science has made, and can make, to society. Criticisms of it for not supplying what is required grew in influence as it expanded over the second half of the twentieth century, not least because this expansion relied very heavily upon state funding. Moreover, during this period, such funding gradually shifted from a patronage to an investment model, so that funders increasingly felt justified, indeed obliged, to try to assess the value of what social science produces in order to determine whether it represented an adequate 'return on public investment' (Gibbons 1999; Demeritt 2000; Nowotny et al. 2003). In this environment, the value and role of social science became a major issue, even more than it had been earlier. And, in the twenty-first century, economic austerity – used as a rationale for severe cuts to public funding and for further marketization of functions that were previously performed by the state (Crouch 2012) – has exacerbated this situation, creating a serious threat to the resources available for social science (Brewer 2013).

In response to this threat, in the UK and elsewhere, political campaigns have been mounted, by organizations and associations representing social science, to demonstrate the value of what it has produced and can produce. The products that social science is typically portrayed as offering include: diagnoses of social problems plus recommendations for their treatment; evidence about which policies and practices 'work'; and empirical or theoretical investigations that document underlying processes and trends. Moreover, the potential or actual practical *impact* of these products is often emphasized. So, for example, as part of a 'Campaign for Social Science' mounted by the UK Academy of Social Sciences, Audrey Osler (nd) offered '10 reasons why you need social science'. Her reasons include: 'Social science can improve our children's lives and education', 'Social scientists contribute to our health and well-being', 'Social science might save your life', and 'Social science can make your neighbourhood safer'. These are very bold claims about the contribution of social science, but I suspect that they accurately capture what most lay people would expect today from public funding of it, and indeed what many social scientists themselves hope it can achieve.

While there is no doubt some truth in claims of the kind put forward by Osler and others, it seems to me that they greatly exaggerate the capabilities of social science. For one thing, they imply a much more direct relationship between the production of knowledge and beneficial policy outcomes than is common. In other words, social research is treated here as *feeding directly into producing policy changes and determining outcomes*. Yet the relationships involved are highly mediated and contingent (Hammersley 2002a and 2013). Equally important, as part of this, it is assumed that social science can produce sound theoretical, explanatory, and predictive knowledge relating to pressing social problems. However, there are questions about whether it can generate the sort of authoritative causal understanding that this requires. Indeed, many qualitative researchers dispute whether causal analysis is possible and/or desirable. And the methodological literature makes clear that such analysis is a very challenging task (for example, McKim and Turner 1997; see Chapter 1).

Osler's claims about the contribution of social science also assume that it can answer value questions, for example about what *counts* as 'improv[ing] our children's lives and education', and about how best to do this. She writes:

> Education research shows that many parents, particularly parents of younger children, are more concerned that their children enjoy school than that they are academic stars. By working with students of all ages to understand their perspectives on schooling, researchers at the universities of Cambridge and Leeds have discovered new insights into what makes effective schools, and what makes for effective school leadership. We just need to listen to children, provide structured opportunities for them to give their views, and prepare adults to really listen.

The implication here is that evidence about children's perspectives, presumably about what they enjoy, ought to form the primary basis of educational policymaking and practice. The task of research is seen as articulating these perspectives and encouraging adults to prioritize them. Yet, we can reasonably ask whether educational goals ought to be determined solely by children's or parents' preferences. Equally, should children's enjoyment be the main purpose of schooling, or ought it to be geared instead, say, to introducing them to new forms of knowledge, or to novel types of experience and activity, or preparing them for their future lives? These are contentious matters of practical evaluation that, in my view, social scientists cannot legitimately claim any distinctive authority to resolve; even though they can provide some of the relevant evidence needed to assess them.

Of course, it is arguable that, in making the public case for social science, doubts about such matters ought to be put on one side. But, even if this is true, it is very important that social scientists are not captured by their own propaganda, forgetting the contested issues it glosses over, especially those about the capacities and role of social science itself. In subsequent chapters I will interrogate some influential assumptions about the current capacity of social science to supply sound explanations, theories and value conclusions. More specifically, my focus will be on whether the task of social science should be causal analysis (an issue that raises especially sharp questions for qualitative inquiry); whether its aim is the production of general theories, or instead explanations for specific, actual phenomena (individual or aggregate); and whether value conclusions can be derived directly from social science evidence and, if not, whether or how they should be included in research reports.

All these are matters about which there is considerable disagreement among social scientists today. There are those who treat the discovery of causal laws as the primary task of social science, for example, this being required to ground 'evidence-based' policy and practice (Oakley 2000). At the other end of the spectrum, many qualitative researchers reject causal analysis, on ethical or political as well as ontological grounds: they deny that causes operate in the social world, and very often regard efforts to engage in this kind of analysis as reinforcing the socio-political status quo and denying human agency. They insist instead that the focus of inquiry should be on describing people's experiences and perspectives, the patterns of social interaction in which they are involved, the discursive strategies they employ, and so on. Similarly, while it is common for social scientists to insist on the importance of theory, there is very little agreement about what that term means – indeed, there are six or seven different senses given to it in common usage (Hammersley 2012c). Finally, while it is widely agreed today that values are inevitably involved in social research, just as a commitment to 'value–freedom' was widely accepted in the past (see Purcell 1973), there is little clarity or consensus about *which* values should be prioritized, about the role they ought to play, or about the rationale underpinning this.

These issues have important implications not only for the public defences that can be made of social research in the face of external threat, but also, and perhaps even more importantly, for how it is practised. In the briefest of summaries, then, this book is concerned with key aspects of the very justification for social science, and of its practice, at a time when it is under considerable pressure to demonstrate its value.

A history of sporadic debate

There has been a long history of debate about these issues across the social sciences. An early example, at the end of the nineteenth century, was a major dispute between representatives of the German and Austrian schools of economics (the *Methodenstreit* or 'methods dispute'). This focused upon whether the aim of that discipline should be to account for the historical development of economic and social institutions in particular contexts or instead to produce general theory about economic laws that apply across all societies and time periods (Agevall 1999; see Chapter 2). And debates about the status and role of such laws have repeatedly occurred in Anglo-American economics (Blaug 1992). A little later, also in Germany, there was conflict over the role of values in social science (the *Werturteilsstreit*, or 'value judgment dispute'), with Max Weber and others criticizing the dominant form of 'ethical economics' (Dahrendorf 1968; Ciaffa 1998; Weiss 2005). In somewhat different form, this issue was also central to Anglo-American discussions around the notion of 'welfare economics' in the early twentieth century, and subsequently of 'cost–benefit analysis' (see Robbins 1935; Hutchison 1964; Little 2002). Moreover, the question of the role of values in economics has been revived more recently, especially by the work of Amartya Sen (see Sayer 2011: 233–5; Putnam and Walsh 2012).

In the discipline of politics, both of the issues mentioned above – the role of theory and of values – were central to US debates surrounding the rise of 'political science' as against older, European forms of political philosophy (Brecht 1959; Storing 1962). And, more recently, the 'perestroika' movement in that discipline has revived concerns about what form research in political science ought to take, and what its purpose is (Flyvbjerg 2001; Monroe 2005; Schram and Caterino 2006). Meanwhile, debates about the role of qualitative case study in this field, which has in recent times been dominated by quantitative method, have opened up questions about the nature of theories and explanations of political phenomena (Ragin 1987; George and Bennett 2005; Rihoux and Ragin 2009).

Taking a parallel trajectory to economics, US sociology started from an approach that combined a scientific with a normative orientation, in large part as a result of the influence of German ethical economics, notably the work of Schmoller, Weber's main antagonist in the *Werturteilsstreit* (see Dibble 1975: 221). But the ethical component came to be rejected in favour of a commitment to 'value freedom' or 'objectivity', only for this to be challenged or redefined by many sociologists later in the century in favour of approaches committed to various political positions.[2] There have also been periodic debates about the proper focus of the discipline, what kind of knowledge it can and should produce. These have juxtaposed, for example, 'positivism' and Critical Theory (Adorno et al. 1976), or 'abstracted empiricism', 'grand theory', and 'middle-range theory' (Mills 1959; Merton 1968; Turner 2009).

More recently, the influence of social and political movements of various sorts – from feminism to the evidence-based practice movement – have also fuelled debate about these matters. So, too, have philosophical ideas from outside the Anglo-American analytic tradition, including phenomenology, hermeneutics, structuralism, post-structuralism and postmodernism. These challenged key assumptions that underpinned earlier discussions: for instance that authoritative theoretical knowledge of the social world and pursuit of 'progressive' social change are possible or even desirable. One aspect of this has been an insistence that conflicts among ethical and political perspectives are intractable, that the issues involved are in an important sense undecidable (see, for instance, Lyotard 1988).[3]

[2]For an influential contribution to this trend, see Gouldner 1962. See the discussion of Gouldner's position, and of other arguments on the same lines, in Hammersley 2000.

[3]In important respects, many of these developments represent a re-emergence of nineteenth and early twentieth-century post-Enlightenment scepticism about grand hopes regarding the progressive role of scientific inquiry, and ambivalence about social progress more generally (Hughes H.S. 1958; Hawthorn 1976; Burrow 2000).

Apparently confirming these postmodernist conclusions, despite recurrent disputes about these fundamental methodological matters there has been little sign of substantial development in understanding them, much less of their being settled. Indeed, there has been a tendency for them to be addressed anew each time they arise, albeit in slightly varying terms, sometimes with relatively little awareness of previous deliberations. And even where earlier discussions have been given attention, they have often been misrepresented. For instance, within sociology, Weber's position on the role of values has been repeatedly misinterpreted (see Chapter 3), as have other contributions, such as Becker's (1967) article 'Whose side are we on?', which is frequently but wrongly treated as a call for scholarly partisanship (Hammersley 2000: ch. 3).

One explanation for the intractability of these problems is, perhaps, that to a large extent the social sciences have, from their beginnings, been caught between conflicting demands. On one side, there has been the model of natural science, this usually being interpreted as requiring a high level of methodological rigour, while, on the other, there have been persistent demands for immediately usable knowledge about social affairs.[4] These two sources of pressure have persisted despite changes in ideas about the nature of the rigour required (for example, moving through positivist, phenomenological, and structuralist conceptions of science, and on to more interpretivist and constructionist approaches to inquiry), and in assumptions about what research can and should supply, and its actual and proper relationship to, or role in, social and political practice (Fay 1975; Hammersley 1995 and 2000).

Social science developed in the shadow of the dramatic success of the natural sciences, in both theoretical and technological terms (Shapin 1996; Principe 2011). Particular social science disciplines, and approaches within them, were frequently stimulated by the belief that, if only the methods of natural science could be applied, similar progress would be made in understanding and resolving political, economic, and social problems (Heilbron 2003). This was, of course, at the heart of positivism in its early Comtean form, and in some of its later manifestations too (see Lundberg 1947). And parallel hopes were sometimes associated with other conceptions of science.

Simultaneously, because social research has frequently been closely related to various forms of practice – with links to political movements, governments, and interest groups of various kinds – it has been exposed much of the time to specific demands for immediate practical knowledge. Indeed, many social scientists engage in research precisely because of their commitment to practical goals, believing that social inquiry is the best means of serving these.

However, from most perspectives, social science has not been very successful in meeting the demands coming from either of these sides: it has often found it difficult to match scientific requirements, on whatever definition; and it has also struggled to

---

[4]On the influence of the natural science model on the development of social science, see Fox et al. 1995 and Mazlish 1998. Haskell (2000) traces early tensions in the USA between commitment to social reform and to science. See also Dibble 1975.

supply the sort of usable knowledge frequently demanded by policymakers, practitioners, political activists, or publics. Moreover, it could be argued that there is a fundamental conflict between these two sets of demands. While natural science has sometimes provided the basis for new technologies, the 'engineering model' of the relationship between research and practice has been found troublesome by most social scientists.[5] Indeed, recognition that there is a tension between what science demands and the provision of useful practical knowledge about the social world has long been recognized. Even in the nineteenth century, John Stuart Mill, writing about economics, distinguished between the sort of abstraction required for scientific inquiry and the more realistic concerns that economists must take into account in order to provide useful practical knowledge (Mill 1874: 140). More radically, neo-Kantians like Rickert and Weber emphasized the fundamental difference between our human interest in the social as against the physical world: that, first and foremost, we are primarily concerned with particular social events occurring in particular places, rather than with abstract theoretical knowledge about social reality. On this basis, they argued that a different kind of science is required in this realm, one that is idiographic in character (Willey 1978).

More recently, of course, there has been an increasing tendency for some social scientists, especially qualitative researchers, to distance themselves from the model of science, to reject it completely, or to seek radically to redefine it (see, for example, Reason and Bradbury 2001; Denzin and Lincoln 2011). This has been prompted, in part, by the perceived failure of social research to achieve the same practical impact as natural science, or the kind of impact that social scientists desired; by doubts about whether the social world is compatible with scientific inquiry; and/or by increasing disenchantment with the socio-political role that science has come to play in modern Western societies.

It might seem that if a different conception of science were to be adopted, or if the scientific model could simply be abandoned, the tension between this and demands for usable knowledge would be avoided, or at least minimized (see, for example, Flyvbjerg 2001). But I do not believe this to be the case. The tension comes, in large part, not from any specific model of the nature of rigorous inquiry but rather from the basic requirement that the likely validity of the knowledge research produces must be above some reasonably high threshold, so that it is generally more reliable than knowledge from other sources (Hammersley 2011a). And this requirement seems to be essential to any justification for research as a specialized activity, and especially for its public funding. Yet that requirement has major consequences for the task facing social scientists, for how long it takes to produce worthwhile research findings, and even for what questions researchers can address successfully; all matters that are very significant for the relationship with practical action, of whatever kind (Hammersley 2002a).

---

[5]For some of the reasons why, see Bulmer 1982 and Hammersley 2002a.

The demand that social science must produce knowledge that is above a relatively high threshold of likely validity makes the task of inquiry difficult in at least two ways. First, and most obviously, it carries significant methodological demands: there is a need for systematic checks to try to ensure that the answers produced to research questions reach the necessary level of reliability, in the commonsense meaning of that term; and, equally important, if knowledge is to be produced through this process, rather than simply a set of disconfirmed hypotheses, some means must be found of generating productive hypotheses that have a strong chance of being true.

The second point is that, given these methodological demands, it is not possible for research to answer all of the questions that face policymakers, practitioners, activists, and publics; many will be beyond its reach at particular times and some probably for ever. Furthermore, social scientific inquiries take a considerable amount of time, and will rarely be fully complete. Indeed, it will often be necessary for social scientists to break down practically relevant questions into more specific ones whose pursuit is more viable, but whose direct practical import may be negligible. In addition, social research often leads to conflicting conclusions, ones that are subject to considerable qualification, and open to reasonable doubt– rather than any clear cumulation of knowledge being generated (Rule 1997).[6] All this has the consequence that, at present at least, most of the time it is very difficult, if not impossible, for researchers to supply the sort of usable knowledge that policymakers or practitioners require, and especially to supply it *when they need it* (Pels 2003). Furthermore, as I have hinted, there will be some questions that are of great importance to practical actors that social science simply cannot answer, within the foreseeable future or even in principle.

Of course, social scientists could avoid the tension between the demand for rigour and that for practically usable findings by adopting a form of deception: rather than deploying the methodological caution that is required, they could simply dress up their conclusions in scientific garb so as to make these convincing to relevant audiences. This may sometimes be done. However, it amounts to a breach of integrity, to a denial of the essential commitments built into research as a specialized, professional activity (Macfarlane 2008; Hammersley and Traianou 2012: ch. 2). Long ago, Max Weber insisted on the importance of such integrity as central to 'science as a vocation': that social scientists must be clear to others, and above all to themselves, about the likely validity of their findings, and about the limits operating upon what they are able to produce.[7]

---

[6]In fact, many qualitative researchers question the very idea of such cumulation, see Hammersley 2013: chapter 10.

[7]What these limits are will vary somewhat between different kinds of research, notably between academic and practical research: see Hammersley 2002a: ch. 6. For a discussion of what research integrity entails, and the threats to it today, see Haack 2013.

This is one of several respects in which I believe that a return to the methodological writings of Weber is of considerable value at the present time; though, of course, in the spirit of integrity this should not be done in an uncritical manner.

Back to Weber?

It is perhaps necessary to point out that Weber's work is relevant to all of social science, not just to sociology – the discipline with which his name now tends to be associated.[8] He lived at a time and in a context where the boundaries between the various social sciences were relatively weak and ill-defined, even more so than they are today. He began with work in the field of legal history, later moving into the study of economic institutions, and then shifted to an interest in, among other things, the role of religion in the development of societies in both the West and the East (Whimster 2007). In the process, he engaged in methodological reflection, and generated a distinctive framework of sociological concepts (Bendix 1960; Schluchter 1981). In addition, he had strong political commitments, and these underpinned his work in important respects – indeed, his approach to all social topics was one in which the political dimension was never far from the surface (Mommsen 1989).

While Weber's legacy has been claimed mainly by sociologists, in the process it has frequently been distorted in important respects. Indeed, Weber has become an ambivalent figure, sometimes viewed as adopting the sort of approach that would today be labelled as positivist, while also widely regarded as the founder of an interpretative approach to social science that stands opposed to the concern with discovering causal laws, whether deterministic or probabilistic (Runciman 1972; Truzzi 1973; Martin 2000). In recent years, a considerable amount of work has been done in trying to gain a sound understanding of Weber's purposes and orientation, against the background of the contexts in which he worked (see, for example, Hennis 1988, 2000a and 2000b; Mommsen and Osterhammel 1989).[9]

As part of this, there has been increased interest in his methodological writings, and these have recently been given a new translation (Bruun and Whimster 2012). Here, especially, the importance becomes clear of understanding the particular

---

[8]Lachman (1970: 2) notes that even though Weber's early work was in the field of economics, that discipline came to bear little trace of his influence. And Loader and Kettler (2002: 81) claim that Weber never called himself a sociologist, though we should note that he was a founding member and active participant in the German Sociological Society. At the same time he is quoted as despairing about 'this damned science of sociology', and as declaring that 'most of what goes by the name of sociology is a fraud' (Radkau 2009: xv). Radkau emphasizes the importance of seeing 'the whole Weber' rather than forcing him into one or other disciplinary framework (p. 1 and *passim*).

[9]Needless to say, perhaps, these investigations have not always reached the same conclusions.

problems he was addressing and the intellectual resources on which he drew (Turner and Factor 1984, 1994; Agevall 1999; Eliaeson 2002). Given our distance from his intellectual and social world, it might be expected that his work would bear little relevance to present-day concerns. And, indeed, a common response to some of Weber's methodological ideas today, most notably to his notion of 'value freedom' or 'value-neutrality', is to dismiss them as outdated. It is here, especially, that a re-evaluation of his work is required. For example, it is worth remembering that his notion of value neutrality was a direct challenge to the then traditional view that social research is normative, a view to which – as I noted – many influential social scientists have reverted in recent times. Early forms of social science operated within a framework of values set by religious commitment, by ideas about natural law, or by forms of positivism or historicism. In many cases, there was little sense of a gap between factual and value conclusions, the first were seen as leading smoothly into the second (as, for example, in the writings of Adam Smith: see Levy 1978; Young 2008). It was only in the late nineteenth century that it started to be insisted that the focus of the social sciences should be restricted to factual matters, these being clearly distinguished from value concerns. Weber's work was very much part of this.

Yet the influence of the belief in seamless reasoning from factual premises to value conclusions stretched well into the twentieth century. For instance, Albion Small, the founder of the first sociology department in the United States, was strongly influenced by the German historical school of economics, with its commitment to a notion of ethical science (see Herbst 1965: ch. 6 and 7; Dibble 1975). Indeed, even after it had become usual to insist that social science should be value-neutral, in practice social scientists frequently produced evaluations and recommendations as if these came directly out of their research (Storing 1962). This reflected not just demands for practically relevant knowledge, but also the persisting influence of taken-for-granted Enlightenment ideas about the role of scientific knowledge in bringing about social progress – ideas that in key respects were secularized versions of older religious notions (see Löwith 1949 and 1965, but see also Blumenberg 1986).

A distinctive feature of Weber's work is that he opposed these ideas, drawing on post-Enlightenment critiques, exemplified most clearly by Nietzsche, that subsequently stretched into existentialism, structuralism, post-structuralism, and postmodernism.[10] What this entailed was the rejection of any assumption that human values are enshrined in the make-up of the universe, in some universal human nature, or in the historical development of human society. In effect, it was a rejection of the natural law tradition that had infused the Enlightenment and the political changes it generated in France – despite their revolutionary character. The core idea of natural law thinking was that there is a coherent rational order built

---

[10]See Owen 1994; Gane 2002; Strong 2002; Owen and Strong 2004.

into human nature or human society which can validate value judgments, thereby making them morally obligatory (Sigmund 1971: viii). By contrast, for Weber, like Nietzsche, values emerge out of particular forms of life that human beings have developed in living on earth, they have no existence or validity beyond this, and they have no *built-in* coherence.[11]

In important respects, Weber was the most resolute and reflective representative of this post-Enlightenment line of thinking, as well as the one whose work is most directly related to social science. He insisted, first of all, that we are faced with choices among conflicting ultimate commitments, so that many issues in life, even the most consequential ones, are undecidable in rational terms (Tuck 1994). It is not necessarily implied that we must make a leap of faith, but rather that we should actively choose to select or construct a meaningful vision of life, to decide which set of values is to be our guide. That this must be done is central to Weber's notion of integrity, which seems to be the only value that he treated as of universal validity. Not only is there no logical means or mode of calculation that can tell us what we ought to commit ourselves to, or what we should reject, but also there is no comprehensive religious or philosophical view whose truth is guaranteed that would provide us with an overarching guide. Weber's attitude towards this situation was not heroically celebratory in the manner of Nietzsche; it was closer to a sense of resignation, that we must cast off our illusions and face reality.

This is a dramatic and challenging form of 'realism'. It has implications for many aspects of human social life, but it is of particular significance in the context of the process of occupational differentiation that has been a characteristic feature of the development of large-scale, complex societies in the West, and elsewhere. Here, on top of a plurality of values that stem from ethnic and religious differences, we find the establishment of conflicting value-complexes within different institutional sectors, forming part of what Everett Hughes called the 'moral division of labour' (Hughes E.C. 1958: 71). The key point here is that in taking on a particular vocation – whether religious, political, or scientific – we must accept a heightened responsibility towards some values and downgrade or sacrifice others (Dreijmanis 2008).

In the case of research, we must devote ourselves as researchers exclusively to the production of knowledge. And given that there is no totalizing perspective – scientific, religious, or political – from which we can decide definitively what is good or bad, right or wrong, we cannot claim to produce authoritative value conclusions. Similarly, there is no theory we can produce that captures the *essential* character of social reality. Rather, whatever knowledge we produce is generated within particular perspectives, each reflecting a particular set of values that picks out what phenomena, and what aspects of them, are relevant for the investigation.

---

[11]Portis (1986: ch. 1) spells out the significance of this rejection of the natural law tradition for Weber's work. For an illuminating comparison in these terms between Weber and key postmodern theorists, see Gane (2002). See also the parallels between Weber's position and that of Stanley Fish (1995 and 2008).

In all these respects, Weber's orientation differs not only from positivist views, such as those of Durkheim, but also from Marxism, and most other approaches that are influential within social science today.[12]

What we find in the work of Weber, then, is an extremely sophisticated assessment of key problems facing social science, and a clear and challenging stance towards them. Moreover, these problems still haunt us. I draw on Weber's work particularly as regards the nature of social scientific explanation (Chapter 2) and in discussing the role of values in social science (Chapters 3, 4, 5, and 6 and the Epilogue). It does seem to me that Weber provided some of the most illuminating and cogent reflections on these matters. However, while this book maps out a position that is very close to his, and outlines its implications, I am under no illusions about the difficulties that it generates.

The chapters

The central concern of this book is what kinds of authoritative knowledge social science can legitimately claim to produce. A first issue here is the concept of causality, since in my view this is essential to any form of social scientific explanation. Social scientists have long been somewhat ambivalent about making causal claims. In Chapter 1, I look at the issue of causation in the context of qualitative inquiry, where it has come to be regarded as especially problematic. I show that, in the past, advocates of qualitative work insisted that causal analysis was the main task of social science, and that case study was the means by which it could be pursued most effectively. However, across most fields today, qualitative researchers typically deny that their goal is causal analysis, because they do not believe that causal relations operate in the social realm, and/or because of political or ethical objections to the pursuit of causal knowledge. I examine the philosophical arguments that have prompted rejection of causal analysis. And I look at how these have influenced some of the main stances qualitative inquiry now takes towards explaining social phenomena. At the same time, I argue that when we examine the strategies that most qualitative researchers *actually* use to produce explanations, we find that these nevertheless involve causal assumptions, defined in broad terms. In effect, what qualitative researchers are rejecting is the claim that there are causal *laws*. However, denying this is compatible with pursuing causal explanations for individual events, actions, or institutions in particular places at particular times. I outline the resources that are available to qualitative researchers, and indeed to all social scientists, in this task: the systematic analysis of empirical data, and the imaginative construction of models of particular social processes

---

[12]This perhaps even includes some that claim to adopt a Weberian approach – for example, in the study of social mobility. See Chapter 5.

on the basis of background knowledge and experience. I argue that it is essential to use both, simultaneously, in developing *and testing* explanatory hypotheses. I also distinguish between the two broad empirical strategies that social scientists employ – within-case and cross-case analysis – looking at their relative strengths and weaknesses, and emphasizing their complementarity. I note, however, that, partly because they do not recognize that they are engaged in causal analysis, qualitative researchers often do not deploy these resources in a systematic and effective way.[13]

Chapter 2 follows on from this, focusing upon whether the task of social scientific explanation is to produce general theories or explanations for specific events. I outline the divergences between these two goals, and how they have been conflated in much qualitative and quantitative work. I then go on to explore the ontological and epistemological assumptions that seem to be built into the work of explanation, suggesting that it is very unlikely that there are theoretical laws that would provide satisfactory generic explanations for the occurrence of particular social phenomena in particular places at particular times. This is because such laws assume the naturally occurring existence of at least semi-closed causal systems in the social world, and that these can be identified through experimental research designs or by some other means – yet neither of these assumptions is cogent. Moreover, if social science is to have practical relevance, its main product needs to be explanations rather than theories – the latter involve abstraction from the concepts and contexts associated with practical action, thereby generating problems in 'translating' theoretical knowledge back into an analysis of what is going on, or will go on, in specific contexts. This connects to recognition of the pragmatic character of explanation: that it always operates within some framework of assumptions about exactly what is to be explained and what would count as relevant factors in explaining it. In seeking to clarify the task of social scientific explanation, conceived in this manner, I go on to examine Weber's views about causal analysis. His focus was specifically upon producing explanations of particular outcomes, or patterns of events, rather than theories about what type of cause produces what type of effect. Nevertheless, he recognizes the role of general ideas, about what people will tend to do and why, in producing explanations, arguing that these should be formulated as ideal or pure types that can be used as resources in seeking to understand the much more complex processes actually found in the world.

Another key feature of Weber's position, already noted, was his argument that social scientists' conclusions should be restricted to factual matters, abstaining from evaluations and prescriptions. This is, of course, at odds with the orientation of much social science today, most obviously that which is committed to a 'critical', activist, or policy science stance. Chapter 3 examines arguments in favour of a

---

[13]I believe that much the same can be said of quantitative researchers, and indeed of those who employ mixed methods. On the problems associated with quantitative analysis, see Hammersley 2012d.

normative or partisan conception of social science, in which the aim is not simply to produce factual knowledge but also to provide authoritative evaluations and recommendations. I argue that the rationales offered for this normative approach are multiple, in conflict, and open to serious question. The main alternative to a normative social science is represented by the principle of value freedom or value neutrality, as developed by Weber. I argue that this principle is not vulnerable to the most common criticisms aimed at it, since these involve misinterpretation. Moreover, even if we reject Weber's relativistic assumption that in committing ourselves to fundamental values we must simply 'choose our demon', there are still strong grounds for arguing that social science ought to limit its goal to factual conclusions. At the same time, it needs to be made clear that this 'value-neutral' orientation is not neutral in relation to all value perspectives, in particular not to those that insist upon full commitment to some set of non-epistemic values across all spheres of activity, including research. In this sense, value neutrality is linked to a particular type of political liberalism. I also address the practical difficulties involved in maintaining a value-neutral orientation, especially in a political climate of the sort that prevails today, in which the production of knowledge is frequently regarded as insufficient on its own to warrant public or private 'investment' in social research: it must be 'usable' and have 'impact'.

Chapter 4 is concerned with one currently influential, and sophisticated, attempt to provide a rationale for a normative social science: that offered by 'critical realism'. This approach is distinctive, compared with most other 'critical' approaches today, in presenting explicit arguments purporting to show that value conclusions can be derived directly from factual premises. I examine in detail the two types of argument that critical realists put forward in support of this. The first relates to what are taken to be the cognitive implications of holding some statement to be true: namely, that people ought to believe it, and that institutions that generate falsehoods must be changed. The second argument is focused on the concept of need, claiming that if we establish that someone has a need of some kind, then the imperative follows automatically (other things being equal) that efforts should be made to meet this need. I show that neither of these arguments is convincing; and that they do not provide adequate grounds for the insistence that social science must be 'critical'. In effect, critical realism, like other forms of 'critical' research, smuggles practical values into what purports to be social scientific analysis.

The chapters up to this point have addressed the nature of social scientific explanation, and the role of values, in *relatively abstract* terms. By contrast, the final two chapters explore how these issues arise in two major substantive topic areas: the study of social mobility and educational inequalities; and research on social unrest, and in particular that concerned with riots in the UK in 2011. The aim here is to demonstrate how the problems discussed in earlier chapters come to the fore when we set out to provide social scientific explanations for important phenomena.

Chapter 5 focuses on attempts to answer the question 'Is Britain (or any other society) a meritocracy?', which has been at the centre of a great deal of research on social mobility. Generally speaking, the conclusion reached, albeit occasionally disputed, has been that Britain – like other societies – is some distance from being a meritocracy, and researchers have set out to document deviations from this ideal and to explain them. However, doubts can be raised about whether this question, as it stands, can be addressed effectively by social science. I show that attempts to answer it breach the limits that a Weberian methodological perspective places upon the sorts of conclusion that social science can legitimately claim to provide. Furthermore, there is a common failure to acknowledge the ways in which analysis of social mobility, and of educational inequalities, generally operates within a particular value-relevance framework – one that is largely taken for granted and is used for making evaluations and recommendations. This structures not just the questions addressed, but also the answers provided, for instance about why there are social class inequalities in school achievement and occupational recruitment. My conclusion is that research can tell us rather less about whether a society is meritocratic – and if not, why not – than is frequently claimed or assumed, and that there are dangers associated with excessive claims in this field, as in others.

The background to Chapter 6 is formed by arguments for public, civic, or 'engaged' sociology: the idea that a *primary* responsibility of sociologists should be to contribute to public discussion of social issues, or even directly to shape policy or practice. As already noted, while these arguments reflect demands from policymakers and funding bodies that social science must demonstrate a significant return on public investment, they also derive from the commitments of many sociologists themselves. A not uncommon formulation of the public contribution that social science can make, especially on the part of lay people, is providing predictions of significant events, such as riots or financial crashes; and criticism of social science has sometimes focused on its failure to meet this need. In practice, the public contributions of social scientists have generally taken the form of *explanations*, and my main focus here will be on some examples of these – the explanations provided by sociologists for the riots that took place during August 2011 in London and other UK cities. Sociological explanations for these riots were often set up in explicit contrast to lay explanations, especially those of politicians. I examine similarities and differences among the various publicly provided explanations, noting that sociologists often supplied conflicting accounts, and that their explanations overlapped with many lay accounts. Moreover, even the lay account that is most obviously at odds with those of the sociologists – that of UK Prime Minister David Cameron and some of his colleagues – can nevertheless be derived from sociological theory. My analysis thus generates doubts about the distinctive character of social scientific knowledge and expertise, and/or about what happens to it when it is 'translated' into statements in the public sphere. In short, the chapter raises questions about the public contribution that social science makes, and can make.

In the Epilogue I return to consider the implications of my arguments for current claims about the capacity and role of social science, and the expectations that are placed upon it, both by social scientists themselves and by external agencies and lay publics. I emphasize that while, against this background, my account is a deflationary one, I nevertheless believe that social science has great importance as a source of factual knowledge about the social world, and that it has the potential to make a significant contribution to public discussion and practical decision-making in these terms. What is at issue is the nature and degree of that contribution. My key point is that, for the potential of social science to be realized, a sober assessment is required of the methodological problems that it faces, and of how these might best be tackled. Equally important is recognition of the limits on what social science can legitimately claim to produce. The focus must be entirely on producing sound descriptions and explanations – social scientists should not be seduced into taking up other tasks that are beyond their distinctive capabilities, not least because this core task is sufficiently challenging and important in itself.

ONE

Causation and qualitative inquiry

The question of whether social science involves causal analysis, and if so what form this should take, has a complex history. There was a time when many of those committed to quantitative versions of social science denied that they were concerned with causation, insisting that their conclusions were limited to discovering correlations (see, for instance, Lundberg 1929: 13). This was particularly common among those employing non-experimental research designs: aware that they were unable to exercise the kind of physical control over variables that is intrinsic to experimental method, they cautioned strongly against confusing correlation with causation, and perhaps even saw no means of going beyond this. But, in addition, in the first half of the twentieth century there were philosophical views declaring that causation had been eliminated from modern physical science, and dismissing it as metaphysical – as involving illegitimate speculation beyond the empirical realm. For example, Bertrand Russell argued that 'in advanced sciences such as gravitational astronomy the word "cause" never occurs', and 'the reason why physics has ceased to look for causes is that, in fact, there are no such things'. He famously concluded that 'the law of causality [...] is a relic of a bygone age surviving, like the monarchy, only because it is erroneously supposed to do no harm' (Russell 1913: 1). Along the same lines, Karl Pearson (1911: vi) called the notion of causation 'a fetish amidst the inscrutable arcana of modern science', insisting that scientific laws are simply patterns of perceived events that have been found to occur repeatedly, with no claim that the sequence is *necessary* or the product of some *underlying force*.[1]

---

[1]These arguments can be traced back at least as far as the scepticism of David Hume, although there is disagreement about what Hume really meant: see MacIntyre 1971: ch. 13; Owen 1999; Beebee 2006; Read and Richman 2007; Garrett 2009. For an account of the emergence of Hume's position from previous developments, and of its subsequent influence in the philosophy of science, see Kurki 2008: ch. 1. It is worth noting that Comte, the inventor of the terms 'positivism' and 'sociology', also rejected

For both practical and theoretical reasons, then, many practitioners of quantitative method in social science, in the early twentieth century, tended to argue that there was no need to make causal claims – that predictive knowledge relying upon systematic correlational analysis was sufficient, and is perhaps all that is possible.

By contrast, at this same time influential defenders of older, and less positivistic, conceptions of social science not only opposed the idea that rigour in social science meant the adoption of quantitative techniques, but also argued that causal analysis is at the core of sociological inquiry. For instance, Florian Znaniecki (1934) rejected 'statistical method' precisely on the grounds that it is incapable of discovering causal relations. He insisted that these take a deterministic form, corresponding to a set of necessary and jointly sufficient conditions – not the probabilistic predictions produced by 'enumerative induction'. He argued that what is required instead is 'analytic induction' through case study, which he claimed *is* capable of discovering causal laws. Others, notably Alfred Lindesmith (1947), developed this method, presenting it as starting from detailed investigation of particular cases, from which a hypothetical law can be generated, this being followed by examination of further cases to test the validity of the hypothesis. Both Znaniecki and Lindesmith treated any single case that did not match the hypothesis as refuting it, and therefore as demanding reformulation of the explanation. This process was seen as continuing until a point is reached where every new case investigated confirms the current hypothesis (see Hammersley 1989: ch. 7 and 8; Hammersley and Cooper 2012).

Another influential voice in the first half of the twentieth century defending qualitative case study against criticism by quantitative methodologists was Robert MacIver (1942). He too argued that the notion of cause is unavoidable in understanding the world, including social phenomena – that what is required for sociological explanation necessarily goes beyond correlation, the observation of 'regular sequences', to refer to productive forces of one sort or another. And, rather than seeing separate factors as each increasing the likelihood or intensity of an outcome to a calculable degree, he insisted that it is necessary to gain a clear understanding of how factors are *interrelated* to form the causal processes involved in systems of social relations.

So, Znaniecki, Lindesmith, and MacIver all rejected the nominalistic retreat into regarding knowledge of correlations as sufficient; though whereas Znaniecki and

---

the notion of causation, even while insisting on the role of laws in scientific explanation (Thompson 1976: 43; see also Turner 2003). On this whole line of philosophical thinking, see MacIver 1942: ch. 1 and 2; and for a more recent account, see Cartwright 2002, 2007. The nature of causation has long been a matter of dispute in philosophy: see Beauchamp 1974; Mackie 1974; Brand 1976; Mohr 1996; Beebee et al. 2009. Some years ago, Tooley (1987: 5) wrote: 'Many accounts of the nature of causation and of laws have been advanced, but none has elicited anything remotely approaching general acceptance'. This remains true.

Lindesmith accepted the traditional scientific conception of causality as involving universal laws, MacIver rejected it. He writes:

> a functional equation is an admirable device to symbolise certain highly general or universal relationships under hypothetical conditions, where, for example, a number of determinate factors or forces are assumed to constitute the structure of a closed system in a state of equilibrium. [However, it] has no relevance to a system that cannot be understood in terms of isolable factors or components. It has no application to a system the changes of which depend in any degree on the impact of factors lying outside it. (MacIver 1942: 52)

Moreover, all these writers believed that causation in the social realm is distinctive as a result of the role of subjective factors, such as perceptions, intentions and motives.

Today, these contrasting positions on the part of quantitative and qualitative researchers, *for* and *against* causal analysis (albeit interpreted in varying ways), have been largely reversed. Quantitative researchers now routinely make explicit causal claims, even while still warning (quite properly) against confusing correlation with causation; and methodologists focusing on such work have given much attention to the nature of causal analysis (see James et al. 1982; Hellevik 1984; Hage and Meeker 1988).[2] By contrast, many qualitative researchers today expressly *deny* the possibility of causal analysis in the social field. Like Znaniecki and Lindesmith, they treat the concept of cause as implying the existence of empirical laws, but *unlike* them they insist that no such laws have been discovered in the social realm and that none exist. They argue that social processes are contingent in character, in the sense that they are heavily dependent upon the agency of actors: that is, on their interpretations, intentions and decisions, *these being highly variable and context-sensitive.*[3]

Qualitative researchers also often treat the idea of social causation as *ethically suspect* and *politically undesirable.* We can get a sense of this from Lincoln and Guba's (1985: 129) statement that: 'if it could be shown that the concept of

---

[2]Hoover (2004) charts a somewhat similar pattern in economics, with the language of cause disappearing from econometrics, but then starting to reappear at the end of the twentieth century. This has been bolstered by some developments in philosophy and statistical theory, designed to provide rigorous means of causal inference from non-experimental data (see, for example, Pearl 2000; but see also McKim and Turner 1997).

[3]See Maxwell (2012: 35) for an outline of these views. There are exceptions to this generalization about the position taken by qualitative researchers today, Maxwell himself being one (see Maxwell 2004a, 2004b, 2012). The situation is rather different in the field of political science. Here a concern with the demands of causal analysis has been central to the development of Qualitative Comparative Analysis (Ragin 2008) and to the defence of case study work more generally (George and Bennett 2005: ch. 7 and *passim*; Bennett and Elman 2006; Gerring 2006). See also Mahoney and Goertz 2006; Goertz and Mahoney 2012.

cause is deficient, the assumption of determinism would be difficult to defend'. It is often argued by qualitative researchers that to adopt a deterministic position dehumanizes human beings, portraying them as – indeed, perhaps inducing them to act as if they were – automatons. A further criticism is that to treat human behaviour as causally determined serves to justify existing social arrangements and to deny the possibility of planned social change. More generally, Lincoln and Guba (1985: 129) comment that 'there are other reasons for [the] causality fetish' besides a positivistic conception of science: 'If causes are the key to prediction and control, knowledge of causes is tantamount to power. This fact may help us to understand why political figures have been willing to support scientific research, in the hope that such inquiry will produce information that can be used to good political effect'. Where Znaniecki, and others, had seen the prospect of social control based upon scientific knowledge as beneficial, these authors, and many qualitative researchers today, see it as oppressive.[4]

In denying that causal analysis can be applied to the social world, qualitative researchers have drawn, explicitly or implicitly, to varying degrees and in various ways, upon several influential philosophical traditions – notably, Kantian and Hegelian idealism, Husserlian phenomenology, and ordinary language philosophy. In the next section I will outline some key arguments they have derived from these sources.

Some philosophical influences on qualitative inquiry

Over the past 50 years diverse philosophical views have shaped qualitative research, and these are partly responsible for generating a disparate array of approaches within it. Here, I will focus on just three broad philosophical traditions that have had a significant effect on how qualitative researchers have set about describing and explaining social phenomena.

To a large extent, the idealist tradition had its origins in Kant's insistence that causality cannot be treated as present *in* the world; that it is, instead, a constitutive principle *through which we understand* that world. Also influential was his argument that it is intrinsic to the very notion of rationality that we have the freedom to act one way rather than another – for example, to treat people as ends not merely as means. In large part, Kant's philosophy was motivated by a commitment to protect the realm of morality from the materialism and naturalism associated with the growth of physical science (Velkley 1989). Hegel subsequently transformed these ideas by abandoning Kant's distinction between noumenal and phenomenal realms (between things-in-themselves and how they appear to us), with the result that from his point of view the world itself is characterized by the sorts of relation typical of thought, rather than those that materialists believe operate among material bodies. He argued that even physical causation is a species

---

[4]In my view, neither position is sensible

of 'logical' relation within a world conceptualized as an evolving whole with its own internal 'dialectic'. Moreover, he saw the task of identifying these relations as depending upon *systematic* interpretation: 'locating' phenomena within the theoretical context of a historical meta-narrative that explains them. Here, theory is treated as an essential means of conceptualizing phenomena, often in a manner that goes beyond, and reveals the distortion inherent in, empirical appearances. This idea was spread within social science particularly through the influence of Marxism and Critical Theory, but it has extended even beyond those who see themselves as belonging to these traditions.[5]

Another important influence on qualitative researchers, from the 1960s onwards, was Husserl's phenomenology, especially through the work of subsequent philosophers influenced by him, such as Heidegger, Sartre, Merleau-Ponty, and Schutz. Husserl defined the philosophical task as rigorous *description* of 'the things themselves', as they appear in our experience, and also of our modes of experiencing them.[6] What are discovered through such investigations are relations operating *within* subjectivity; this time (by contrast with Hegel) a subjectivity that is universal rather than historically developing, and individual (albeit transcendental) rather than collective. Some qualitative researchers have taken over these ideas (often modifying them considerably in the process), for instance seeking to *describe* people's perspectives, patterns of social interaction, etc., *as these appear in the world*; in other words, seeking to portray these phenomena *in their own terms* rather than from some broader perspective in the way that both positivist and Hegelian/Marxist science do.

Interestingly, both the idealist and the phenomenological traditions generated more or less the same problem in the course of their development, as regards their support for non-causal interpretations of human social life. This was that the distinction originally drawn between internal and external relations came to be challenged or undermined. In the case of idealism, once Marx had turned Hegel's dialectic back on to its feet (Marx 1873/1970: 20), the focus of inquiry became social relations in a material world, rather than within a developing 'world spirit'; and it is hard not to see Marx's account of capitalism as attributing causal relations (see Ruben, 1979: 118–26). In the case of Husserl, once his followers became primarily interested in *being-in-the-world* rather than in the transcendental core of individual subjectivity, the same problem arose. It came to the surface, for example, in the disagreement between Sartre and Merleau-Ponty as to whether human actions are simply a matter of free will, any denial of this being treated as bad faith, or are always necessarily biologically, historically, and socially located, and therefore caught up within some kind of causal nexus (see Gutting, 2001: 203–8). Sartre effectively conceded this point in his later work.

---

[5]As an illustration of the terminological complexities of the philosophical field, it is striking that Pearson, the positivistic advocate of the 'grammar of science', labelled his own position a form of idealism (Pearson 1900: vii). What he meant was that he was committed to phenomenalism, like some other positivists at the time, such as Mach.

[6]Like Hegel, Husserl abandoned Kant's distinction between noumena and phenomena.

The third, and final, influence I will mention is the sort of 'descriptive meta-physics' (Strawson 1959) that was the concern of much ordinary language phi-losophy in England in the 1950s and 1960s (see Anscombe 1957; Peters 1958; Melden 1961). Here the focus was on how concepts, including those relating to human action such as 'reason' and 'cause', are used in ordinary language-use, the assumption being that studying this allows us to understand their meaning, and how their misuse can confuse us. This involved resistance to attempts to treat everyday meanings as the defective realization of some single, underlying formal logic; or to regard them as imperfect reflections of the world that they are sup-posed to conceptualize, or as mere epiphenomena – whether deriving from brain functioning or from social processes (such as the mode of economic production). In the very nature of this kind of conceptual analysis, reasons must be seen as internally related to the behaviour for which they are held to account, so that one cannot treat the two as separate phenomena, even less as exhibiting a *general* rela-tionship – assumptions that are normally treated as essential components of any notion of causality. Furthermore, it came to be argued that the giving of reasons must itself be viewed as a form of action, for example, one that is directed towards the tasks of justification or excusal, and this means that the statements produced must be seen as forming part of this action, so that reasons must become context-sensitive and contextually variable linguistic products, rather than motivating factors that exist inside people's heads.

Qualitative approaches to explaining social action

All of these philosophical ideas tended to lead to a denial that human actions and institutions are produced by causal processes, in favour of conceptualizations portraying them instead as constituted by relations of an 'internal' – intelligible or meaningful – character. And it was also usually argued that these must be grasped through forms of understanding that are quite different from the methods used by natural scientists. At the same time, these ideas generated a diversity of orienta-tions among qualitative researchers, rather than a single one. I will outline three broad common tendencies that illustrate some of the main lines of variation.[7]

Intentional explanation. Some qualitative researchers take people's accounts of their intentions and motives largely at face value, and treat these as playing the key role in generating social phenomena. This is characteristic of some 'biographical' approaches, though it is not limited to these.[8] Underpinning this sort of approach, often, is the idea that we cannot assume that the environment that actors experience

---

[7]In practice these are sometimes combined in various ways.

[8]For outlines of biographical approaches, see Bertaux 1981; Atkinson 1998; Roberts 2001; Bornat 2008.

corresponds to what is specified 'objectively' by social scientific analysis: there may be discrepancies not just in terms of what is salient but even in the very character of what is perceived and how it is interpreted. Moreover, participants' understandings of their surroundings, and indeed of themselves and their own actions, may change over time, rather than being fixed, stable, or standard. Thus, it is argued that – in any attempt to explain people's actions – the first task is to document their own understanding of themselves, of their actions, and of their world, rather than assuming that the motivational process corresponds to some pre-given and standard sociological model identifying objective causal factors. Moreover, often, description of these understandings is judged to be sufficient in itself for the task of explaining actions.

More than this, it is often argued that there is a problem concerning how the sort of 'objective' factors that are prioritized in many social scientific accounts (whether appealing to societal values and norms, interests arising from social divisions, or whatever) can be related to the perceptions and understandings of participants, in such a way as to show how these factors structure their behaviour. Some qualitative researchers have concluded that 'objective' and 'subjective' perspectives represent different, incommensurable 'realities'; or, indeed, that there is no such thing as objectivity, simply multiple subjective perspectives. One formulation of this is the idea that people are 'experts in their own lives', which has become a common position in the field of Childhood Studies (see, for example, Christensen and James 2008). This is often underpinned by an ethical commitment to the importance of *respecting* people's understandings of themselves and their world, rather than claiming that science can produce a superior account, one which identifies forces shaping people's behaviour, of which they are unaware, or assigns motives to them that they would disavow.

Explanation in terms of mutual shaping. A second, rather different, sort of approach to explaining social behaviour that can be found among qualitative researchers is illustrated by the arguments of Lincoln and Guba (1985). In place of the notion of cause, whether interpreted as referring to a set of necessary and jointly sufficient conditions, or in probabilistic terms to the presence of some factor that increases the likelihood or intensity of a particular type of outcome, they argue that the focus should be on systematic relations among a large number of factors that 'simultaneously mutually shape' one another.[9] It is argued that these relations are not deterministic but contingent, and are 'circumstances-relative' (1985: 152). As a result, any knowledge we have of them can only amount to making '*plausible imputations*'. Moreover, which elements we include in our focus will depend upon our purposes, not only upon the structure of relations among the elements within the causal nexus. Lincoln and Guba (1985: 152) write that 'Understanding results

---

[9]At one point these authors suggest that there is 'an infinite number of mutually interacting shapers' (Lincoln and Guba 1985: 156).

from an appreciation of the myriad mutual shapings that are synchronously ongo-ing, and abstracting from that complexity a subsystem that serves the investigator's needs'. This understanding is 'shaped in equal proportion by the investigator's pur-pose and the phenomenon's presentational aspect'.[10]

Lincoln and Guba's account of causality differs from the first approach, to some degree, in the emphasis it gives to understanding the social relations in which people are involved, as a prerequisite for describing and explaining their behav-iour. But the most important difference is that there is no suggestion that we must analyse these relations purely from *within* participants' perspectives. In this respect, the approach is analogous to older arguments in favour of pattern models of explanation (Diesing 1972; Williams 1976) and to more recent reliance upon approaches like actor network theory and activity theory (Engeström et al. 1999; Law and Hassard 1999).

Reasons as rhetorical. The final stance I will discuss is very different from the other two. This is the idea that it is misleading to think of motives, or for that matter of other potential causes, such as interests or value-commitments, as forces operating *on* or *within* individuals that *drive* their behaviour. Rather, these phe-nomena are linguistic or discursive in character, and are socio-culturally gener-ated and deployed in order to make sense of and act in the world (Mills 1940; Blum and McHugh 1971). To apply a particular label to an event – for example, to describe a death as a murder, rather than as an accident – is to mobilize a whole set of other categories that must be filled, as far as possible, with relevant features from the situation concerned: there must be a murderer, a situation in which this could occur, a weapon or other means by which the victim was killed, and a motive. The label also potentially stimulates a series of responses – shock, out-rage, fear, calling the police, mounting a search, questioning those involved, and so on. Rather than assuming that a label, such as 'murder', simply reflects reality and has consequences as a result of this, we can notice that the mobilizing effect of the labelling occurs whether or not it comes subsequently to be treated as true or false. Given this, it is suggested that the focus of analysis should be on how people attribute perceptions, intentions, motives, etc., both to themselves and to others. It is argued that research must examine how people formulate motives and other purported causes of behaviour – how these are attributed, challenged, etc., in processes of social interaction or within texts of various kinds; in other words, emphasis is shifted to the 'discursive construction of social reality'.

In some early versions, this approach incorporated causal explanation: 'vocabu-laries of motive' were treated as directing material causes down one line of action rather than another. An example is Sykes and Matza's argument that ideas about blame and responsibility serve as 'techniques of neutralization', allowing peo-ple to engage in criminal behaviour that they would otherwise have rejected as

---

[10]For a somewhat similar epistemological position, see Eisner 1992.

morally proscribed (Sykes and Matza 1957; Matza 1964; see also Cressey 1953). However, more recently, there has been a strong tendency to abandon this causal component, in favour of a more radically constructionist position.[11]

An assessment

While all three of these approaches distance themselves from causal analysis, if we look more closely at what they entail we find that they are by no means entirely successful in avoiding it. The first two approaches still retain some notion of cause, if we interpret this in a broad sense as referring to factors (including perceptions, intentions, motives, social relations, etc.) that generate one kind of action rather than another, so that what results is not simply a matter of coincidence (see Mohr 1996: 13; Kurki 2008: ch. 6). Only the third approach, and then only in its radical constructionist form, appears to abandon the notion of causation completely. Moreover, even here, as we shall see, there are questions about whether, *in practice*, causal claims are completely escaped: they may still arise, for example, in seeking to explain why one vocabulary of motives, or one discursive strategy, is adopted, and/or in documenting the *effects* of actors' adopting these.

So, despite frequent disavowals, much qualitative research *is*, in effect, still concerned with putting forward causal explanations for why or how something occurred, or with offering accounts of the consequences of some event, intervention, etc. At the same time, perhaps because there is not usually an explicit commitment to or focus on causal analysis, none of the approaches outlined provides an entirely satisfactory basis for understanding what this involves, or for producing sound causal accounts. I will look again at each approach in turn.[12]

---

[11]A key source for this whole approach is the work of Kenneth Burke, see Overington 1977. See also Mills 1940. While for Burke and Mills there was no question that there are phenomena existing independently of particular discursive acts, so that labels could turn out to be false, later exponents of this set of ideas often seemed to abandon this assumption. See Bruce and Wallis 1983 for a critique of this approach. Sharrock and Watson 1984 respond, and Bruce and Wallis 1985 reply. See also Housley and Fitzgerald 2008. For other versions of this argument, in a different field, see Laffey and Weldes 1997. It is striking to compare this attitude towards motive with that of MacIver, for whom motives are genuine causal factors, albeit ones about which it is difficult to provide conclusive evidence (see MacIver 1940). There have recently been counter-trends to the discursive turn in the form of psycho-social approaches to the study of human behaviour. For a response to these developments from within a constructionist perspective, see Wetherell 2008.

[12]There have been a number of calls for qualitative researchers to engage explicitly in causal analysis, on the argument that quantitative research has been founded upon a defective, Humean conception of causation which reduces it to observable regularities (see, for example, Kurki 2008). While there is some truth in this diagnosis, in my view it is often based on too sharp a distinction between regularity theories and other ways of understanding causation.

The first one treats people as having direct knowledge of what they are doing and why. And it emphasizes the importance of our grasping of how they see the world, and themselves, if we are to be able to understand their intentions and motives. Up to a point, there is much to be said for this. Those approaches that deny self-knowledge – whether behaviourism, some form of structuralist sociology, or discursive psychology – fly in the face of what it is surely reasonable to accept as true: if we were to doubt that we can have self-knowledge of some sorts, we would inevitably be pitched into complete epistemological scepticism, since there are few other sorts of knowledge that we treat as generally more reliable.[13] That said, this does not mean that people's accounts of their intentions, motives, perceptions, etc. should be accepted at face value, or treated as always sufficient for explaining what they do and its consequences. We are all aware that we can be mistaken about our own behaviour, even about what we actually did, and certainly about our motives – such doubts are not an invention of depth-psychology. Similarly, we may not understand much about how the situations that prompted our actions were generated, yet this may be relevant both to explaining those actions and (even more obviously) to accounting for their consequences. Here, too, we can see that there is scope for research to produce more adequate explanations (in some sense) than those which we ordinarily produce as actors.

Turning to Lincoln and Guba's account of causality, this clearly has the advantage of emphasizing the importance of understanding the social relations in which people are involved, and in a way that is not restricted to viewing these exclusively from *within* participants' own perspectives. It is also surely true that patterns of social action are shaped by a wide range of factors, rather than being under the determinate control of one or two. Also, these authors' acknowledgement of the role of the analyst's purpose and perspective in selecting causal factors is to be welcomed. However, Lincoln and Guba do not provide much guidance about how we should go about generating and assessing hypotheses about the causes or effects of particular patterns of social relationship. They themselves write that 'there is a great difference between finding a statement persuasive and being able to say *why* it is persuasive. The development of appropriate criteria represents an intellectual task that is, at the moment, beyond us, but that, we are persuaded, will turn out to be doable' (Lincoln and Guba 1985: 157). Moreover, while they recognize the role of the analyst in selecting from a very wide range of social relations, they do not give much indication as to how this ought to be done.[14]

---

[13]The form of argument I am using here, about certainty, is to be found in Wittgenstein 1969. Discursive psychologists appeal to other parts of Wittgenstein's work (particularly to his *Philosophical Investigations* (1953)) to justify their position (see, for instance, Edwards 1997).

[14]In Chapter 2, I outline Weber's notion of value relevance which, it seems to me, provides a sound understanding of the proper basis for the selectivity necessarily involved in analysing causal relationships. See also Mackie 1974 and Roberts 1996.

As regards the third approach, in its constructionist form it seeks radically to detach itself from the whole business of causal analysis, in favour of a focus on relations that are internal to particular discourses or modes of discursive practice.[15] However, generally speaking, it fails to make good its escape. Take, for example, Potter's (1996) version of discourse analysis, and specifically his concept of 'stake-inoculation'. This points to the way that people often preface a judgment they are putting forward by indicating why they have no stake in its being true. An example would be when someone says: 'I'm a member of the Conservative Party, but I can't deny that the gap between rich and poor in the UK today has become too great'. Built into Potter's account here are implicit causal claims: it is assumed that this strategy of stake inoculation is adopted because it generally has the effect of disarming one sort of countermove that audiences may make to dismiss what the speaker is about to say (in the example above, accusations such as 'you must be anti-capitalist'). In other words, the concept presupposes that actors believe that use of this strategy will have this disabling effect (that *they* assume a causal relationship). Moreover, besides the analyst attributing this causal assumption to actors, he or she also assumes that it is precisely *because* of this belief that actors use stake-inoculation strategies: that there is a causal relationship between belief and use here.[16] In addition, it seems to be taken for granted that the effect of stake-inoculation will actually be, much of the time, to close off, or at least to make interactionally difficult, the moves anticipated, and that this is not happenstance but is to do with its *systematic effect* on hearers.

As should be clear then, in practice, albeit usually implicitly, qualitative researchers almost always rely in their descriptions and explanations upon the idea that causal relations operate in the social world. Indeed, very often they are concerned, for instance, with the ways in which various objective factors – such as social status or class, sex or gender, ethnicity, and so on – shape people's circumstances, attitudes, and behaviour. Given this, it is not surprising to find the frequent use of verb forms that imply causal relations – such as 'influence', 'shape', 'leads to', or 'results in'. And, even though qualitative researchers generally avoid terms that imply strong causality, such as 'determine', these are nevertheless occasionally employed (Hammersley 2008c). In fact, escaping from causal analysis would require a major re-specification of the task of social science, for example along the lines of ethnomethodology (Button 1991), and even this may not be successful in avoiding it.

---

[15]In its less constructionist form it offers a model of one important sort of causal process, one that is similar to that found in Weber's arguments about the role of religion in facilitating the rise of capitalism (Weber 1948: 280).

[16]Potter and his colleagues would almost certainly deny that they attribute any such beliefs to the people they study, but in my view these minimal views about agency cannot be avoided in the sort of analysis in which they engage: see Hammersley and Treseder 2007: 286–8.

How are we to explain the fact that, while qualitative researchers today frequently deny that causation operates in the social world, they nevertheless engage in causal analysis? One explanation is that they cannot answer the sorts of question they address without doing so. Another is that what they are rejecting is not causal analysis *per se* but, rather, particular interpretations of it, notably those that demand the specification of a set of necessary and jointly sufficient conditions, and/or those that treat documenting causal relations as necessitating the use of statistical analysis.

Furthermore, it is perhaps because they usually do not explicitly recognize that they are engaged in causal analysis that qualitative researchers rarely deploy systematically the full range of strategies required to generate, and especially to test, causal interpretations. They often rely upon just one of these strategies and may not even use this in a very systematic fashion. In effect, many of them seem to assume, much of the time, that identifying causes is relatively straightforward: that conclusions about these can be simply drawn from what people report about their intentions or motives, or that they can be directly observed at work in interactional processes, that they can be read off from the identification of discursive practices, and/or that currently influential theories will supply privileged insight into them (see Hammersley 2012b).

In the next section I want to examine, in broad terms, the resources that are available to qualitative researchers, and to social scientists more generally, for identifying causal relationships and thereby for providing sound explanations of social phenomena.

Strategies for causal analysis

While the aim of causal analysis is to document real world processes, we have no *direct* access to these via perception.[17] Nor can we derive knowledge of them from empirical evidence *in a strictly logical or calculative fashion*.[18] Instead, we have to rely upon two sorts of resource:

---

[17]Maxwell (2012: 38) and others (see Connelly 1998) have argued that it is possible to *observe* causal relations. There are undoubtedly occasions when the perceptual evidence is so strong as to be beyond reasonable doubt. One of the examples that Maxwell uses, appealing to Scriven 2008, is that of a hawk taking a pigeon. However, in my view this is not a useful paradigm for most of the causal relationships with which social scientists are concerned, where the perceptual evidence can only support much less certain lines of inference. Also treacherous here, of course, is any assumption that what is perceived is simply given and therefore automatically true. The existence of optical illusions warns against this. Furthermore, see Mohr (1996: 43) and Strawson (1985) on the argument that it is actually physical feelings rather than vision that is basic for understanding causation.

[18]Some use of statistical analysis seems to operate as if this were possible, and the same may be true of the ways in which Grounded Theorizing and Qualitative Comparative Analysis are sometimes employed.

- *Imaginative construction of plausible models* of relevant causal processes that could be involved in the situation(s) we are studying. This will draw upon past experience of other situations felt to be similar in significant respects, on analogies and metaphors that appear to offer illumination, and on thought experiments concerned with assessing whether the outcome would have been different if some element of the situation had varied. These imaginative processes may be stimulated by reading appropriate literature, even including fictional material.
- Equally important is the *analysis of empirical data* about relevant cases. This is essential for both the generation and the development of explanatory ideas (abduction or retroduction), *and* for testing their likely validity.[19]

It is very important to emphasize that the imaginative and empirical aspects of causal analysis are intimately interrelated: indeed they are complementary. Empirical analysis feeds the process of imaginative construction of causal models, and also serves as a corrective to it, but cannot on its own identify causes. If the two become separated, or if one is given priority, causal analysis is likely to be less successful. Excessive emphasis upon imaginative construction of causal models leads to speculative accounts that may bear little relationship to what happens in the world. On the other hand, excessive stress on empirical analysis tends to result in superficial accounts that do not capture the causal processes involved: it must be remembered that empirical data can only serve as *signs* of real-world processes – these must be *interpreted*, and it is necessary to make this a deliberate and thoughtful process.[20]

There are two broad forms of empirical analysis available to qualitative researchers, and indeed to social scientists more generally, in seeking to identify causal relations: within-case and cross-case analysis. It is worth noting that these are strategies we all use to a degree in everyday life, where we are inevitably often concerned with identifying causal relations. And qualitative researchers have long relied upon them – albeit, as already noted, often only partially and not always very systematically. These two strategies involve the following:

---

[19]The terms 'abduction' and 'retroduction' appear to have been introduced by Peirce, see Fann 1970. However, they have come to be used in a variety of ways that depart from his usage. In particular, whereas Peirce treated abduction/retroduction as just one of three types of reasoning required in science, it is now often presented as if it were self-sufficient: see, for example, Coffey and Atkinson 1996: 155–6. Blaikie (2000) treats these terms as referring to different research strategies, but once again they are viewed as self-sufficient.

[20]I am not claiming any novelty for the view presented here. Something like it can even be found in Comte (Thompson 1976). However, it does seem necessary at the present time to reiterate what is involved, since in my view there are many examples in social science today both of excessively speculative accounts and of ones that effectively treat data as speaking for themselves.

- *Within-case analysis* takes the form of detailed investigation of features and processes within a particular case, over some period of time (short or long), examining patterns of co-occurrence, of co-variation, and/or of sequence, relevant to putative causal processes. Generally speaking, it involves examining cases where the outcome that is of interest actually occurred, to look at what preceded it or what is otherwise associated with it, and to document participants' understandings of themselves, their situation, and their behaviour that might be relevant to any explanation. The aim is to use the data to think about what processes could generate the outcome, and also to test out ideas about this.
- *Cross-case analysis* involves systematic comparison of several cases, perhaps a large number, looking for patterns of co-occurrence or co-variation between outcome or effect variables and potential causes. All cases within a population, or some sample designed to be representative of it, may be studied, or cases may be selected for investigation strategically; for example, focusing upon those where candidate factors, or combinations of factors, are present and absent, or are at different levels of intensity, and where the effects of confounding factors can be discounted. Researchers might also investigate cases where what they suspect is the key factor is present to find out whether the outcome also occurred in those cases. The patterns discovered through comparing cases can suggest what causes what, and will also enable us to *test* our ideas about this to some degree.

As my discussion indicates, each of these empirical strategies can be used to produce data that will both generate explanatory ideas and test the validity of hypothetical explanations of what happened in particular cases. Moreover, usually neither can provide conclusive evidence on its own:

- Given that it is not usually possible simply to observe causal relations, within-case analysis can only offer suggestions, stronger or weaker, that a particular type of causal relationship is operating, or rule out some otherwise plausible hypothesis.
- Similarly, cross-case analysis alone can rarely provide entirely convincing evidence about causal relationships, in part because it is not usually possible to devise comparisons that enable all of the potentially relevant factors to be taken into account.[21]

Even when these two strategies are used together, they will not produce absolutely conclusive evidence, but they may well provide the resources for generating convincing explanations. To maximize the chances of this, they need to be used in a systematic way.

As regards within-case analysis, this requires seeking to document all relevant internal processes of a case in sufficient detail, and to check inferences about the potential causal processes involved against information from the case. Where cases are large and internally differentiated, considerable work may be required to gather all of the relevant information. With cross-case analysis, there must, once again, be an effort to ensure, as far as possible, that all the relevant information from each case has been collected, and that this is reliable; though, generally speaking, less information will be collected about each case and there will be less chance to check its

---

[21]This is what Ragin 2008 refers to as the problem of 'limited diversity'. See also Ragin and Sonnett 2004.

reliability, as compared with what is possible in within-case analysis (Hammersley 1992: ch. 11). In addition, there need to be systematic efforts to find and use data from whatever relevant comparative cases are available. To the extent that it is feasible, comparative cases must be studied in such a way as to identify *complexes* of factors that operate together, and to rule out competing hypotheses (see Ragin 1987). Moreover, as part of this it is necessary to identify the different functions that causal factors can play, for example, as background facilitator or as trigger (see Roberts 1996). Finally, in the use of both strategies there needs to be clarity about the limitations of the data collected, and of the inferences that can be drawn, as regards the likely validity of the answers being proposed to research questions.

A great deal of qualitative research relies primarily, if not exclusively, upon within-case analysis. Furthermore, while there is often imaginative use of data to produce likely explanations, there is frequently a low emphasis upon systematically testing these candidate accounts. As noted earlier, this perhaps arises from underestimating the difficulties involved in reliably drawing conclusions about causal relationships. It also probably stems from the fact that qualitative studies often focus on a wide range of *descriptive and explanatory* issues simultaneously, for instance with the aim of providing a rounded account of the case(s) being investigated (Hammersley 1992). There is considerable tension between the breadth of focus adopted and the depth of the analysis that can be carried out.[22]

Qualitative researchers do also sometimes use cross-case analysis, comparing cases that are similar and different in relevant respects. Indeed, this is built into Analytic Induction, Grounded Theorizing, and Qualitative Comparative Method. However, not only is appeal to these methods – especially in the case of Grounded Theorizing – much more frequent than systematic deployment of them, but also each method has weaknesses as a form of comparative analysis (Cooper et al. 2012). In my view, there is particular scope for improvement in the use of cross-case analysis within qualitative studies, though the challenges this entails, not least in logistical terms, should not be underestimated.

Conclusion

In this chapter I began by noting that there had been a shift over time in the attitudes of qualitative researchers towards causal analysis: from explicit commitment on the part of many in the first half of the twentieth century to rejection by most qualitative researchers in most fields today. I looked at key philosophical ideas that had influenced this change, and at some common current approaches

---

[22]It should be noted, however, that the trade-off here is no simple matter, once we recognize that causal analysis requires understanding how multiple factors may work *together* in producing an outcome, and acknowledge the importance, for grasping how this process operates, of the contexts in which it takes place.

to the tasks of description and explanation. At the same time, I suggested that, in practice, most qualitative researchers still make causal claims, but that their hypotheses are often not developed and tested very effectively.

I then outlined the two main resources for use in causal investigation: imaginative construction of causal narratives and the analysis of empirical data. I also discussed the two empirical strategies that can be used to discover causal processes – within-case and cross-case analysis – stressing that these are both essential and complementary. While use of these resources does not guarantee success, they are all that is available to any social researcher. And how well they are executed can increase or decrease their effectiveness significantly.

Qualitative case study has both strengths and weaknesses in pursuing causal analysis, as compared with more quantitative approaches. It can provide detailed understanding of what goes on within cases that may enable productive explanatory hypotheses to be developed and tested. And, in cross-case analysis, it may allow strategic selection of cases to facilitate both the development and assessment of causal explanations. However, complementarity operates at this level too: combining qualitative work with quantitative analysis, both within and across cases, can improve the chances of reaching sound causal conclusions.

In my judgment, there is some way to go before social science can realize its potential in this respect, and there is too much complacency on the part of many about what is currently being achieved. This has been a persistent problem. Writing in 1942, MacIver reported:

> The writer made a survey of the articles dealing with [a variety of] subjects as published over a period of years in journals of sociology, psychology, economics, political science, and education. In the great majority of instances either no grounds or quite inadequate ones were given in support of the causal imputations they presented. Sometimes there was displayed a meticulous care in the refinement of statistical indices or in the calculation of correlation coefficients, followed by a sweeping, unguarded, or wholly unwarranted conclusion regarding the causal nexus. Sometimes a selective description of conditions attendant on the phenomenon was the only basis for quite definite imputation. Sometimes cases or examples were offered showing the presence of the alleged cause, as though that were sufficient to establish its causal relation to the social phenomenon. Not infrequently an order of priority or importance was assigned to a number of 'causes' with little or no attempt to justify or even to elucidate this rating. Occasionally an investigator ventured so far as to give numerical weights or percentages of 'influence' to the various 'factors'. When several authors dealt with the same social phenomenon they differed considerably regarding its causation. [...] The almost complete lack of any well-considered methodology was very noteworthy. (MacIver 1942: 73–4)

It is hard to avoid drawing the same conclusion about much social research today. And, as I have made clear in this chapter, MacIver's damning judgment is as true of qualitative as it is of quantitative work.

TWO

The problem of explanation in social science: a Weberian solution?

In the past, a common starting point for discussions of social science explanation was the model of causal laws in physics (for a classic example, see Nagel 1961). This methodological ideal is much less influential today, but there is a feature of it that has been retained in the thinking of many social researchers which needs examination: the idea that the primary goal of social science is to produce theoretical propositions having general scope.[1] While most contemporary social scientists reject, or at least downplay, the possibility of discovering universal or even historical laws of social life, they do not usually present their work as entirely concerned with producing idiographic accounts of particular phenomena; and, even when they do this, in practice they often make more general claims. For instance, the 'thick descriptions' offered by many qualitative researchers almost always involve general theoretical arguments that go beyond the particular phenomena described, and indeed this seems to be part of the purpose of thick description (Hammersley 2008a: ch. 3). Similarly, the conclusions of survey research are often presented as causal models that represent stable relationships among variables that will be found much more widely than in the specific sample studied, or even than in the population from which it was drawn.[2] There are, however, important questions that may be raised about the nature of any theories that social science can produce, about the 'logic' of inquiry which generating them

---

[1]There are, of course, exceptions among social scientists in this tendency to give priority to producing theories, most notably Max Weber (see Ringer 1997). For him, the main task of social science was to produce explanations for particular, value-relevant phenomena, and he insisted that more abstract theoretical characterizations of social phenomena were only of value as tools in producing explanations. I will explore his ideas later in this chapter.

[2]In much the same way we find advocates of case-based methods seeking to position themselves *between* the nomothetic and idiographic orientations: see Byrne 2009: 152.

demands, and about the relative priority of and relationship between theory-building and the task of explaining particular social phenomena.

Theorizing versus explaining

There is a clear distinction to be drawn, at least in principle, between what I have referred to elsewhere as *theorizing* and *explaining* (Hammersley 1992). Theorizing involves identifying the causes or consequences of a *type* of object, or of variation in some property possessed by some *type* of object. It therefore relates to an open-ended range of phenomena (those belonging to the relevant type), this including those that have occurred, those that may be occurring and those that could occur, in many times and places. By contrast, I take 'explaining' to mean accounting for the occurrence and/or characteristics of some particular object, event, or feature – or some specific set of objects, events, or features – that actually occurred at, or are actually occurring in, a particular time and place.

It is worth elaborating on the differences involved here. The focus for *theorizing* is the *type* of phenomenon, or the *kind of variation*, that the theory is to account for. Interest in actual cases is entirely secondary to this: they are of concern solely in so far as they exemplify this type of phenomenon, or variation in it, in a manner that facilitates understanding, or point to ways in which a current conceptualization of it needs to be revised. In other words, for the activity of theorizing, *which* cases are of interest, and *what aspects of each case* are focused on, depends upon the theory. Furthermore, the type categories or dimensions involved may be reconstructed during the course of theorizing, and this could alter what counts and does not count as a case, and therefore what actual cases are worth investigation. The intrinsic significance of particular cases is irrelevant; indeed, those that are focused on could be of little interest in any other terms.

By contrast, in *explaining* something, using the word in the narrow sense I am employing here, our starting point is always some aspect of a particular set of phenomena (one or more) that have actually occurred or are in the process of occurring, *and that are of interest in themselves* (directly, or indirectly through their connection to something that *is* of direct interest). Of course, these phenomena can only be described using categories, and all categories are general in character; in other words, they imply multiple possible instances. The phenomena of interest may even be identified as instances of a *single* general type, though frequently we use *combinations* of general categories to try to make sense of any particular phenomenon of interest. The key point is that, in the task of explaining, the explanandum – located in the particular case or cases investigated – is the anchor. Furthermore, while it is possible that here too there may be reconceptualization, in that we may come to see the phenomenon to be explained in quite a different way from how it was understood at the start, nevertheless our primary interest continues to be in some aspect of what actually happened in that particular place at that particular time, or in particular places at particular times.[3]

There are forms of social research, albeit sometimes ones that today are regarded by many social scientists as marginal, that are *quite explicitly* directed either exclusively towards *theorizing* or exclusively towards *explaining*. A clear example of the first is experimental work concerned with developing and testing social psychological or sociological theories about processes in human groups (see, for instance, Berger et al. 1972; Hare 1976; Levine and Moreland 1990). An illustration of the second is the work of historians and some historical sociologists (see Roberts 1996; Abrams 1982) or qualitative researchers using biographical methods (Bornat 2008). However, much social science pursues both of these goals – theorizing and explaining – simultaneously, recognizing no sharp distinction between them. This is true of both quantitative and qualitative work.

Thus, a great deal of survey research is directed – in immediate, practical terms – at accounting for the occurrence of examples of some type of event that have happened within a specified population, the latter consisting of a set of cases existing during a particular period of time and usually in a particular socio-geographical region. In the terms introduced here, we would describe such research as concerned with *explaining* what happened, or what is happening, in an aggregate of actually existing cases. However, as I noted earlier, very often *theoretical* conclusions – about relations among the variables studied that are assumed to hold beyond the population concerned – are also put forward in survey research. For example, studies of social mobility usually investigate rates of mobility within samples drawn from particular cohorts, in a particular national society, during specific time periods, but they are also frequently concerned with identifying what has caused any changes in mobility within a national society over a longer time period, and what causes changes in levels of social mobility more generally in societies of the type concerned.

So, there are at least three kinds of 'generalization' that are frequently involved or implied in these studies:

- From the sample of people studied in the particular cohort to the cohort as a whole.
- From this cohort to other cohorts within the same national society before and after it. Thus, the experience of one or two cohorts in a century may be used to draw conclusions about social mobility patterns across that whole century.

---

[3]It is important to note that the time period and the socio-geographical spread of the phenomenon to be explained may be relatively small but it could be quite large: from a decision made at some specific place and time by a single person, at one extreme, to a much larger phenomenon, such as a socio-political revolution, at the other. It is also common for much social science to be concerned with aggregates of objects or events located in particular regions during particular periods.

- From evidence about what happened in a particular country over a particular time period to some theoretical conclusion; for example, about 'social mobility in industrial society'[4] or about social mobility processes even more widely.

The first two types of generalization do not go beyond the task of explaining, but the third one does. However, the distinctive character of theoretical claims is rarely addressed in this kind of work.

In short, in terms of the distinction drawn earlier, while practically speaking research on social mobility seems to be directed primarily at producing descriptions and explanations of what happened at particular times and places, theoretical conclusions are also often implied or stated as conclusions. Furthermore, the requirements for validating these are frequently not met. And this is characteristic of a great deal of non-experimental quantitative work, not just that which focuses upon social mobility (Hammersley 2012a).[5]

Much qualitative research is similarly catholic in its intended product. Very often, a single setting is investigated or a relatively small number of people are interviewed, but the conclusions drawn usually extend beyond that situation or set of people studied; even if the intended scope is not always clearly specified. Moreover, when justification for this 'generalization' of the findings is provided, it typically involves, explicitly or implicitly, an appeal to what can be referred to as theoretical inference; in other words, inference about the likely validity of some theory, rather than generalization to an extant population of cases (see Mitchell 1983; Yin 2002; though see also Schofield 1989). Much the same is true of case-based or configurational approaches like Qualitative Comparative Analysis (see Ragin 1987, and Rihoux and Ragin 2009). Here, too, there is an ambiguity about whether the goal is a theory about the types of phenomena being investigated or the use of comparative analysis to illuminate causal processes in particular cases (Hammersley and Cooper 2012). And there are serious questions about how theoretical inferences are to be justified effectively within qualitative case study work, and beyond (Hammersley et al. 2000).

A range of attitudes can be taken towards the roles of theorizing and explaining. These include:

---

[4]This is the title of an influential early study of social mobility in US sociology (Lipset and Bendix 1959) which not only seeks to document mobility patterns in the United States, but also makes broader theoretical claims, for example about 'the consequences of social mobility' for social stability (see p. 6 and Chapter 2).

[5]The views of Goldthorpe (2007) offer an illuminating illustration. While offering a sophisticated discussion of the methodology of non-experimental quantitative research, he nevertheless conflates theorizing and explaining, and in this way and others in my view greatly underestimates the methodological problems involved in the kind of research that he champions.

1. That the two tasks are, in fact, identical: to develop a sound theory about a type of outcome is itself to produce an adequate explanation for all instances of that outcome.
2. That developing and testing theories is the only appropriate task for academic social science: the production of explanations is the province of *applying* scientific knowledge, and therefore is deemed to be a separate matter.
3. That explaining and theorizing are quite different but equally legitimate tasks for social science. Indeed, it may be argued that they are interdependent: developing an explanation for what happened in a particular situation or set of cases may suggest more general theoretical ideas about what causes what; and, in turn, sound social science theories are essential as resources for producing an adequate explanation for phenomena occurring in particular places and times.
4. That explaining particular outcomes is the prime task of social science, and, while this relies upon general ideas about what usually causes what, these ideas do not always (or usually) need to be tested – in effect, they are assessed through their use in particular explanations. Nor does it always (or ever?) enhance the validity of an explanation if formal testing has been carried out.
5. That explaining particular events, outcomes, etc. occurring in particular places and times is the only task for social science, and this does not involve any reliance upon general theoretical ideas about what causes what. In other words, there is no role whatsoever for theorizing.

I am going to make a couple of assumptions at this point which narrow down these options. First, there seems to me to be no good reason for declaring the production of explanations to be outside the scope of social science or as subordinate in importance. This rules out at least the second attitude listed above. Secondly, I will assume that any explanation involves counterfactual assumptions and thereby some notion of what generally causes what. This rules out attitude five.

I suggest that choosing among the remaining options requires, above all, clarification of the nature of explanation as a research goal, in the context of social science, and this will be my focus in the remainder of the chapter.[6]

The two sides of explaining: the contextual/pragmatic and the ontological

There are two aspects to the task of explanation, as I am using that term here, and both need to be given attention. The first can be referred to as its pragmatic or contextual character. What I mean by this is that any explanation is an answer to a particular question, posed against some background, and addressed to a particular audience or set of audiences.[7] In order to understand and assess any explanation

---

[6]This chapter indicates a shift in my own thinking away from Option 3 (see Hammersley 1985) towards Option 4.

[7]In academic work some vagueness about these matters is probably unavoidable, but I have argued elsewhere that the primary initial audience should be colleagues in the relevant research community (Hammersley 2012a).

we need to be aware of these contextual features. In other words, explanations are not *simply* re-presentations of what happens in the world, of what caused what; they do not *capture* reality 'in itself', they are always answers to some question (or set of questions) *about* reality.

However – and this introduces the second aspect of the task of explaining – explanations *are* nevertheless intended to be representations of the world. In other words, social science explanations are not just fanciful or fictional answers to particular questions, they are intended to be true: to bear a relation of correspondence (in some sense) to the specific phenomena to which they refer.[8] This second, ontological, aspect of explaining indicates that the nature of the phenomena being explained, and the causal relations in which they are implicated, are of considerable importance: if we are to provide sound explanations, it is necessary to document relevant aspects of their character. I will consider each of these two aspects of the task of explaining in more detail.

The contextual character of explanations

A good place to start here is at what would conventionally be regarded as the opposite end of the spectrum from physical science: with the sorts of explanation that are produced in everyday social interaction. The contextual character of these explanations is obvious: they are given, expected, and occasionally demanded, on specific occasions, in the context of particular activities or lines of action, often in response to specific events, and normally for particular audiences and purposes. Furthermore, what is taken to count as an explanation, and as a good or adequate explanation, will depend heavily upon these contextual features.[9]

The contextual character of everyday explanations has sometimes been presented as a reason for why they are unsatisfactory in scientific terms. Thus, Mill (1843–72: 331–3) suggests that while such explanations are often appropriate for practical purposes, *scientific* explanations must identify all that is necessary and sufficient for a specified type of outcome to occur. Along the same lines, Znaniecki describes the contextual character of everyday explanations as allowing 'arbitrary and vague approximations' with which science 'cannot be satisfied' (Znaniecki 1928: 310). From this point of view, it is demanded that scientific explanations

---

[8]The conclusion, sometimes derived from Nietzsche, that the perspectival character of 'knowledge' means that all accounts are false is itself false. It would only be true if truth were restricted to accounts produced by a 'view from nowhere' (Nagel 1986), or an 'absolute conception of reality' (Williams 1978: 64–5, and *passim*). But there is no good reason to assume this. On the complexities of Nietzsche's views on truth, see Clark 1990.

[9]On the issue of everyday accounts, see Scott and Lyman 1968; Lyman and Scott 1970; Hewitt and Stokes 1974.

be 'complete', 'fundamental', or 'universal', in a way that everyday explanations are not. Above all, their form and adequacy must *not* be relative to circumstances.

However, the idea that there could be explanations that are all-purpose in character, that are complete in some absolute sense, or that capture what is fundamental from all points of view, is open to doubt. I suggest that it would be better to say that social science must provide explanations that are appropriate to *its* purposes as an activity, just as those in physics or in history should be appropriate to the requirements of *those* disciplines. However, what this means is not entirely straightforward, given the current diversity of social science, and it generates particular problems in inter-disciplinary or post-disciplinary contexts.

As already indicated, a key aspect of the pragmatic or contextual character of explanations is that they are always answers to particular questions – in other words, they are erotetic. In his book *Forms of Explanation*, Alan Garfinkel uses a well-known joke to illustrate the point:

> When Willie Sutton was in prison, a priest who was trying to reform him asked him why he robbed banks. 'Well', Sutton replies, 'that's where the money is'. (Garfinkel 1981: 21)

Garfinkel points out that it is not unusual to find that different social science inquiries claiming to investigate the same topic actually address rather different questions, much in the manner that Sutton's answer is a response to a different question from the one the priest intended. The scope for this joke is created by what Garfinkel refers to as the 'relativity of explanation'. He clarifies this idea by talking about explanatory frames. Thus, the explanatory frame behind the priest's question was as follows:

> Why does Sutton *rob* banks [rather than earning money legitimately]?

Sutton's answer operates within a different frame:

> Why does he rob *banks* [rather than robbing other sorts of establishment]?

Other writers have made the same point, using slightly different terminology (see van Fraassen 1980: 142–3; Woodward 1984; Henderson 1993 and 2002; Risjord 2000; and Khalifa 2004; Lipton 2004). For example, Lipton presents an explanation as an answer to a question 'why P rather than X?', labelling P as the 'topic' of the explanation and X as the 'foil'; whereas Henderson (2002: 335) treats the latter as indicating the contrast class. In the example from Garfinkel above, the foil or contrast is what is enclosed in square brackets. Risjord (2000: 71–2) identifies the independent components of a why-question as consisting of topic, foil(s), and a relevance criterion which specifies how an answer must differentiate between topic and foil(s). The key point from all this is that there are always many questions that could be asked about the same object, these varying with the frames, foils or contrasts employed, and what would count as an appropriate answer will necessarily differ across these.[10]

A second respect in which explanations are contextual is that, even within the same frame, *which* factors are selected as part of an explanation depends not just upon assessments of what-could-have-caused-what, but also judgments about what would count as a worthwhile answer to the question. In fact, there are potentially an infinite number of factors that could be identified as causes of any event. There will usually be several immediate factors, each of which will itself have been a product of a *complex* of factors, and the same is true for each of those factors, and so on. Moreover, there is also scope for variation in the level of abstraction in dealing with each of these factors, so that they could be formulated in different ways. For example, in principle, the rural unrest that took place in Surrey in 1649, giving rise to the Digger movement, could be formulated in terms of local groups responding to local grievances generated by a local conjuncture of trends, such as the declining fortunes of manorial tenants (Gurney 2007: 35–6), but *potentially* it could also be treated as, say, an instance of class struggle in England (see Hill 1992) – members of the lower classes reacting against medieval restrictions (for instance, against those protecting deer in grounds that were claimed to be part of Windsor forest) – or explained in other ways.[11] These types of explanation are not necessarily incompatible, but one may be selected rather than the other for particular purposes. It can be misleading when disagreements that stem from researchers' use of different explanatory frames are treated as if they were about the facts of the matter.

Equally important, in both ordinary life and historical accounts, explanations can vary in terms of whether they are synchronic or diachronic, and in their degree of elaboration. Thus, one response to the call for an explanation could be a list of factors that are treated (in effect) as having all operated simultaneously (a synchronic account). A quite different response would be to provide a story, a causal narrative, indicating what led up to the event which is to be explained – the operation of a particular *sequence* of factors – perhaps over a relatively long period of time

---

[10]Equally important, following Lipton (2004: 36–7), it is worth noting that in answering a causal question we assume that the topic to be explained involves reference to an event that actually occurred. As Russell (1990: 2) points out, this parallels Perry Mason's favourite rule of law: 'the prosecution must first prove *corpus delicti*'. Similarly, in providing an answer to a causal question, we assume that the explanatory factors we appeal to were actually present 'in the case' and that they had their normal causal generative force. This too is an assumption whose validity will often need to be checked. These apparently trivial points must be given attention. It is not unknown for explanations to be put forward for what never actually occurred, or for factors to be cited that were not actually present in the case concerned.

[11]On the historiography of explanations for the English Revolution in general, see Richardson 1977. My point here is about the *range* of types of explanation that could be offered, no assumptions are made about the validity of any particular type of explanation.

(a diachronic explanation). For example, if someone is asked how she became an agnostic, even though born into a religious family, she might say: 'I've always had a sceptical turn of mind and have tended to challenge authority'. Alternatively, she could provide a *narrative* recounting a series of biographical events (an argument with a dogmatic religious teacher, a death in the family, etc.), which eventually resulted in a loss of religious faith.

The choice between these two types of explanation also emerges in the context of academic work, exemplified, for example, by the very different explanatory strategies employed in survey analysis and much historical sociology.[12] But, as I noted earlier, the basis for making the choice is less clear here, since pragmatic situational constraints on what would be an appropriate answer do not operate in the same way. Different kinds of explanation may tend to be put forward in different fields, but there is often little clarity about the grounds for this variation. Often, practices seem simply to reflect presuppositions about how a particular discipline, or a particular approach within a discipline, is 'normally' pursued. If we could assume that the different social science disciplines were directed at genuinely distinct forms of knowledge, this might not be a problem, but it is hard to see them like that. Their character is, to a large extent, a contingent product of history, so that they take somewhat different forms at different times and in different countries.

For these reasons, there is usually considerable scope for selecting different explanatory factors in answering social science questions; and, to reiterate, this selection process cannot be based solely upon what factors actually have causal power since the set of factors of this kind is potentially infinite in extent. This is especially true if negative conditions are allowed as part of explanations, as Roberts indicates:

> In fact if one allows the *absence* of certain [factors] to be a necessary condition, then the number of conditions that must be enumerated [as possible causes] is limited only by a person's imagination. One might even insist on including the fact that a comet did not destroy the earth a moment before [the event to be explained occurred]. (Roberts 1996: 90, emphasis added; see also Mohr 1996)[13]

---

[12]However, we should note that historians often supply both kinds of explanation. They generally provide narrative or diachronic accounts, but may also offer synchronic summaries. For instance, Roberts (1996: 98–9) points out that in tracing the events that led up to the First World War, a historian is likely to note the role of nationalistic ambitions at various points, on the part of various agents, which may result in a summary explanation that emphasizes this factor. Worden (2009: 69–76), in the midst of a largely diachronic explanation of the process and outcome of 'the English civil wars', pauses to provide a more synchronic account concerned with the factors that favoured and hampered each side.

[13]Qualitative Comparative Analysis is distinctive among social science approaches in including the absence of factors as a potential cause: see Ragin 1987: 39–41.

It is important to note that their contextual nature does not render explanations arbitrary constructions: there are reasonable and unreasonable judgments to be made about what are and are not appropriate, productive, or interesting questions to ask, and about what are and are not relevant answers or explanations, as well as about what are true answers; and there will often be a great deal of agreement about what is irrelevant or unreasonable. At the same time, there is also almost always considerable room for reasonable disagreement about what a particular question is asking for, or *should be* asking for, and/or about what ought to be foregrounded and what backgrounded in answering it; as well as about what are the most important causal factors to be included in any answer. I suggest that the scope for disagreement is particularly great in social science, as against more practical contexts. In the latter, what sort of explanation is required, and how elaborated it needs to be, appears to be routinely resolved on the basis of judgments about what is appropriate to the situation; and should any mis-judgment of this occur subsequent interaction will often lead to the explanation being restructured so as to make it more appropriate.[14] By contrast, practical relevancies and constraints do not operate in academic contexts in the same way, and there are often no very well-defined, widely agreed, or clearly justified alternative requirements in place.

Given this, it is worth examining a little more closely what sorts of consideration operate in the context of everyday interaction to narrow down the field of relevant explanatory factors that can provide answers to causal questions. Frequently, the concern may be with who is to blame for some outcome, or the focus could be upon identifying causal factors which can be acted on to prevent or remedy a problem. A classic illustration of the latter focus was provided by Collingwood:

> If my car fails to climb a steep hill, and I wonder why, I shall not consider my problem solved by a passer-by who tells me that the top of a hill is farther away from the earth's centre than its bottom, and that consequently more power is needed to take a car uphill than […] along the level. All this is quite true; what the passer-by has described is one of the conditions which together form the 'real cause' […] of my car's stopping […]. But suppose [a car mechanic comes along], opens the bonnet, holds up a loose high-tension lead, and says: 'Look here, […] you're running on three cylinders'. My problem is now solved. I know the cause of the stoppage. It is the cause, just because it has not been 'arbitrarily selected'; it has been correctly identified as the thing that I can put right, after which the car will go properly. If I had been a person who could flatten out hills by stamping on them, the passer-by would have been right to call my attention to the hill as the cause of the stoppage; not because the hill was a hill but because I was able to flatten it out. (Collingwood 1940: 302–3)

---

[14]Of course, on some occasions there may be genuine disagreement about what is appropriate.

Moreover, it is not just in general everyday contexts that there are usually established considerations in operation that can provide a basis for selecting explanatory factors. The same is true in some more specialized contexts, for example in legal settings (see Hart and Honoré 1985), and legal reasoning about causation was an important model for Weber, as we shall see.

But, as I have said, it is less clear what considerations should operate to narrow down the scope of potential answers in the case of academic social science. At least, this issue cannot usually be resolved in the relatively routine and unproblematic way that it is in most everyday social interaction, where the explanation concerned is often intended to serve a specific function. Moreover, differences in assumption about these matters underpin some of the major academic disagreements that take place: the explanations being put forward by different researchers are sometimes not competing ones but are instead designed to answer different questions, or the same question under different assumptions about what should be foregrounded and what backgrounded in answering it (see, for example, Hammersley 2008b: 550). For this reason, clarity about these matters – about what question is being addressed, and what it is believed would count as a relevant and reasonable answer – is much more necessary in academic work than it usually is in everyday explanation. Yet, in fact, these matters are often neglected.

In an excellent discussion of historical explanation, Roberts (1996) identifies a number of guidelines that seem to inform historians' selection of causal factors. These correspond to some extent to those already mentioned as shaping ordinary, everyday explanations. Here, too, there may be a concern with responsibility and blame. Historians are often concerned with identifying who or what was responsible for a particular historical event, whether in the sense of who intended it, or of who brought it about through negligence, or who was in a position to and should have acted to prevent it happening. For instance, there have been recurrent historical debates along these lines about the causes of the First World War (Henig 1989; Showalter 2006). Roberts discusses some other considerations too: in particular, he notes that causes which are unusual or abnormal events in some sense are especially likely to be selected or prioritized in historical explanations (Roberts 1996: ch. 5 and *passim*).

There are a couple of conclusions that can be drawn from this discussion of the contextual character of social scientific explanations. First, as already emphasized, it is necessary for researchers to be explicit about the considerations that have shaped which question has been addressed, of the many that could have been asked about the same topic, *and* about which explanatory factors have been given attention and why. This is not always done. A second point is that, in the case of academic research, what question to address, and what explanatory factors to select as relevant, has to be determined in relatively abstract terms that relate to the current state of, and key problems in, a particular discipline, or some other epistemic enterprise. In addressing this issue, Lindesmith (1981) refers to 'the principle of limited inquiry', indicating that the aim cannot be to incorporate all of the factors that play a role in producing an outcome:

> Thus, the explanation of malaria does not include the earth's rotation on its axis as a causal factor despite the fact that the disease is spread mainly during the night and the hours of dusk. Similarly, while common sense might conclude that the atomic explosions of Nagasaki and Hiroshima were caused by political events in Washington, such an assertion makes no sense in physics. (1981: 91)

While Lindesmith refers to disciplinary perspectives here, in fact his two examples illustrate rather different principles according to which some set of causal factors is foregrounded and others backgrounded. In the case of the explanation for malaria, what is crucial is a concern with finding a means of prevention or treatment, reflecting the applied character of medical research: the rotation of the earth is irrelevant not least because we can have no control over it, in much the same way that knowing about gravity does not help in getting a car up a hill. By contrast, in the case of atomic explosions, the governing principle is not practical: it is to do with what is and is not relevant to the discipline of Physics, rather than to policy issues surrounding the deployment of atomic weapons. One way of understanding this is to say that in Physics the focus is on particular types of causal system that are central to the discipline. Of course, a question that arises as regards the social sciences is whether there are bounded causal systems within the social world that can determine the questions addressed and how they should be answered, in the manner that is apparently possible in Physics.[15] This takes us straight to the other aspect of the task of explanation mentioned earlier, the ontological.

The ontological side of explanation

The central point I want to make in this section is that all forms of explanation involve assumptions about the parts of the world to which they relate, assumptions that may be true or false. Furthermore, whether these assumptions are accurate may well have consequences for their success. In exploring the implications of this for social scientific explanation, I want to begin in the opposite way from the previous

---

[15]For an argument that these are present in physical reality but not elsewhere, see Ellis 2008 and 2009. See also Homans' (1967) argument that there are psychological but not social laws. Mill (1843–72) seems to have taken a similar view. Note that it might be argued that systems *are* available in the phenomena with which much medical research deals, but that nevertheless these systems do not set the terms for medical research, since their boundaries are not isomorphic with the focus demanded by the pragmatic concern with finding a cure or a preventative measure. This means that even if there were causal systems in the social world, they might not be the best basis for setting our questions and framing our answers. This is the stance that Weber adopts.

section: in other words, with the natural science model. While there is considerable dispute about the nature of explanations or theories in the natural sciences, an influential view has long been that they involve the identification of a set of necessary and jointly sufficient conditions. Another way of formulating this, already hinted at, is to say that they assume the existence of closed or semi-closed causal systems.[16]

Where such systems operate there may be no difference between theorizing and explaining: to explain any particular outcome we could simply identify the particular *type* of causal system that produces this *type* of outcome. Thus, the problems surrounding the contextual character of explanation – namely, how to determine which questions to ask and which potential causal factors to treat as relevant to any answer – would be solved by ontology: it could be argued that only those questions about what caused what can be answered that correspond to an operating causal system, and the task would then be to discover whether any particular question falls into this category:

> If it does *not* fall into that category, then it is a false question.

> If it *does* fall into this category, then the task is to investigate the nature of the corresponding system, and the factors that must be included in the explanation are simply the key components of this system.

A classic example of a closed or semi-closed system in this context is a moving spherical object on a flat plane (for example, a ball on a billiard table) hitting another object of the same type; here, the effect can be inferred (to a large extent) from the fixed characteristics of the type of object concerned and its environment. With some natural systems of this kind, the pattern of relationships involved is discoverable via uncontrolled observation. The standard case here is the solar system: the movements of the planets can be observed to be regular, and we can explain these very largely in terms of a relatively small number of factors, primarily the gravitational pulls associated with the sun and the planets themselves. However, causal systems that can be detected by uncontrolled observation seem to be relatively rare even in the physical world. So, generally speaking, natural science relies upon experimentation to exercise

---

[16]A further alternative formulation could be in terms of natural kinds. Note that there is an important sense in which the treatment of the physical world, as made up of standard and eternal types of object involved in fixed relationships, may probably misleading if we adopt a very long-term perspective: the physics of the Big Bang are probably very different from the kind of physics we need to understand the universe today. This is an idea that was central to Peirce's philosophical system: he argued that 'Nature may [...] change, even in its most entrenched fundamentals. Thus, even if scientists were at one point in time to have conceptions and hypotheses about nature that survived every attempt to falsify them, this fact alone would not ensure that at some later point in time these same conceptions and hypotheses would remain accurate or even pertinent' (Burch 2010). Nevertheless, differences in *degree* of stability can be very significant in epistemological terms.

physical control over causal factors so as to reveal causal systems that would not otherwise be easily or rigorously identifiable.

It is important to note that successful experimentation depends not only upon it being practically feasible to isolate the operation of the relevant set of factors from those that obscure the relationship, but also involves the requirement that a relatively small set of factors *actually does* largely determine the relevant type of outcome. As already noted, natural scientists do not assume that there is a causal system operating in relation to all of the categories that could be used to conceptualize physical phenomena; to the contrary, a central part of the task of science is precisely to *discover* outcome conceptualizations that capture the products of causal systems. Initial ideas may need to be reformulated until they come to represent the typical outcome of a particular type of causal system. This process of reformulation often involves movement away not just from commonsense categories – for example, 'water' no longer means what we take it to mean in everyday life, becoming instead a liquid with the chemical composition H_2O – but also from human relevancies and interests. This has implications for the subsequent use of scientific findings: 'translation' back into practical, everyday terms will often be required, and may not always be straightforward.[17]

This form of explanation, with its underlying assumptions about causal systems, has often underpinned the thinking of social scientists, even when they have recognized that it is an ideal they cannot closely approximate. Experimental research in social psychology, sociology, social policy, and economics generally adopts this model explicitly, and applies it relatively directly. Interestingly, this conception of explanation also formed the basis for an influential critique of 'statistical method' within sociology in the first half of the twentieth century. Proponents of 'analytic induction', notably Znaniecki (1934) and Lindesmith (1947), criticized statistical analysis because it did not set out to identify causal systems but was preoccupied instead with measuring the relative contributions of a collection of factors to the *likely* occurrence, or intensity, of some pre-defined outcome (see Chapter 1). Analytic induction is specifically founded upon the idea that naturally occurring semi-closed causal systems can be discovered in the social world, and that these are the proper basis for social psychological and sociological theories.[18]

---

[17]There is an important qualification that needs to be made here: all causal systems operate on the basis of background conditions, and any (necessarily futile) attempt at a complete explanation would have to include all of these (Mackie 1974). Of course, some of what are taken as background factors at one particular time may previously have been important for the operation of the system, and some that are not currently treated as important may come to be regarded as important in the future. However, in relation to physical causation, there will be many factors that are always treated as part of the 'normal' background, and therefore as not in need of attention.

[18]On analytic induction, see Hammersley 1989: ch. 7 and 8, and Hammersley and Cooper 2012.

Znaniecki's critique was, and is, correct in claiming that much non-experimental quantitative work in the social sciences is designed to determine the relative contributions that various factors make to the likelihood of a given type of outcome or to the level of this outcome variable, employing one or another mode of correlational analysis to do this. Involved here is a 'weaker' conception of causation than that involved in the natural science model adopted by experimentalists and early advocates of analytic induction, since here the contributory factors need be neither necessary nor jointly sufficient. The focus, instead, is on the degree to which the presence of a particular factor, or its operating at a particular level, increases the probability of a particular type of outcome, or level of outcome, across a specified aggregate of cases.[19]

Interestingly, much *qualitative* social science also relies upon a comparatively 'weak' conception of causation, and indeed often employs an approach that is rather similar in form to the non-experimental quantitative approach just outlined, even though it does not employ statistical techniques. Thus, while there is rarely any attempt to *measure* the degree to which a factor contributes to the likelihood or intensity of an outcome, judgments are nevertheless often made about what the major factors are that tend to produce a type of outcome (see Hammersley 2012b). By contrast, analytic induction is rarely employed by qualitative researchers today; nor do the assumptions about the operation of semi-closed causal systems associated with its early champions even seem to be adopted by more recent supporters of this approach (see, for example, Becker 1994 and 1998; Hammersley 2008a: ch. 4).

One reason for most social scientists' reliance upon models of explanation that involve weaker assumptions about causal processes is, of course, the difficulty or impossibility of using experimental method in studying many social topics, for both practical and ethical reasons.[20] However, it has also frequently been argued, especially by qualitative researchers, that there is a deeper problem – to do with the open and contingent character of human action (see, for example, Blumer 1969; Hammersley 1989 and 2008a: ch. 2; see also Bhaskar 1978). In other words, it is suggested that the very nature of the social world rules out the possibility or value of experimentation. The argument here may be that a form of 'soft' rather than 'hard' determinism operates (Matza 1964) or that the concept of causality cannot be applied to the social world at all (see Chapter 1).

Very often, these arguments have involved something like the archaic contrast between nature, on the one hand, and a semi-divine humanity, on the other, so that human beings are seen as, at most, only partially subordinate to causal laws and therefore as having freedom and responsibility. However, the point need not be formulated in this anti-naturalistic fashion (see Dennett 2003). Instead, it can be proposed that human beings form part of a natural world that displays a

---

[19]Whether this can be done successfully, and if so how, is open to dispute. See Turner 1948 and Hammersley 2012a for a discussion of some of the problems.

[20]Of course, these difficulties also occur in some areas of natural science.

variety of sorts of causal relation, and that, in many areas, there are few, if any, underlying closed or even semi-closed systems operating – in other words, there are few, if any, outcome types that are controlled in a regular fashion by a small set of factors. Instead, it may be argued, we have much more complex processes in various respects. Relevant alternative conceptions from other scientific fields that have been drawn on to make this point include the 'teleological' causation involved in plant growth (Waddington 1977) and complexity theory (Byrne 1998). The key point, though, is that if, on either anti-naturalistic or naturalistic grounds, we accept that in the case of human social action there is an important degree of openness and therefore indeterminacy involved, this does not make explanation impossible, but it does mean that it will not conform to the model of natural science explanation I outlined earlier, in which theorizing and explaining amount to the same activity; a model which seems to guide a great deal of social science whether or not it recognizes its failure to meet the requirements involved.

Interim conclusion

Once we move away from theories concerned with identifying necessary and jointly sufficient conditions, the importance of the distinction I drew earlier between theorizing and explaining re-emerges, and it becomes necessary for any study to make clear which task is being tackled. More than this, though, questions may arise about whether theories are the most desirable product of social scientific work or indeed about whether theorizing is possible in social science: do the many explanatory ideas that social scientists typically draw on need to be systematically developed and tested as scientific theories? Can they be?

If causal processes in the social world are of a weaker kind than the natural science model assumes, involving considerable contingency and uncertainty, including that stemming from agents' decisions, then it is not clear that the ontological preconditions for theorizing exist. This means not only that testing theoretical hypotheses would be difficult (even aside from ethical and practical restrictions), but also that, even if they can be tested, theories that survive falsification will not necessarily serve us any better than those that have *not* been tested, or perhaps even than those that have apparently been falsified. The proper conclusion from all this may be that the explanatory ideas on which social scientists rely should be seen as, at best, only plausible and potentially useful causal narratives, whose applicability in particular cases should always be assessed. In other words, they do not have validity in any general sense beyond their being functional in particular explanations.[21]

---

[21]This might be seen as fitting into the long tradition of treating the status of theories as instrumental or even fictional: see, for example, Vaihinger 1923 and van Fraassen 1980. However, my position here is still a form of ontological realism: it asserts that causal processes *do* operate in the world, even if not in the form of closed systems. At the

In terms of the five options I outlined earlier, this suggests that the fourth one is correct: that explanation, not theorizing, is the exclusive task of social science, and that the theoretical ideas employed in this do not need testing, though there is certainly a role for careful conceptual clarification and for their development into explicit models, with comparative analysis playing an important role in this. Whether this is the correct answer to the problem remains to be seen. However, it is quite close to the position developed by Max Weber in his methodological writings (Weber 1949; see Turner and Factor 1994; Ringer 1997; Agevall 1999; Eliaeson 2002; Bruun and Whimster 2012). Furthermore, given the contextual character of explanations, Weber may also be right that social science explanations must be framed within value-relevance frameworks (Hammersley 2011a, see ch. 8 and 9). In terms of the two principles of limitation that I extracted from Lindesmith's discussion, this would imply that social science is closer to medical research than to Physics. However, by contrast with medical research, the 'relativity' of explanations, as regards relevance not truth, would need to be given much more explicit recognition in social science. This is because, at face value at least, the appropriate framing of the topics investigated, and of what answers would be relevant, is likely to be much more open to disagreement in the broader social field, since a *range* of (potentially conflicting) practical values is involved, not just health.[22] Furthermore, if the argument presented here is correct, the explanatory ideas on which social scientists must rely are very different in epistemic status from those used by medical researchers, most of the time.

So, there are good reasons to doubt the operation of even semi-closed systems in the social world. Moreover, even if there were such systems, without the capacity to engage in experimentation it might be very difficult, if not impossible, to detect them. Also, as with the case of medical research, these would not guarantee to provide us with findings that have socio-political relevance. So, how to proceed? I suggest that Weber's methodological writings provide useful guidance.

Weber to the rescue?

Weber's methodological writings, as well as his substantive research, took place against the background of a considerable body of nineteenth-century German scholarship in the socio-historical sciences concerned with the origins and development of social, political and economic institutions (see Turner and Factor 1994;

---

same time, while what I am proposing has some affinity with those approaches, whether influenced by 'critical realism' or 'analytical sociology', which are concerned with identifying stable generative mechanisms (see Bhaskar 1978; Hedström and Swedberg 1998), it differs from them in questioning the generic character of such mechanisms.

[22]Health is, of course, a complex value, one that shades into 'quality of life', thereby generating some scope for discrepant value frameworks even within medical research.

Agevall 1999). Some of this had been stimulated by the practical legal and political tasks arising, first of all, in the aftermath of Napoleonic control of Prussia and
other German states, and then in the unification of Germany; which involved
drawing on Roman Law to coordinate and develop standard institutional forms
and practices across what were previously independent German states with very
different traditions. Particularly significant for Weber's work was the emergence
of a historical approach to economics alongside the historical approach to law
characteristic of Savigny and others, and the flowering of German historiography
more generally.

There were two major crises in the field of economics that significantly shaped
Weber's work. One was the *Methodenstreit*, or 'battle of the methods', between representatives of German historical economics, notably Schmoller, and the Austrian
school, led by Menger, who had developed marginalist theory (see Agevall 1999:
61–9). Weber was trained as a lawyer and legal scholar but he had a particular
interest in the study of economic institutions; the links between legal, economic
and political scholarship were, in any case, strong in Germany at the time. While
his approach was primarily influenced by the German historical school, he had
some sympathy for the arguments of Menger, and in effect his work mediated
between the two approaches.[23]

German historical economics rejected the concern of British classical economists
with identifying abstract laws that apply at all times and places, for example about
supply and demand – along with the laissez-faire and free trade policies that were
taken to derive from this approach. At the same time, much German nineteenth-
century scholarship in this field *was* concerned with identifying *historical* laws,
about the development of economic and social institutions, which were claimed
to be analogous to those of natural science. Weber argued that this position
involved a fundamental methodological inconsistency. He applied the ideas of
neo-Kantian philosophers, notably Rickert, who distinguished between the nomothetic or generalizing method employed by natural scientists, in which the aim is
to identify universal laws, and the idiographic or individualizing method appropriate to the socio-historical sciences – where the task is to describe and explain
specific socio-historical events, processes and structures, their development and
change, taking account of distinctive local circumstances.[24] Weber insisted that
social science must focus on explaining individual, socially located phenomena
rather than seeking nomothetic laws, not least because it is such knowledge that
is of direct socio-political relevance. So, while he followed Menger in seeing an
important role for theory, he believed that this must take the form of developing

---

[23]What was involved in this mediation is by no means straightforward, as Agevall (1999:
ch. 5) makes clear. He took some elements and rejected others from both sides, creating
a novel methodological position. See also Eliaeson 2002.

[24]The distinction I have employed between theorizing and explaining derives from this.

ideal types, rather than the specification and testing of laws. Ideal types were to serve as techniques that could be used to identify relevant singular causal relations operating in the situations being studied. So, for Weber, the task of causal explanation is not a matter of trying to capture what are the essential and universal determinants of some type of outcome, or of producing a complete explanation for the occurrence of some particular outcome (in the manner proposed, for example, by Mill). Rather, the focus is on the identification of singular and value-relevant causal relations that explain what occurred in particular places at particular times.

Weber did not rule out the possibility that there are semi-closed, universally operating, causal systems in the social world, but, in line with other neo-Kantians, he argued that, even if these exist, the development of knowledge about the laws governing them would not provide the kind of understanding demanded by our practical interest in the social world, since that interest necessarily involves a primary concern with phenomena in their individuality rather than their generic character (Ciaffa 1998: 51–3).[25] As a result, Weber explicitly addressed the issues arising from what I have called the contextual character of explanation, and the question of how causal relations are to be identified. I will discuss these two aspects of his methodological work separately.

Framing explanations

The other crisis within economics around this time, in addition to the *Methodenstreit*, was the *Werturteilsstreit*. This was concerned with the role of values in social science, and Weber played a central part in it. There was a strong tendency within some sections of the historical school to treat values in teleological terms, as intrinsic to particular institutions, notably the state. While Hegel's meta-narrative about the dialectical realization of human ideals over the course of history, and the role of the State in this, was generally rejected, Ranke and other German historians and social scientists nevertheless treated nation-states as embodying particular cultural

---

[25]It is perhaps of some significance that Menger (1985) distinguishes between theoretical, historical, and practical sciences, all three orientations being found within the field of economics, and playing their own specific roles. It seems likely that Weber saw his work as falling into the third category, on analogy with the role of legal scholarship (see Weber 1949: 42), although he would perhaps have drawn no distinction between this category and that of the historical sciences. Of course, a concern with individual phenomena is not restricted to the social sciences: in applied science and technology the primary focus – for example, why did the bridge collapse? – may well take the form of explaining rather than theorizing, in the terms I am using in this chapter. Here, too, the selection of relevant causal factors will not be determined by the boundaries of some causal system but will take place on the basis of the sorts of criteria mentioned earlier: likely responsibility, avoidance of a similar problem in the future, what normally occurs, etc. As already noted, medical research could be another example of a practical science in this sense.

ideals, and as being engaged in a struggle with one another for the supremacy of those principles.[26] Similarly, much German economic analysis treated institutions as involving the teleological realization of particular ideals. Here, in effect, a kind of evolutionary functionalism prevailed, whereby institutions were seen as developing in ways that met functional requirements, but with a crucial role for the State in facilitating this.[27] Thus there was taken to be a direct inferential route from analysis to policy recommendations. It was in this way that those working in the German historical tradition 'resolved' the issue of what questions social science should ask and how they should be answered: if it can be assumed that, for example, the state embodies a particular ideal, then that ideal can be used as a criterion for determining which questions are important to address in socio-political analysis, and what would be relevant answers to them.

Weber and others challenged this infusion of values into social science: they declared that no value conclusions can be derived exclusively from facts about the nature or development of social institutions. And they insisted that, given this, in their research and teaching, social scientists must strive to be neutral in relation to practical values. Indeed, much of Weber's later substantive work can be interpreted as an attempt to reconstruct previous accounts of the development of social institutions in the West in non-teleological terms (Turner and Factor 1994). So for Weber, social science had to aim at being value-neutral: it should not treat values as built into the nature of the world in such a way that their validity could be regarded as a matter of fact; it should restrict itself to factual conclusions; and it should seek to minimize any bias coming from the value commitments of the researcher. However, at the same time he argued that it had to be guided by assumptions about *value-relevance*. In other words, value principles must be used to identify the phenomena to be investigated and to provide the framework within which explaining why they have the forms that they do, and/or for identifying their consequences, takes place. In this approach, value-relevance frameworks are a way of dealing with the infinite plurality of potential causes and potential consequences that exists: only those that are of significance from the point of view of some particular value-relevance framework, adopted for working purposes in a particular study, are selected for attention. In other words, these frameworks determine what questions should be asked and what would count as relevant answers; and different studies may well adopt different frameworks.

---

[26]As a politician, Weber shared this perspective. As summarized by Baehr and Wells (2002: xii), he believed that: '[…] the future promised a ceaseless global struggle over material resources and alternative modes of life. Only the most industrially competitive, politically dynamic, and assiduously hardheaded nations had a chance of becoming – or remaining – great powers and great cultures'.

[27]See Turner and Factor's (1994: ch. 3 and *passim*) discussion of the work of Ihering, which they treat as having been a very important influence on Weber.

It is necessary to recognize the radical implications of Weber's views here. He argues that the social phenomena investigated by social scientists and historians are not well-defined objects that already exist prior to investigation, in the way that, say, different kinds of rock exist independently of the process of geological study. Rather, these phenomena – for example, the French Revolution, modern capitalism, industrialization, secularization, etc. – are *constituted* through the analyst's use of value-relevance categories. In addition, cultural categories will have been employed by the people actually involved in the events being studied, thereby shaping those events. Weber notes that these will have been present 'in the minds of the persons living in that epoch as an ideal to be striven for in practical life or as a maxim for the regulation of certain relationships' (Weber 1949: 95; Rogers 1969: 22). While such ideals and norms are clearly of great significance in understanding the events concerned, Weber insists that the historian and social scientist may employ other value-relevant categories as well, ones that reflect later concerns. As a result, social scientists may select and formulate events in different ways from those of participants, though the latter's categories cannot simply be ignored – they may be an important factor in shaping what was done and what resulted.[28]

It is worth trying to illustrate what is involved here. If, for example, we are interested in explaining some aspect of the English civil war (or, it may be better to say, civil wars) in the early seventeenth century, there are several events that we would immediately recognize as forming part of this phenomenon, such as the raising of an army by Parliament or the execution of the King. But there are many others whose links to these, and to the notion of a civil war, are more uncertain, for instance the prayer book riots in Edinburgh during 1637. Indeed, there is scope for disagreement even about exactly when the civil war(s) started and ended. There are also, of course, questions about how we should conceptualize the whole phenomenon, and these are signalled by differences in the labels used to characterize this set of events. Using the phrase 'civil war' tends to make military matters the central feature. By contrast, to talk of the 'English Revolution' gives a rather different slant, and also redefines somewhat the boundaries of what would be relevant events. Even here there can be further variation, depending, for example, upon whether a

---

[28]Of course, past events are constructed and reconstructed in collective memory in various ways. The work of historians and social scientists simply represents a distinctive form of this. The epistemological position underpinning Weber's approach here is constructivist in a Kantian or neo-Kantian sense: phenomena are always at least partly a product of mind. However, it is not clear whether Weber adopted the radical constructivism of some neo-Kantians, whereby the material worked on plays no role in shaping the outcome, or where it is assumed that no such material exists: see Friedman 2000 and Gordon 2010. For a sophisticated Kantian approach to this issue that is also realist, see Code 1987. There is an interesting parallel in this respect with Durkheim, see Turner 1995.

Marxist or some other conception of revolution is adopted. It is also possible to see these events as a 'Puritan Revolution', emphasizing the religious dimension, and this would constitute them in a different way again.[29]

So, there is much scope for disagreement about the identification and conceptualization of historical phenomena, and much the same is true of the social phenomena that are likely to be the focus of social scientific study. Moreover, the tasks of identification and conceptualization are often intimately linked to ideas about how the phenomena, or aspects of them, can be explained. But the key point here is that this is not the only type of consideration that shapes and should guide these processes – also involved are questions of value-relevance. The crucial point that Weber makes is that there are always alternative value-relevance frameworks within which any field of events can be defined and understood. And that this will significantly affect the explanations produced.[30]

So, in the terms introduced earlier, value-relevance frameworks determine both what questions are to be asked about the events and what would and would not count as relevant explanatory factors – in other words, as answers to those questions. To elaborate, if we are interested in the English Civil War, we might be concerned with explaining any or many of the following things: why the disputes which led to it occurred (for example, over the rights of the King as against those of Parliament), why they turned into war rather than being resolved in other ways, why the two (or more) sides formed up in the way that they did, why the outbreak of war occurred when it did rather than earlier or later, why a civil war occurred in Britain at this time but not in France or some other country, and so on. As regards the identification of explanatory factors, there is a huge range of these that have been discussed by historians, whose relevance and importance varies according to which of the questions just outlined are being addressed; but also, more broadly, according to what value-relevance framework has been adopted. For Weber, the appropriate value-relevance framework for his own substantive work was shaped by a relatively coherent set of concerns that were central to German politics at the time he lived. But Weber writes: 'Inasmuch as the "points of view" from which they can become significant for us are very diverse, the most varied criteria can be

---

[29]On the issue of the different names for these events, and their implications, and for an excellent account of the events themselves, see Worden 2009: 1–2 and *passim*. On different interpretations of the English Revolution, see Richardson 1977. For a more recent study that examines changing views of Cromwell, see Worden 2002. There are those who have been accused of denying that any great change happened in these years in social terms, notably Laslett 1971.

[30]But, it must be insisted, the differences in approach that arise do not derive *solely* from this. I am not denying the significance of what caused what, or of the more subtle aspects of this: what was necessary, what increased the likelihood of a particular type of event happening, what combination or sequence of factors seems to have had causal power, and so on. All this goes back to my discussion in the first half of this chapter.

applied to the selection of the traits which are to enter into the construction of an ideal-typical view of a particular culture' (Weber 1949: 91; Rogers 1969: 18–19). He recognized that in other times other questions, and other answers to the 'same' question, would be relevant.

From Weber's perspective, then, what I referred to earlier, following Lindesmith, as 'the principle of limited inquiry' should be applied *in social science* by the adoption of value-relevance frameworks, rather than by attempting to identify closed causal systems. This is the respect in which social science is closer in character to legal or medical research than to Physics. This raises questions, of course, about the distinctive character of the various social science disciplines. There does not seem to be any obvious relationship between specific value-relevance frameworks and particular disciplines. Weber notes the distinctive set of concerns that guides economics, or at least theoretical economics (and even this has varied – see Hutchison 1964), but it is much less clear that each of the other social sciences is associated with a single distinctive value-relevance framework. Indeed, value-relevance seems likely to cut across disciplines, as currently constituted – in other words, to demand *inter*-disciplinary investigation.

At least in principle, Weber's notion of value-relevance serves as a potential solution to the problems arising from what I have called the contextual or pragmatic character of social scientific explanation. We should note, though, that it leaves important questions unresolved. In particular: how should social scientists decide which value-relevance framework to adopt for any particular study? Should this be a matter of personal commitment, of adopting the dominant viewpoint (if there is one) within a discipline or within the surrounding society, or of taking over the preferences of research funders or other stakeholders? More fundamentally, does determining these matters come under the professional responsibility of the researcher, or can and should they be decided by others, for example through some democratic process or by the market? Crucial here is how the role of researcher is to be defined – for example the extent to which, and ways in which, it should take a professional form.[31]

Identifying causal relations

Weber also provides us with a way of trying to deal with problems arising from what I called the ontological aspect of social science explanation. The issue here is: if we cannot employ experimental methods, for practical and ethical reasons and/ or because there are no closed causal systems at the social level, how are we to, or indeed can we, determine what caused what in a way that meets the requirements

---

[31]For an attempt to characterize and justify the character of academic social science in these terms, see Hammersley 2011a.

of science, or of any reasonably rigorous form of inquiry? Even if, like Weber, we are primarily interested in explaining, rather than theorizing, there is still the problem that candidate explanations rely upon counterfactual assumptions. How are we to determine which of these are true and which false?

In focusing on identifying singular causal relations rather than on discovering causal laws, Weber is in line with the orientation of most historians and, *in practice*, most social scientists engaged in non-experimental quantitative and qualitative social science as well. Thus, for Weber a cause was not 'a sufficient condition for the occurrence of the effect; [but rather] a factor that, in conjunction with background conditions, is comparatively likely and thus "adequate" to bring about the outcome, rather than other possible alternatives' (Ringer 1997: 3–4). In other words, starting with some set of conditions that might be thought of as bringing about the outcome, we can treat one of these as an adequate cause if without it the probability is that the outcome would not have occurred, or its presence made the outcome much more likely to occur. The focus, then, is on 'adequate causation', and adequate causes are to be identified by making assessments concerning the 'objective possibility' or probability of a particular factor producing the outcome, a factor that has been identified as value relevant. Primary reliance is placed here on thought experiments, though Weber also saw comparative analysis as playing an important role (Turner and Factor 1994: 129–30).[32]

Turner and Factor and others have shown how Weber's thinking about causation came out of the legal tradition in which he had been trained. He saw a direct correspondence between the two fields. In determining legal responsibility, and therefore liability, we need to identify the factors that contributed to the occurrence of some event, and (against this background) to weigh up the contribution

---

[32]For a detailed discussion of Weber's approach, see Heidelberger 2010. Thought experiments and fictions are, of course, used in physical science (Sorenson 1992; Suarez 2009). They involve the manipulation of what is known from past experience in order to clarify and test the plausibility of various possible explanatory factors: concocting counter-examples to definitions and laws, expanding the domain of explanatory ideas to explore their implications, developing metaphors and analogies, imagining some things as absent to see what difference it might make, and so on. This is very much in line with what Weber says about the development of ideal types, as regards abstraction, exaggeration and stylization. The sort of thinking that comes under the heading of thought experiment occurs, and must occur, throughout all stages of the research process, including when new data are being analysed. The assessment of hypotheses must involve judgments about plausibility: about how well the new data fit or do not fit with our existing interpretations and with our general experience. If it does not fit, this is not grounds for rejecting the new data and the inferences we have drawn from them of course, but neither is it grounds for simply jettisoning the explanatory ideas from past experience that seem to be at odds with the data. We need more evidence, and we need to think about what could be wrong with the data or with our explanatory ideas or with our interpretations of past experience that have led to the conflict. In short, thought experiment blends into the use of new data in important ways (see Chapter 1).

of the defendant's act to the outcome. Weber uses this as a model for how the historian should approach causation. In other words, he treats the task of historians and social scientists in identifying whether some value-relevant cause seems likely to have produced the outcome they are seeking to explain as analogous to the task of a court in trying to determine an agent's responsibility for some offence (Turner and Factor 1994: 124).[33]

His ideas here are derived to a large extent from those of the physiologist von Kries, who had turned from his own field to the issue of identifying causes in legal deliberations; although Weber also draws on various other legal theorists, notably Radbruch (see Heidelberger 2010). Von Kries challenged the dominant legal theory of causation within German jurisprudence at the time. According to this theory, 'responsibility attached to those actions that were necessary conditions of a harmful result' (Turner and Factor 1994: 126). He sought to remedy a key problem with this approach: that it extended liability too widely and resulted in various *ad hoc* devices being used to reduce its scope. The crucial concept offered by von Kries, designed to replace these devices, was 'objective possibility': the aim was to rule out those actions where the odds of their producing the result were absurdly low. In other words, a certain degree of probability – 'adequate causation' – had to be reached before liability could be ascribed.[34] Use of the concept of 'probability' here did not imply that 'objective possibility' was to be determined on the basis of data about statistical regularities in some relevant population. Rather, according to Weber, it was based upon 'nomological knowledge'. Weber does not spell out what this means but the term generally refers to conceptions of physical, logical, or even customary laws or law-like patterns. In these terms, he insists that ideal types must be 'objectively possible', in other words 'plausibly motivated', which he also formulates as '*adequate* from the nomological standpoint' (Weber 1949: 92).

This seems to be what he refers to elsewhere as 'adequacy at the level of meaning', for example identifying patterns of action that are intelligible in the sense that either we can see that they are likely to follow from commitment to a particular goal or that they exemplify a particular value commitment and would (other things being equal) be carried out by anyone with that commitment.[35] Weber does not regard such ideal types as hypotheses in themselves, but rather as templates for the construction of hypotheses, both supplying potential explanations and

---

[33]He specifies that this is in terms of civil rather than criminal legal liability: see Turner and Factor 1994: 187–8, note 5.

[34]On the relationship between probability and objective possibility, see Agevall 1999: ch. 7. These terms seem to be used interchangeably in this tradition.

[35]This brings the notion of 'adequacy at the level of cause' close to 'adequacy at the level of meaning' (see Eliaeson 2002; see also Runciman 1972), whereas in the past this distinction has often been treated as the fulcrum upon which radically different interpretations of Weber have hinged.

also allowing us to identify deviations from what would rationally be expected in terms of a particular ideal type, that are caused by other factors. Ideal types are necessarily no more than approximations to reality, because of the complexity and mixed motivation of most human action, and their aim is not to capture reality in its complexity, but rather to provide a means of identifying particular value-relevant causal relations.

Given this 'interpretative' stance, what seems to provide the general component in social scientific explanation for Weber are not causal laws that have been systematically tested, but ideal types that take the form of rational models about what people with particular types of commitment or goal in particular types of situation are likely to believe, feel, and do. These models are constructed on the basis of background personal experience as well as through socio-historical investigation – of the phenomenon to be explained and of others that might be relevantly similar and different. However, their construction also involves the refinement of this experience through careful abstraction, thought experiment, and systematic conceptual analysis.[36]

Weber sees the construction of ideal types as an essential part of the process of generating explanations. He takes as his key model here the abstract concepts used by economists, such as the theory of marginal utility.[37] He describes these concepts as offering us:

> An ideal [i.e. an idealized] picture of events on the commodity-market under conditions of a society organized on the principles of an exchange economy, free competition and rigorously rational conduct. This conceptual pattern brings together certain relationships and events of historical life into a complex, which is conceived as an internally consistent system. Substantively, this construct in itself is like a *utopia* which has been arrived at by the analytical accentuation of certain elements of reality. Its relationship to the empirical data consists solely in the fact that where market-conditioned relationships of the type referred to by the abstract construct are discovered or suspected to exist in reality to some extent, we can make the *characteristic* features of this

---

[36]This argument was used in the immediate literature on which Weber drew in German historical economics, notably that of Roscher: see Agevall 1999: 51. The justification for reliance upon such ideal types is presumably along the lines of Vico's and Dilthey's argument that in studying human beings we have sources of knowledge that are not available in studying physical objects, and that this can compensate to some degree at least for the unavailability of experimental control.

[37]The epistemological or methodological status of 'economic laws' has long been a matter of dispute within economics, see Blaug 1992: ch. 3. It is also worth pointing out that Weber did not see himself as putting forward some new method here but rather as analysing or explicating what historians and social scientists have previously and necessarily done, albeit often imperfectly, with a view to identifying how they could improve their work; namely, by rendering the concepts on which they rely more internally consistent and more explicit, and perhaps also by being clearer about why one set of concepts has been employed rather than another.

relationship pragmatically *clear* and *understandable* by reference to an ideal-type. This procedure can be indispensable for heuristic as well as expository purposes. The ideal typical concept will help to develop our imputational skill in *research*: it is no '*hypothesis*' but it offers guidance to the construction of hypotheses. It is not a *description* of reality but it aims to give an unambiguous means of expression to such a description. (Weber 1949: 89–90; Rogers 1969: 17; Bruun and Whimster 2012: 124–5)[38]

Weber elaborates on the construction of ideal types by taking a contrasting example to that characteristic of contemporary economic theory: the medieval 'city economy'. He writes that this concept is not formed as:

an average of the economic structures actually existing in all the cities observed but as an ideal type. An ideal type is formed by the one-sided accentuation of one or more points of view and by the synthesis of a great many diffuse, discrete, more or less present and occasionally absent concrete individual phenomena, which are arranged according to those one-sidedly emphasized viewpoints into a unified analytical construct. (Weber 1949: 90; Rogers 1969: 17; Bruun and Whimster 2012: 125)

What seems to be involved here is an imaginative reconstruction, in terms of what would seem rational for people in the circumstances, given certain assumptions about their goals, interests, perceptions, etc. But this must be done on the basis of considerable knowledge of examples that approximate more or less closely to the type. So the task of the analyst in constructing ideal types is to identify what it can reasonably be expected that people would believe, feel, and do, given certain assumptions about them. This is the point where *Verstehen* plays its role.[39]

It is important to recognize that multiple ideal types could be used to examine the same patterns of behaviour. Even in the case of *homo economicus*, Weber insists that:

it is possible, or rather it must be accepted as certain, that numerous, indeed a very great many, utopias of this sort can be worked out, of which *none* is like another, and *none* of which can be observed in empirical reality as an actually existing economic system, but *each* of which however claims that it is a representation of the 'idea' of capitalistic culture. (Weber 1949: 91; Rogers 1969: 18; Bruun and Whimster 2012: 125)

---

[38]I have used the translation appearing in Rogers 1969, which seems to involve some slight modification from that appearing in Weber 1949, because this seems to me to be the most easily understandable. I have included references to both these sources, and to the more recent translation by Bruun and Whimster 2012, which probably represents what Weber actually wrote more closely.

[39]Eliaeson (2000) argues that what Weber meant by *Verstehen* was not empathetic understanding, but rational understanding in terms of means–ends schemas, as represented in ideal types. However, I suspect that it went beyond this to include relevant cultural knowledge.

What seems to be driving Weber's argument here is not simply the neo-Kantian idea that all study involves selection and formulation of material, but the ontological assumption that the sheer complexity of human social relations, at least when viewed as individual social phenomena in the way that our value interests demand, makes any attempt to grasp them 'as they are' impossible. At one point he writes that:

> those 'ideas' which govern the behavior of the population of a certain epoch i.e. which are concretely influential in determining their conduct, can, if a somewhat complicated construct is involved, be formulated precisely only in the form of an ideal type, since empirically it exists in the minds of an indefinite and constantly changing mass of individuals and assumes in their minds the most multifarious nuances of form and content, clarity and meaning. Those elements of the spiritual life of the individuals living in a certain epoch of the Middle Ages, for example, which we may designate as the 'Christianity' of those individuals, would, if they could be completely portrayed, naturally constitute a chaos of infinitely differentiated and highly contradictory complexes of ideas and feelings. (Weber 1949: 95–6; Rogers 1969: 23; Bruun and Whimster 2012: 128)

Weber believed that both thought experiments and comparative analysis could assist us in the construction of ideal types, and also in using these to develop hypotheses to account for particular concrete events. Furthermore, what is involved here, in part, is a matter of engaging in counterfactual inference to assess the likelihood that a particular set of factors played a significant causal role in bringing about the outcome. Weber writes:

> Our real problem is [...]: by which logical [i.e. scientific] operations do we acquire the insight and how can we demonstratively establish that such a causal relationship exists between those 'essential' components of the effects and certain components among the infinity of determining factors. Obviously not by the simple 'observation' of the course of events in any case, certainly not if one understands by that a 'presuppositionless' mental 'photograph' of all the physical and psychic events occurring in the space–time region in question – even if such were possible. Rather, does the attribution of effects to causes take place through a process of thought which includes a series of *abstractions*. The first and decisive one occurs when we *conceive* of one or a few of the actual causal components as modified in a certain direction and then ask ourselves whether under the conditions which have been thus changed, the same effect (the same, i.e., in 'essential' points) or some other effect 'would be expected'. (Weber 1949: 171; Bruun and Whimster 2012: 173–4)

But it must be emphasized that what is involved is not the use of thought experiments and comparative analyses to identify laws, not even probabilistic laws.[40]

---

[40]Weber insists that it is not possible to *calculate* the probabilities involved here: 'One naturally cannot in any way arrive by this operation at an estimate of the relationship between these two possibilities which will be in any sense "numerical"' (Weber 1949: 182; Bruun and Whimster 2012: 180).

Rather, these analytic strategies are being used to facilitate the process of explaining what occurred in some actual case or set of cases: the task is explaining rather than theorizing, in the terms outlined earlier.

The implication of Weber's argument seems to be that where we identify behaviour that could conform in an approximate way to a rational model enshrined in an ideal type, it may supply hypotheses directly to explain whatever outcome it is that we are concerned with explaining. We examine actual behaviour in terms of how closely it approximates to this type and from this we determine how far this rational model, and the motives associated with it, can explain the actual behaviour that is observed. I suspect that Weber's insistence that ideal types are not hypotheses reflects his belief that, generally speaking, no single rational model will apply, because the motivation of human behaviour is usually a product of a mixture of factors, so that the actual explanatory hypothesis that we need to generate will combine one or more ideal types with other explanatory ideas, for example about habitual or traditional behaviour. He did not believe that the discipline of psychology could help us much with these other ideas, and that often we will already have the resources necessary from our own experience in the world, combined with reading about other times in history and about other societies. It seems that Weber had a very pragmatic view of socio-historical explanation: the task is not to grasp 'what really happened', either in its fullness or even in essential terms. This pragmatism stems in part, no doubt, from his view that the social sciences are practical in character: they are designed to illuminate the way ahead for decision-making, notably for those involved in national policymaking. But it also arises from his recognition of the sheer complexity of social processes, especially when we are dealing with large-scale socio-historical phenomena. Furthermore, Weber adopted an extremely cautious view of the likely validity of causal interpretations of human actions in social science (Turner and Factor 1994: 156–65).

Nevertheless, Weber regarded this kind of knowledge about the world as making a very important contribution to policymaking: it is essential if realistic goals are to be adopted, and reasonably effective means of pursuing them found. He insisted that practical decisions must be informed by knowledge of the situation involved, rather than simply being a matter of value-commitment. This was central to his advocacy of an ethics of responsibility. He seems to have regarded this kind of 'realism' as the most important practical contribution that social science can offer (see Bruun 2007: 250–9; see Chapter 4).

While Weber provides us with an interesting model of what historians and social scientists typically do to some degree, and what they *should* do, there are difficult issues that arise from this aspect of his approach. A major one concerns the nature of the general assumptions about what causes what that underpin judgments about objective possibility and adequate causation; whether the validity of these needs to be secured independently; and, if so, how this could be done. He seems to have believed that this was neither necessary nor possible, but clearly there are issues concerned with how we are to determine what are appropriate ideal types for particular purposes.

There is also an important question to be asked about the nature of the thinking that is required in constructing ideal types. Clearly, they are partly determined by the value-relevance framework adopted by the researcher. But to the extent that the aim is to construct types that will facilitate causal analysis, they must capture accurately at least some aspect of the courses of action or institutional practices being studied. This suggests, and Weber's discussion confirms, that there is an inductive aspect to generating ideal types, in a loose sense of that term. There is a role here for studying not just the particular phenomena being investigated, but also those that might be judged similar and different in relevant respects. Hence, in part, the need for comparative analysis, and this was of course one of the main strategies employed in much of Weber's substantive research (see Buss 1999).

Conclusion

In this chapter I have explored some important aspects of the character of social scientific explanation. I drew a distinction between theorizing and explaining, the first concerned with discovering relationships among *types* of phenomena or variables, the second aimed at identifying a set of factors which account for the occurrence of a particular feature or outcome in a particular place and time. In subsequent discussion, I focused mainly on the task of explaining, on the grounds that there seems no good reason to deny that producing explanations is a reasonable goal for social science, and there are some grounds for believing that it is the most important task. At the same time, I recognized that any explanation relies upon counterfactual assumptions and thereby on some general notions about what types of factor cause what types of outcome, or what variation in causal variables causes what variation in outcome variables. I discussed two problems that face the task of explanation: that many different questions can always be asked about the same phenomenon; and that an infinite number of causal factors can be identified for any outcome. Given these problems, some reasonable means must be found of selecting what question to ask and of foregrounding some factors and backgrounding others in seeking to answer that question.

I examined the claim that theorizing (interpreted as the identification of necessary and jointly sufficient conditions) can solve these problems. From this perspective, only outcome typologies or variables that correspond to semi-closed causal systems should be the focus of social scientific investigation; and the relevant factors to be focused on are those belonging to the system that produce variation in the outcome variable. By these means, the problems involved in explanation would be resolved indirectly and ontologically, as it were. However, there are reasons to believe that theorizing is not possible in the social sciences: because it seems unlikely that there are closed, or even semi-closed, systems in the social realm and/or because the main means of discovering them, experiments, cannot generally be used.

In the second half of the chapter I examined Weber's proposed solution to the two problems facing social science explanation. For him, which research questions are to be addressed, and which causal factors given attention, is to be determined via the explicit adoption of a value-relevance framework. The implication of this is that, even if closed causal systems operate in the social world, the explanatory factors that must be given attention are unlikely to be selected solely from within just one of them, because this will not serve practical purposes well. However, while value-relevance seems to offer a promising solution to these problems, questions remain about how researchers ought to decide which value-relevance framework to adopt in a study, or indeed about whether this is always a decision that *they* should make.

As regards the ontological aspect of explanation, there are challenges concerning how we can determine which value-relevant factors played a significant causal role in bringing about the outcome to be explained. Weber provides a thoughtful and elaborate answer to this question, and it may well be that this is the best approach available. However, its limitations, clearly recognized by Weber himself, must be borne in mind. We should also note that, if Weber is correct, a great deal of what currently passes for social science must be judged futile, in searching for theories, as well as seriously inadequate in its failure to employ explicit value-relevance frameworks and systematically elaborated ideal types in the production of explanations.

THREE

On the role of values in social research

As we saw in the Introduction, the role of values in social science has been a focus for disputes, recurrently, across the social sciences – albeit without any consensus being reached. At the same time, it seems that it is an issue that has been largely ignored *in practice* by most social scientists much of the time. Yet it is an important topic because it carries implications both for how research ought to be carried out *and* for its proper relationship with politics, policymaking, and the various kinds of occupational practice that it is frequently seen as serving – such as those in health-care, education, social work, and elsewhere.[1]

The issue is a complex one, and very different stances have been taken towards it. In this chapter, I will begin by outlining currently influential arguments proposing that social science can and should be normative, partisan, or 'perfectionist' (Root 1993): in other words, that it should produce value conclusions – practical or political evaluations (including critiques) and recommendations. For reasons I will explain, in my view these arguments are unconvincing. I will also address some of the criticisms that have been made of the principle of 'value-neutrality' as the guiding ideal of social science. My conclusion will be that this principle is more subtle than is generally assumed, and avoids most of these criticisms. Indeed, I will suggest that, along with the twin concept of value-relevance, it provides the only viable

---

[1]What Hutchison (1964: 13–14) says about economists in the first half of the twentieth century – that despite little agreement on the issue it was rarely discussed in any *sustained* and open-minded way – can also be said of social scientists more generally through into the twenty-first century; and this despite considerable diversity in orientation among them in ways that are relevant to the issue. There has, of course, been a significant shift from a purported adherence to the principle of value-neutrality, on the part of many social researchers in the past, to rejection of that principle by most today. Yet, this has generally occurred without careful attention to the arguments on both sides, despite some key discussions of the issue, of strikingly different kinds, such as those of Storing 1962; Hutchison 1964; Gouldner 1973; and Putnam and Walsh 2012.

framework for social science. At the same time, I will examine the respects in which even research operating on this basis is not neutral in relation to all value perspectives. And I will conclude by considering some of the practical difficulties likely to be faced by social scientists today were they to try to abide by this principle.

Proposals for normative social inquiry and their weaknesses

There are those who insist that social research must be normative: that it should be directed towards answering value questions about what is desirable or undesirable, right or wrong; about what must be changed, or (more rarely) preserved; about who is, and is not, responsible for what; and so on. However, advocates of this position differ significantly among themselves as regards the substantive values to which they believe inquiry should be committed, and in *how* they see commitment to these values being justified (where they give attention to this more fundamental issue).

The various strands of 'critical' research – geared directly to challenging inequality or oppression – clearly fall into the category of normative inquiry (Hammersley 1995: ch. 2). But there are approaches coming from other, often very different, political directions that must be placed under this heading as well. Challenger (1994: 1) mentions some examples:

> Voegelin, Strauss, and Wolin as well as more contemporary social thinkers such as Robert Bellah, Alasdair MacIntyre, Jürgen Habermas, and Hans-Georg Gadamer are concerned that the separation of ethical issues from science is, in large part, the reason why mainstream social science is suffering a crisis of relevance today. The result of this positivistic dictum in the twentieth century is a science of society bereft of significant achievements, as well as societies that lack the help they might have expected from a science linked to normative concerns.

The views of the thinkers mentioned by Challenger spread across much of the theoretical and political spectrum. Furthermore, and at first sight surprisingly given the dismissive reference to positivism in the extract above, Challenger goes on to argue that Durkheim advocated a normative sociology: concerned with diagnosing the ills of contemporary, 'transitional' forms of society and prescribing a remedy for these. And, in important respects, this characterization of Durkheim's orientation is true (see Bellah 1973). Within economics, there are similar normative stances to be found, often centring on treatment of economic welfare as equivalent to the common good (see Hutchison 1964; Vickers 1997; Putnam and Walsh 2012).

Aside from explicit championing of normative inquiry, in *practice* a great deal of social science presents value conclusions. Indeed, this often occurred even when commitment to value-neutrality was declared (Storing 1962; Hutchison 1964). Sometimes, the valuational character of the conclusions is left implicit and/or is ambiguous – as with much use of words like 'inequality', 'social change', and 'discrimination', which carry evaluative load even when their primary reference is factual (see Foster et al. 2000). The use of these and other terms in value-laden ways by researchers may stem from their assuming that the value conclusions they reach follow automatically from the factual evidence they have produced, or at least from this combined with their own value commitments, which they take for granted.[2] Yet there is little justification for this, and very often the conclusions put forward are sharply contested by other social scientists. Of course, these challenges are frequently themselves dismissed as arising from ideological bias, the result being that the value disagreements involved are not examined in any productive way.[3]

Where attention *has* been given to the process of drawing normative conclusions from factual evidence, there have been appeals to a variety of types of justification: to notions of religious or natural law (Strauss, MacIntyre); to other conceptions of objective values, for example deriving from a teleological account of the development of human society (as in the case of Hegel or Marx); to a concept of society as an organism, knowledge of whose static and dynamic functioning legitimates judgments about health and ill-health (Comte, Durkheim); to some logical argument from 'is' to 'ought' (as, for example, with Bhaskar); to a claimed moral consensus underlying apparent disagreements, on which social scientists can rely in deriving value conclusions (see, for instance, Wootton 1950: 126–7); or to a process of deliberative democracy through which objective value conclusions can, in principle, be reached (as with Habermas).

However, all of these rationales for the derivation of value conclusions from factual evidence are open to serious question. Problems with the notion of natural law have long been recognized: without appeal to some kind of speculative metaphysics, religious or secular, it is hard to see what support there could be for believing that there is a form of law, or a set of universal rights, that has intrinsic validity above and beyond the everyday world of positive laws and norms. And the metaphysical justifications offered conflict with one another.[4] Other arguments for the objectivity of values have also been subjected to major criticism (see Mackie 1977; Blackburn 1993; Fisher and Kirchin 2006), and the Hegelian and Marxist versions of this position have been largely abandoned, even by Marxists.[5] Positivist reliance upon the

---

[2]Sayer (2011: 229) suggests some reasons why 'critical' researchers today are 'coy' about their values.

[3]For one example among many, see Tooley 1997 and Ball and Gewirtz 1997.

[4]On natural law theories, including recent attempts to revitalize the argument, see Murphy 2011. For the history of these theories, see d'Entrèves 1951 and Sigmund 1971.

[5]On Hegel's and Marx's ethics, see Wood 1990 and Lukes 1985, respectively. With the exception of the critical realists, 'critical' researchers today seem to have largely abandoned any attempt to demonstrate the validity of the value assumptions on which they rely, and this despite, or perhaps as a result of, post-structuralist and postmodernist critiques.

idea of society as an organism has been rejected by most modern sociologists, and with good reason (Baert 1998: ch. 2). Bhaskar's attempt to derive 'ought' from 'is' fails, like earlier attempts (see Chapter 4). The idea that there is some underlying moral consensus to which appeal can be made may have some validity, in that across many societies there is agreement on what are regarded as fundamental values: the preservation of life, cooperation with others, justice, and so on. However, when it comes to giving relative priority to these values, and to interpreting them in particular cases, there are profound disagreements across *and within* cultural traditions (Berlin 1981 and 1990; Larmore 1987; Gray 1995: ch. 2) – and it is at this level that any normative social science must operate. Finally, Habermas's attempt to resolve the problem has been subject to effective critique (Lobkowicz 1972; Rienstra and Hook 2006; Sayer 2011: 227–8; see also Habermas 2003). My point is not that these various ideas have no value, but that all of them are open to very serious question; and that they are incompatible with one another. As things currently stand, at least, they offer no foundation for a normative social science.

Instead, I suggest that we must recognize that while factual evidence from research is often important in reaching value conclusions, such conclusions necessarily also rely upon value principles whose acceptance is to a considerable degree independent of factual matters, and is certainly not derivable in a logical or calculable fashion from a single, mutually consistent set of premises whose validity is simply given or is a matter of consensus. Instead, multiple, conflicting value principles are involved, and this, along with the need for them to be *interpreted* in relation to particular situations, almost always generates considerable potential for disagreement. Disagreement that is not easily resolvable (Hanson 2009), and that social science can make no distinctive claim to resolve.

Of course, the problem of moving from factual investigation to value conclusions may not always be a severe one *in practice*. This is true, for example, of research that is specifically geared to serving particular groups of practitioners, for instance, being designed to evaluate some development in policy or practice largely within the framework of the assumptions that those practitioners adopt in their work. Examples of this would include inference from facts about an increase in patient recovery rates, in the context of medical research, or about a rise in children's reading achievement levels, in educational inquiry, to the conclusion that improvement has occurred. Even here, though, it is still important to recognize that a value framework, and in particular ways of applying it, are involved; and that discrepant judgments are always possible. In the examples mentioned these may arise through adopting different assumptions about 'quality of life' after illness or about the nature of literacy. Moreover, I suggest that especially when it comes to academic research – in other words, inquiry that is not geared *directly* to serving practical activities (Hammersley 2011a) – the problematic and uncertain nature of any move from factual premises to value conclusions ought to lead us to restrict the research task to factual investigation. I will expand on the reasons for this below.

Value-neutrality as a principle

The alternative to normative social science is the idea that the social scientist should strive to adopt a 'value-neutral' or 'value-free' orientation. This is sometimes attributed to positivism – as we saw in the case of Challenger (1994: 1; see also Habermas 1988: ch. 7). And it is true that this idea can be found within that tradition: there are strands of positivist thought that draw a sharp distinction between 'facts' and 'values', insisting that value conclusions cannot be derived solely on the basis of factual premises, an argument that can be traced back at least to Hume. Examples from the nineteenth century would include John Stuart Mill's writings on economics – Mill counting as a positivist on most definitions of that term – indeed – he was directly influenced by Comte.[6] However, as already noted, at the same time there was also an important strand within positivist philosophy that sought to derive value conclusions from factual evidence, for example by reducing them to the calculation of sum totals of happiness or utility, as with Bentham's utilitarianism, or by drawing an analogy with the role of physiology in determining bodily health. Along these lines, Durkheim, following Comte, claimed that only one set of moral judgments will be rationally defensible when we have full scientific knowledge of a situation and its foreseeable future: 'it is never possible to desire a morality other than that required by the social conditions of a given time. To wish for a morality other than that implied in the nature of society is to deny the latter, and, consequently, oneself. [...] We cannot choose a criterion by an act of decision: we can only observe it and derive it from the facts' (see Lukes 1973: 426).[7] Given this, the positivist parentage of the principle of value-neutrality is rather ambiguous. And, in fact, the most developed version of the argument for this principle, that of Max Weber, drew on neo-Kantianism rather than upon positivism.[8]

---

[6]There is some uncertainty about the precise nature of Mill's position, since there is variation in what he writes in different places (Hutchison 1964: 27–9). One has to turn to later writers, such as John Neville Keynes, for a version of this position that is more clearly defined, this perhaps prompted by the emergence of what Freeden (1986) has called 'the new liberalism', and the need to distance economics from laissez-faire ideology. Hutchison notes that the earlier tradition of economic thought, exemplified by Adam Smith and the Physiocrats, did not draw any distinction between economics as a science and as an art, or between positive and normative economics, since it relied upon a concept of natural law – 'the simple system of liberty' – that had no need of such distinctions.

[7]What Durkheim says here about whole moralities may be true, but I suggest that it is not true of particular moral judgments.

[8]There have been debates about the extent to which Weber was influenced by neo-Kantianism, and specifically by Rickert, but see Burger 1987 and Oakes 1988. On neo-Kantianism more generally, see Willey 1978; Köhnke 1991; and Gordon 2010.

Partly as a result of uncertainties about its genealogy, and perhaps also because of problems with Weber's mode of writing, and translations of his work, what the concept of value-neutrality is taken to mean has varied significantly, and interpretations of it on the part of critics have often deviated sharply from Weber's position.[9] In particular, many critics have taken the term 'value-neutral' or 'value-free' at face value, as implying the claim that researchers can and should be entirely free from the influence of, or should be neutral towards, *all* values.

This has rightly been rejected, on at least four grounds, namely that:

1. Research inevitably has some goal, notably pursuing knowledge, and what is pursued must be assumed to be of value – otherwise it would not be regarded as warranting any expenditure of energy or of other resources. Given this, by its very nature, research cannot be free from, or neutral towards, all values.
2. In committing themselves to the principle of value-neutrality, advocates are necessarily treating this principle as of normative significance, yet by doing so they are simultaneously departing from value-neutrality. In other words, there is a performative contradiction built into the position.
3. In pursuing inquiry, social researchers typically take *ethical* values into account (minimizing harm to participants, respecting their autonomy, etc.), and they clearly *should* do this. However, in doing so, here again, they are departing from value-neutrality: they are pursuing research in a way that is not 'value-free'.
4. Finally, commitment to the principle of value-neutrality, as neutrality towards *all* values, seems to require researchers to eliminate all of the value-commitments that they have acquired during their lives, or at least to eliminate any influence these values might have on how they do their research. Yet this is clearly impossible, and efforts to achieve it are almost certainly undesirable.

It cannot be denied that, on the face of it, the terms 'value-neutrality' and 'value-freedom' invite the interpretation that what is proposed is that researchers should be unaffected in their work by any values. And the four criticisms I have outlined demolish that position. But this interpretation does not correspond to what most advocates of value-neutrality mean by this term, and certainly not to what Weber intended (see Keat 1981; Bruun 2007).[10]

Weber's position – most, but not all, of which I will adopt here – treats the principle of value-neutrality as requiring simply that the conclusions of research be restricted to factual (rather than value) claims, and that any distortion of the research process by the researcher's own value commitments, or those of others, be minimized.

---

[9]From early on, Weber found himself challenging objections that he regarded as deriving from a failure to grasp the arguments he had presented (Weber 1949: 10). Bruun 2007 provides a detailed and accurate account of those arguments. On subsequent interpretations of Weber's work, see Derman 2012.

[10]There are additional problems relating to the term 'neutrality'. Montefiore (1975) has discussed the meaning of this word and related ones, such as 'disinterestedness'.

Defining the goal of research exclusively as the pursuit of factual knowledge marks Weber's position off from attempts to treat inquiry as having some additional or alternative goal, such as to improve social outcomes of one sort or another, to 'emancipate' or 'give voice' to some category of person (women, children, the working class, ethnic minorities, sexual minorities, the 'disabled'), or to challenge or 'trouble' the socio-political status quo. In so far as the words 'research' and 'inquiry' have any standard meaning, they surely refer to the pursuit of knowledge, not to these other goals. Of course, we may well carry out research in the belief that producing knowledge through research will serve other goals; indeed, this would be true of most researchers. But motives for engaging in an activity are quite different from its goal. The latter guides what is done *within* the activity, whereas the motives for pursuing it relate only to why we entered upon it in the first place, and perhaps also to why our effort has been sustained. And, while inquiry can be subordinated to other purposes, I take it that the defining feature of research, *as a specialized activity*, is that it is not, and should not be, subordinated to any other goal (see Hammersley 2004b) – in much the same way that a doctor's concern with the health of a patient should not normally be subordinated to other considerations, for example to ensuring that the maximum number of people are available for work in an economy or to reducing the burden of the elderly on society.

This interpretation of value-neutrality is immune to all four of the criticisms outlined earlier. As regards the first, 'value-neutrality' means neutrality in relation to practical, that is non-epistemic, values. It is quite clear that for Weber science is a 'vocation', existing alongside other vocations in the modern world (for instance, to politics or to some form of religious life), and that any vocation necessarily involves value-commitment. In the case of research, the commitment is to epistemic values, to knowledge and truth. Furthermore, Weber recognizes that the particular questions that a researcher addresses are set, in part, by reliance upon other value assumptions, notably about what is and is not an important issue. However, he insists that while these assumptions determine what would be worthwhile research questions and what would be *relevant* answers to them, the assumptions do *not* determine what would be *valid* answers or how investigation of the issue should be carried out.

With respect to the second criticism, commitment to value-neutrality does not require the researcher to act solely on the basis of facts, or even exclusively upon epistemic values. All that is necessary is that he or she treats the production of factual knowledge as the sole operational goal – in other words, the only goal that efforts are made to realize *through* the way in which the research is carried out. Hence, while commitment to the principle of value-neutrality is a normative matter, this is not self-contradictory.

The third point – that researchers take account of ethical considerations in pursuing knowledge, and should do so – also does not count against the principle of value-neutrality, as formulated by Weber. As already noted, this principle does not require that non-epistemic values play no role in inquiry, only that they must not constitute its operational goal. Epistemic values – notably truth – are *intrinsic* to the research process precisely because they define its goal (the production of knowledge), along with what may be required in order to pursue this effectively (for instance, objectivity). By contrast, ethical considerations represent an *external* constraint on how knowledge ought to be pursued, albeit a very important one (Hammersley and Traianou 2012).

Responding to the final criticism, it is necessary to point out that the principle of value-neutrality only requires that researchers strive to minimize the danger of practical values *distorting* the conclusions reached in carrying out research. It does *not* demand that researchers find some way of avoiding all influence from such values. Indeed, practical value commitments can be productive in opening up lines of investigation, suggesting fruitful explanatory ideas, and so on. Once again, then, the principle of value-neutrality, properly formulated, does not succumb to this criticism.

So, the standard criticisms I have outlined do not apply to the principle of value-neutrality, as originally intended by Weber at least. However, there are other criticisms sometimes made of this principle that need discussion. One is that it sets up a dichotomy between values and facts, treating them as constituting two realms that are completely separate from one another; when, in fact, values and facts are entangled in various ways (Putnam 2002). Like the other criticisms already discussed, this is inaccurate in relation to Weber's position. It is central to his concept of value-relevance, and to his notion of an 'ethic of responsibility', that values and facts are intimately interrelated even though they are different in character.

Another criticism, one that requires rather more discussion, is that the principle of value-neutrality implies that value conclusions are irrational – simply a matter of personal preference or taste – by contrast with factual conclusions, which can be rationally determined; and that this position has damaging implications for both public policymaking and research itself, given that these are necessarily based upon value commitments (Putnam 2002; Sayer 2011). Here, Weber's argument that fundamental values are a matter of non-rational commitment is treated as an essential feature of the value-neutrality position, so that if this argument can be shown to be defective the whole position is held to be undermined.

In response, we can start by noting that, while (perhaps drawing on Nietzsche) Weber did believe that we must simply commit ourselves to fundamental values, rather than adopting them solely on the basis of argument and evidence, he did *not* conclude from this that all value judgments are wholly non-rational. He saw the *derivation* of specific value judgments from fundamental value principles as properly open to rational guidance and evaluation (Bruun 2007). Indeed, I think he believed that researchers could play an important role in showing what value-conclusions follow, in relation to particular cases, from given value principles.

Equally significant, he emphasized the importance, in making practical decisions, of taking account of the facts of the situation (even when these are unfriendly to one's value commitments), rather than making utopian or excessively optimistic assumptions about what can be achieved. This kind of 'realism' is the crux of his distinction between an ethic of conviction and an ethic of responsibility (Bruun 2007: 250–9).[11]

It is true, nevertheless, that there are serious problems with Weber's idea that value judgments are derived from ultimate principles about which there can be no rational deliberation.[12] There are some grounds for arguing that deliberation about value issues is open to rational examination in a deeper way than Weber allowed. For instance, we might replace his hierarchical model of deriving specific value judgments from fundamental principles with a 'flatter' model of a web of assumptions, involving both facts and values.[13] While some assumptions in a web of belief will be more strongly embedded than others, none need be entirely fixed and beyond rational appraisal. Relatedly, some value assumptions may be closer to the interface with facts than others. Indeed, it might be argued that while a particular principle may serve as foundational in some justificatory contexts, in others it will legitimately be treated as itself dependent upon other assumptions.

In these terms, it is better to treat our thinking as relying upon networks of value principles, theoretical ideas, substantive value judgments, and empirical assumptions about the world, all of which depend upon and influence one another, in various ways and to various degrees that are context-dependent. Moreover, as this indicates, each value principle has to be interpreted in terms of its possible substantive instantiations – in other words, according to what it would mean in particular contexts. Usually, there are one or more standard cases associated with each principle – indeed, these are essential to give it meaning – but these will change over time and across justificatory contexts. Indeed, they are open to modification on each occasion a value principle is applied to a concrete situation.

---

[11]We should note that, at the same time, he also recognized that there are occasions when, even while recognizing the likely consequences of our actions, we must take a stand on our principles: see Gane 2002: 66–79.

[12]In effect, like Nietzsche, he abandons Kant's assumption that there is a single, coherent set of values that can be derived from the very nature of rational thought. Instead, he recognizes competing principles ('gods' or 'demons') among which we must choose *while at the same time acknowledging that others can be legitimate*. The problem here, in my view, is that in rejecting the idea that there can be demonstrable knowledge of what is good and bad, what ought and ought not to be done, and so on, the false dichotomy between demonstrable knowledge and *mere subjective opinion* seems to be taken over, instead of recognizing that what is involved is a continuum.

[13]For one influential use of a web model in epistemology, see Quine and Ullian 1978. Rather different uses can be found in Haack 2009 and Williams 2001.

Whether or not this alternative conceptualization is sound, the most important point I want to make is that, even if we abandon this part of Weber's position, we can still recognize that there is a considerable difference between what is required in coming to reasonable value conclusions, on the one hand, and what is needed to reach sound factual conclusions, on the other. Furthermore, this difference is sufficient to warrant restricting research to factual inquiry.

One argument here is that any factual question, if it is well formulated, has a single correct answer, whereas value questions do not – however well-formulated they are. It is not that all answers to value questions must be treated as equally valid – there are certainly answers that would generally and rightly be judged quite wrong. But there is almost always scope for several answers that are reasonable, among which it may be difficult to decide, and about which people will disagree. This partly reflects the fact that, unlike factual questions, value issues rarely involve judgment in terms of a single criterion: multiple criteria must be taken into account – relating to different aims, interests, and other considerations – and these will often generate conflicts that can only be resolved by adopting some compromise, with substantial scope for different views about what kind of compromise would be best. Equally important, as already noted, the implications of each relevant principle have to be interpreted in ways that are appropriate to the situation concerned, and there may be competing reasonable interpretations here too. Finally, it is important to recognize that some differences in opinion about value issues stem from the fact that people occupy very different positions in society, and therefore have divergent interests, concerns, attachments, etc. Contrary to the arguments of some ethical theorists (notably Kantians and utilitarians), we are not obliged always to reach value conclusions from a universalistic perspective (Larmore 1987). Indeed, the obligation may run the other way (Maclean 1993).

It is true, of course, that when people address a value question they do frequently behave as if they believed that there were just one right answer to it, and that they know what this is. However, I suggest that in most cases it is clear to any moderately thoughtful person that there are conflicting arguments that are reasonable in principle, each having some virtues; and that there is often no easy means of reconciling them.[14] Indeed, we will sometimes be *forced* to recognize that there are other reasonable points of view by noticing inconsistences in our own stance across different occasions. For example, many UK politicians praised those people who went out on to the streets attacking the authorities in Middle Eastern countries in 2009 and 2010, in what was dubbed the 'Arab Spring', but

---

[14]As already noted, what may be required instead is some sort of compromise, but there is still room for disagreement over how much each of the various principles involved should be compromised.

later condemned rioters on the streets of London in 2011, and in Belfast in late 2012 and early 2013. They would, of course, point to differences in the kinds of action involved and in the circumstances, as the reason why they responded in contrasting ways. But, as soon as we start to address such differences, we find that they can be interpreted and 'weighed' differently, and that we do not have any very determinate means of doing this, so that conflicting but reasonable evaluative conclusions can be reached about the same set of events.[15]

While it is true that factual questions are sometimes apparently open to more than one possible right answer, I suggest that this is always because there is significant ambiguity or vagueness in the terms in which they have been formulated. To the extent that this can be eliminated, and doing this may certainly be challenging sometimes, there will be just one right answer to each of them.[16] It is, of course, the case that we can never, with justification, be absolutely certain that the answer we have provided to any factual question is the true one. And at any particular point we may not be able to decide among competing alternatives with any confidence. Nevertheless, in pursuing factual inquiries we *do* typically assume that there is a single true answer that is knowable, and this assumption plays an essential role in such inquiry, and is sound.

All this lays the ground for my argument that in the case of factual inquiry there is some hope of reaching a single definitive conclusion that can be given authoritative warrant, whereas this is not the case with value questions. We can acknowledge that what is involved here is a difference in *degree* of difficulty, but still insist that the difference is sufficient to justify restricting research conclusions to factual matters. Indeed, if we recognize that even factual inquiry about social affairs is extremely difficult to pursue successfully, not least because the evidence and inferences on which we must rely are often of uncertain validity, and always fallible, there is even more reason for researchers to concentrate entirely on *this* task rather than *also* taking on the *even more challenging* one of seeking to reach value conclusions in a way that carries intellectual authority.

Moreover, it is not just that taking on the larger task would result in less time and other resources being available for factual inquiry, important though that is, but also that it would increase the danger that the value-commitments, interests, etc. of the researcher would distort the inquiry process. There will be an inevitable *tendency* to be more favourably disposed towards factual conclusions that are compatible with, or offer support for, what we judge to be the best value conclusion, and to reject those we view as linked to opposing positions. In other words, if one is not only trying to produce sound factual knowledge, but also to

---

[15]Needless to say, what is and is not reasonable is a matter of judgment and of degree. There is no escape from this in relation to either factual or value conclusions.

[16]This will require clarification of the presuppositions that underpin the question and frame the sort of answer required, see Chapter 2.

further a political or practical cause, there will be occasions when these goals pull in opposite directions – whether the researcher is aware of this or not; and one result will be an increased chance of factual error.[17]

Of course, this is not the only source of error or kind of bias operating on researchers, nor is it an inevitable result, but it *is* a significant risk. And it should be noted that such bias can be unconscious and difficult to detect. At the same time, there is certainly no reason to claim that people who declare themselves to be, or even believe themselves to be, acting in accordance with the principle of value-neutrality are necessarily unbiased. The principle of value-neutrality or objectivity, on the interpretation I am using here, is one that we have to work hard to live up to, and we will probably never entirely succeed in doing this.

Finally, there is a political aspect to the epistemological argument just outlined about the relative difficulty of producing a single correct or reasonable answer to value questions, as opposed to factual ones. It is necessarily the case that social scientists claim some authority in putting forward the findings of their research. At a minimum, they are presenting what they produce as more likely to be true than answers to the same questions from other sources. Indeed, unless social scientists can legitimately claim greater reliability for their conclusions, in this sense, it is hard to see what warrant there could be for the work they do, and for its public funding. Let us assume that this authority is justified in the case of factual conclusions – though we should note that doubts are sometimes raised about this, even by researchers themselves. The key point is that it is *a great deal more questionable* that researchers, in the natural or the social sciences, can legitimately claim similar authority in relation to value issues. Moreover, any attempt to do this risks undermining both democracy and liberal governance. This has been highlighted, for example, in discussions of the implications of positions like that of Comte, where science is treated as potentially resolving all issues about how people should live and how they should be governed (Wernick 2001). As we saw earlier, drawing value conclusions on the basis of factual evidence alone is not possible – value assumptions are necessarily involved as well (see also Chapter 4). But on what authority can researchers claim to decide which practical values should be prioritized on particular occasions in producing evaluations and recommendations about social issues and public policies, and how these values should be interpreted in particular cases? It seems to me that there is no warrant at all for this, and that presenting value conclusions as if they derived from research amounts to

---

[17]This is not to deny that there are potential costs associated with detachment from commitment to practical values in social inquiry, not least that the knowledge produced may be less immediately relevant to practical concerns. Furthermore, my argument here is not against inquiry that is geared to practical commitment, this can often be of great value. My objection is to substantive academic research taking this form (Hammersley 2011a). Indeed, methodology, including the kind of inquiry in which I am engaged in this book, is itself a form of normative rather than value-neutral inquiry.

an abuse of its authority. Moreover, even when they are not presented in this way, audiences will often treat the evaluations and recommendations made by social scientists as having been validated against alternatives solely or primarily on the basis of the facts established by research, when this cannot be the case. Or, alternatively, if disagreeing with these evaluations and recommendations, they are likely to reject the factual as well as the normative components of research reports. Either way, the capacity for rational public debate is undermined.

No one should over-extend, or be allowed to exaggerate, her or his legitimate claim to distinctive knowledge and understanding under the mantle of science. Thus, just as occupations like medicine must not exceed their authority in pronouncing on matters outside their realm, so too social researchers should not claim expertise in drawing value conclusions about what is good or bad in policy or practical terms, or about what ought to be done.[18]

The limits of neutrality

We have seen that the principle of value-neutrality does not require that researchers seek to be neutral in relation to all values: only non-epistemic ones, and then only as regards the *goal* of research. Moreover, in adopting research questions, researchers necessarily rely upon non-epistemic values to determine what issues are of interest and importance, and these will frame the answers that are judged relevant. What this makes clear is that, on a Weberian interpretation, there are very significant limits on what 'neutrality' means.

In addition, the principle of value-neutrality does not bar researchers from engaging in politics or other practical activities. They may certainly do this under the auspices of other identities, notably that of citizen. But, even as researchers, the principle of value-neutrality allows them to engage in political and organizational activities designed to preserve the conditions required for research to operate effectively or for it to flourish: for instance, seeking to protect or increase the resources available for research (resources that could, of course, always be used for other purposes), and/or demanding certain types and levels of freedom to carry out inquiry and publish their findings. It should be noted that the authority researchers claim here is not scientific, at least not in the same sense that they can claim scientific knowledge on the basis of research evidence. Instead, the normative claims are based upon researchers' practical experience in doing research and on their commitment to the value of knowledge and inquiry. Moreover, their expertise in this respect is properly restricted in its scope to what is entailed in and required by the activity of research. It is similar to the authority that other occupations, and the organizations representing them, can

---

[18]The danger here is one aspect of what Strong (1979) referred to as sociological imperialism.

legitimately claim: to determine what is required if they are to be able to pursue *their* tasks effectively.[19]

There is also a deeper sense in which research governed by the principle of value-neutrality cannot be neutral in relation to all value perspectives: it cannot adopt this attitude towards any that reject the adoption of a value-neutral stance (as defined earlier), even for the specific purposes of research. Examples would include religious, ethical, or political views that seek to enforce a single set of goals and evaluative criteria as the overriding priority across all or most human activities. Such views may also threaten other specialized orientations, including those of doctors or lawyers, demanding, for example, that they serve 'the national interest', the dictates of the Party or of the Church, etc.

I have argued elsewhere that, contrary to Root (1993), there is a legitimate parallel with liberal political philosophy in this respect (Hammersley 1995: ch. 8 and 2011a: 183). That philosophy prescribes neutrality on the part of the state towards conflicting substantive values, but it cannot be neutral towards *all* value perspectives, notably those that specifically deny the toleration that liberalism demands. However, the fact that there are limits to liberal-neutrality does not undercut its value: liberal states still offer *more* toleration of a *wider range* of views and forms of life than other types of regime.

Moreover, at least one of the arguments that has been used to justify liberal-neutrality on the part of the state is also relevant to the principle of value-neutrality in the context of research. This is that it allows scope for the exploration of unconventional views and practices that could turn out to be of general value (Mill 1869). Thus, research communities that include members having diverse religious, ethical, and political orientations are more likely to produce sound knowledge than those whose members all adhere to more or less the same value perspective. This is because such diversity will highlight biases that would otherwise have gone unnoticed, and will also counter any tendency to treat some particular value-relevance framework as the only possible or legitimate one.

It is worth noting that there is another theme in Weber's work relevant to the discussion here, aside from his Nietzschean notion of 'choosing one's demon'. He argues that while we are free to select a particular ethic to govern our lives, how we will fare in the world will vary depending upon the relationship between this ethic and prevailing social conditions. More specifically, Weber's position seems

---

[19]It has occasionally been argued that such defence or promotion of the interests of research necessarily entails commitment to a particular form of society. On some interpretations this is a commitment to liberalism, on others to discursive democracy. However, such arguments tend to exaggerate what is involved: the conditions required for research to flourish are not specified by any single political philosophy, and do not relate to all of the aspects of social life relevant to such philosophies. Moreover, these conditions are matters of degree: it is not the case that research can only operate under a single type of political regime, but rather, at most, that it is easier under some types than others.

to have been that if we want to participate in, and even shape, modern Western society, then we have to recognize and adapt to its character, not least to the processes of rationalization that have occurred within it, and that continue to shape it; and to work from within these to preserve what otherwise might be lost, in other words to try to prevent the door of the 'iron cage' closing (Gane 2002). Indeed, Weber has been interpreted as arguing that often we have an *obligation* to engage with reality in this way (Bruun 2007: 255). Thus, even if, in principle, we would prefer to be involved in a form of inquiry that is normative as well as factual, and that tackles the most important value questions, we must recognize that we live in societies in which there is now a great deal of specialization; with each specialized occupation necessarily adopting a value orientation that reflects its specific role and responsibilities, thereby downplaying value considerations that might be judged at least as important, or even more important, from other angles. Part of what I referred to earlier as Weber's 'realism' seems to me to amount to an acceptance of this consequence of specialization, and a willingness to work within it (see Weber 1919/2012). At the same time, there may of course be extreme occasions when we must abandon this attitude because the situation faced is so severe in its ethical demands from some other point of view. For example, there may be emergency situations where we should abandon the role of researcher in order to intervene on ethical or political grounds. But to view the world as in a continuous state of emergency, whether permanently or until some great transformation is brought about, is not compatible with social science governed by the principle of value-neutrality.

It may even be that Weber saw social science as an essential component of the modern world, and as playing a key role in injecting a sense of realism into practical decisions of all kinds, especially in the realm of politics. This would fit with his insistence that social scientists must have integrity, and must teach it to their students: they must devote themselves, in their work, solely to the task of documenting facts relevant to policies and practices, and be prepared to recognize facts that are unfriendly towards their own commitments and preferences. Furthermore, they must publish these facts with honesty and courage in the public sphere, whatever the personal consequences.

Practical problems in adhering to the principle of value-neutrality

Even if it is accepted that adherence to the principle of value-neutrality is desirable for researchers, it is nevertheless important to recognize the practical difficulties that this can cause, especially in present circumstances. These arise, most obviously, at the points of contact between researchers and those playing related roles: funders of research; university managements, ethics committees, etc.; gatekeepers and other people in the settings being studied, or from whom data are to be elicited; and audiences for research reports, including the media and agencies seeking advice that is 'evidence-based' (governments, charities, commercial firms). The problem is that these others will often expect, perhaps even demand, that researchers go beyond producing value-relevant factual knowledge. Evaluations and recommendations will frequently be expected or called for, though of course this does not mean that any that are provided will automatically be accepted as authoritative. More than this, factual conclusions will often be treated by lay people as immediately indicating particular value conclusions, with the authority of research being used to promote them. Given this, there may be resentment at any insistence by researchers that such conclusions do not follow automatically from their findings, and that quite different ones are also compatible with the research evidence. Such insistence may also be seen as proving that research is of little value.[20]

Of course, these problems are partly generated by the adversarial character of the public sphere in modern Western societies, this tending to promote a conflation of fact and value, and indeed resistance to drawing the distinction. Moreover, it is not just that there will be these external demands and objections to researchers' adherence to the principle of value-neutrality, but also that those demands and objections may well be backed up by powerful negative sanctions.

While friction between specialized occupations and their environments is inevitable, along with some internal conflict and diversification generated by this, there can be variation in how serious this is, and in how it is managed. This will be determined not just by the power resources available to the different parties, but also by the cultural environment within which relationships at the interfaces between one occupation and others must operate.

In recent decades, conflicts between researchers and external agencies have been sharpened by the growing influence of an instrumentalist cultural discourse which denies that research knowledge (or anything else, including art and literature) has any value in itself, claiming that it is only of value if it assists in the achievement of practical goals of one sort or another. Indeed, if research appears to be an obstacle to the pursuit of such goals, it may be viewed as actually of negative value, and efforts made to discredit it. This makes it extremely difficult for researchers committed to the principle of value-neutrality to promote the value of their work effectively. Hutchison (1964: 190) remarks: 'Effective persuasion [of those 'unversed in the finer normative-positive distinctions in economic terminology'] often requires, or at least in the short run can often be powerfully assisted by, blurring and not emphasizing the distinction between normative and positive [...]'. Yet, if social scientists do this, they undermine the integrity of their own position.

---

[20]Very often, these conflicts between occupations and their funders and clienteles have echoes *within* the occupation, with different segments of it adopting different 'solutions' to these conflicts. This is one source of the fragmentation now to be found within social science.

Moreover, researchers are increasingly in competition with think tanks and other organizations that are only too willing to supply what is demanded, and who often show little compunction about melding facts with values. Given all this, it is no accident that current public campaigns mounted by research organizations in support of continued state funding of social science do not observe the restrictions imposed by the principle of value-neutrality (see the Introduction).

Another feature of the cultural environment that causes problems in this context is the prevalence of what has been referred to as 'the hermeneutics of suspicion' (Gadamer 1984). In effect, this involves treating Hume's (1888: 415) argument that reason is governed by our desires as leading to a blanket dismissal of all knowledge as biased, including that produced by researchers. Or, rather, this radical scepticism is typically applied selectively: to lines of argument to which the speaker is opposed. This scepticism is given traction because there is always scope for raising doubts about the validity of any knowledge claim, given that all such claims are fallible. The key point is that this sceptical climate leads to doubts about the validity of research knowledge: it comes to be seen as little more than a weapon to be deployed or destroyed, depending upon the function it will serve on the political battlefield. In these terms, we can see advocacy of partisanship *within* research as, at least in part, simply a reflection of this outside environment. Yet it threatens to turn research reports into political pamphlets disguised as objective accounts.

Conclusion

In this chapter I have argued that, while the idea that social science should be normative has become increasingly influential, so that few social scientists today would claim to adhere to the principle of value-neutrality, the rationales for this view are weak. Moreover, much criticism of the idea of value-neutrality is based upon a simplistic interpretation of what it requires. I argued that even if we abandon Weber's assumption that value judgments derive from a necessarily *non-rational* choice of fundamental values, there are still strong reasons for insisting that the goal of social research should be restricted to the production of value-relevant factual knowledge, rather than being extended to include value conclusions, such as practical evaluations and policy recommendations.

I went on to acknowledge that the principle of value-neutrality cannot be neutral towards all value perspectives: that it is inevitably in conflict with any religious, ethical, or political perspective that insists upon the universal priority of some set of non-epistemic values across all realms, including research. Finally, I noted the practical difficulties that face any attempt to sustain commitment to value-neutrality in societies, such as those in the West today, where an instrumentalist attitude towards inquiry and knowledge prevails, along with a scepticism that is deployed against 'hostile' information.

Nevertheless, it seems to me that it is important for social scientists to affirm the principle of value-neutrality, and to adhere to it as far as is possible. While they can make a justifiable claim to be more able to produce reliable factual conclusions about some issues than lay people, they have no basis for claiming that they have a distinctive capability to resolve value disagreements, and therefore to validate evaluations and prescriptions. They can provide factual evidence that may be used in deliberations about these matters, and clarify the implications that could follow from particular values; but to go beyond this under the auspices of social science is to claim illicit authority, and it is also likely to damage the enterprise by increasing the chances of error in the conclusions reached. It is true that there are strong pressures to exceed the proper limits operating on social science, both external and arising from social scientists' own motives and interests. But these must be resisted.

FOUR

From facts to value judgments? A critique of critical realism

A growing influence within social science over the past few decades has been critical realism (Collier 1994; Archer et al. 1997). This is committed to a scientific approach that is explicitly concerned with producing theories that identify causal relationships. However, my focus here is on its 'critical' character. There is, of course, an important sense in which all research should be critical: it should subject knowledge claims to scrutiny. However, the phrase 'critical realism', and the notion of 'critical social science' more generally, goes beyond this. It requires that the social phenomena being studied, and the societies in which they are found, themselves be subjected to criticism – on the basis of research. In my view, this conception of social science is mistaken (see Chapter 3).[1]

A distinctive feature of critical realism, by contrast with most other recent versions of critical social science, is that it offers an explicit rationale for how value conclusions are to be derived directly from descriptive and explanatory evidence. Very often, the nature of this form of inference is not made clear in critical research: features of the operation of social institutions are presented as if their undesirability, and the need to change them, were immediately obvious.

---

[1] It is perhaps worth pointing out an ambiguity in the meaning of 'critical' and 'criticism'. In some contexts, for example that of literary criticism, 'being critical' means 'subjecting something to assessment', and such assessment can result in positive as well as negative judgments. Yet, it is built into the notion of critical realism, and of critical social research more widely, that the aim is to diagnose what is *wrong* with some institution or with the wider society, and sometimes also to identify remedies. While I am not going to pursue the issue here, there is reason to pause before accepting the legitimacy of a process of evaluation whose required outcome is always negative.

Yet, while the value judgments concerned may often seem uncontentious to both 'critical' researchers and their main audiences, value assumptions are nevertheless involved, and they are ones that would be rejected by many people. Given this, their validity should not be assumed; doing so would itself surely amount to adopting an uncritical stance.

Of course, historically, within the 'critical' tradition, there has been an influential rationale available for drawing value conclusions from factual evidence: that offered in the work of Marx. Versions of Marxism influenced by Hegel have relied upon a teleological account of the development of the world from which, it is claimed, value conclusions can be drawn directly – in much the same way that is possible within an Aristotelian perspective. In this respect, both Hegel and Marx are opposed to ethics in the more usual Kantian sense. For them, any conclusions about what is good or bad, or what ought to be done, should be derived from an understanding of the nature of the world, not from some separate, abstract realm of rationality or values. In fact, they treat the belief that there is such a separate realm as an aspect of the alienation generated by the dialectical development of human social life.[2] However, generally speaking, critical researchers today do not place explicit reliance upon the sort of teleological meta-narrative promoted by Hegel and the early Marx. Indeed, this has long been subjected to fundamental criticism and largely abandoned even within the Marxist tradition, with the arguments of neo-Kantians, pragmatists, structuralists, and post-structuralists providing the resources for this at various times.

Critical realism offers an alternative rationale for a 'critical' orientation, via the notion of explanatory critique: the idea that criticism of social phenomena can be derived directly from sound explanatory models of them.[3] And just as Marx and Hegel had opposed Kantianism, so too some critical realists have challenged the sort of non-naturalistic ethics which became influential in the twentieth century, according to which value judgments are portrayed as subjective and perhaps even irrational. Indeed, quite falsely, they often portray this view of ethics and politics as the only alternative to that offered by critical realism.[4]

---

[2]On the positions of Hegel and Marx in relation to ethics, and concepts like justice and need, see Wood 1981: part 3, 1990 and 1993; Buchanan 1982; and Fraser 1998.

[3]Accounts of this aspect of critical realism are to be found in a variety of places: Archer et al. 1997: 233–57 and Part III; Bhaskar 1979: 56–103, 1986 and 1991: Appendix 1; Collier 1994: ch. 6; the entry on 'explanatory critique' and other related entries in Hartwig 2007. For assessments, see Lacey 1997 and 2007, and Sayer 1997 and 2007. For an earlier attempt on my part to grapple with this issue, see Hammersley 2002b. In a recent paper Elder-Vass (2008) has examined Bhaskar's arguments about this in some detail, including his later appeal to meta-reality.

[4]See, for example, Sayer 2011. For overviews of the range of meta-ethical views now available, and assessments of them, see Fisher and Kirchin 2006. Note that even views

There are two main arguments to be found within critical realism underpinning the notion of explanatory critique – in other words, designed to justify the drawing of value conclusions from factual evidence alone.[5] The first has the following components:

1. If we establish some fact about the world, we are simultaneously implying that other people ought to believe it. So, right at the start, we have a model for deriving an 'ought' from an 'is'.
2. If we can show that beliefs incompatible with this fact are systematically generated by a particular social institution, then criticism of that institution automatically follows, other things being equal.

In this way, it is claimed that evaluative and prescriptive conclusions can be drawn directly from factual evidence established by social science. This first set of arguments is sometimes described as 'cognitive', because it relates to beliefs.

The second set of arguments is non-cognitive, in the sense that it concerns other aspects of human life. It runs as follows:

- If we establish that someone suffers from an unmet need, such as the absence of food, then it follows automatically, other things being equal, that action should be taken to meet this need.
- In addition, if it can be shown that the frustration of a need is not only generated by some institution but is necessary for the reproduction of that institution, then the conclusion follows (other things being equal) that the institution should be changed.

Again, this is presented as an example of deriving a conclusion about what is wrong, and perhaps also about what ought to be done, *solely from a statement about what is the case.*

I will assess each of these arguments in turn.

The cognitive argument

At the start, it should be made clear that this argument does not succeed in the strict logical deduction of a value conclusion solely from factual premises (even aside from the inclusion of a *ceteris paribus* clause).[6] In the first component, the conclusion (that any statement of fact ought to be believed) only follows by assuming a value principle to the effect that we ought to believe what is true, and

---

about ethics within analytic philosophy in the first half of the twentieth century were more varied than is often assumed, see Bevir and Blakeley 2011.

[5]In what follows, I will rely to a considerable extent on Collier's (1994) account of Bhaskar's position.

[6]There is also an issue about whether *ceteris paribus* covers only variation in factual conditions or variation in value assumptions as well.

not what is false. It could, of course, be argued that this value principle is deeply entrenched within, or even constitutive of, human social life,[7] so that the assumption of this principle is trivial. I certainly agree that this value is constitutive for the goal of any kind of inquiry, but there are questions about whether it applies across the board.[8]

There is another, and more significant, problem with the first component of the cognitive argument. This is that, as fallibilists, we should distinguish between a factual knowledge claim being true *and our belief that it is true*.[9] It may – in practical, even if not in strictly logical, terms – follow automatically from the fact that some factual claim is true that people ought to believe it. However, to declare that a knowledge claim (let us call it 'P') is false does not, in itself, amount to declaring that belief in the truth of P is wrong; this would only be true in the present tense and in the first person. Thus, *past* belief in the validity of P cannot be judged wrong on the grounds that P has *now* been disproven. After all, prior to this time, there may have been reasonable grounds for believing P to be true. Moreover, this indicates a more general point: that there is an important distinction to be drawn between the *rationality* of believing and the *validity* of the beliefs held.

Even more importantly, it *does not* follow automatically from the fact that I have come to the conclusion that statement X is true that others ought to believe it. It could equally follow that they ought to decide that I am mad for believing such a thing. The only way to bridge this gap is to assume that we can know with absolute certainty that a statement is true, so that the conclusion can be derived from this that everyone ought to believe it. For example, it might be argued that there is a scientific method whose use *guarantees* true conclusions. However, once we recognize that we can never have absolute knowledge of this kind, the argument fails. And, given that critical realists adopt a fallibilist epistemological position, they cannot use this strategy to support the cognitive argument.

Given all this, it does not follow from the fact that social scientists claim to have established the validity of some knowledge claim that other people ought to believe it. Indeed, as rationalists we might expect, and hope, that they would exercise their own critical faculties rather than simply deferring to the authority of social scientists, especially since much of what is currently put forward as social scientific knowledge is open to serious dispute. Yet, for the cognitive argument to

---

[7]For a genealogy along these lines, see Williams 2002.

[8]These include those put forward by William James about what it is good to believe, in his critique of W.K. Clifford's insistence that we should only believe those propositions for which we have strong evidence (James 1909; Hollinger 1997). Nietzsche, notably in *Beyond Good and Evil*, is of course an even more trenchant critic (Nietzsche 1886/1972).

[9]There is variation in the meaning of the word 'fact' in everyday usage that can cause misunderstanding. It can mean 'matters of fact as against matters of value', 'well-established knowledge rather than speculation', or 'what is true as against what is false'. Clearly, these distinctions are not isomorphic. In this book I am using the first one.

hold we must assume that social science is capable of producing knowledge whose validity is beyond all possible doubt, and should therefore simply be accepted.

It is also important to remember that even in the case of a belief whose truth is accepted there may still be room for reasonable disagreement about its scope, about the situations to which it applies. Very often, people may accept the general validity of some knowledge claim, but argue that despite appearances it does not apply to the particular cases with which they are concerned. This can simply be special pleading, but it need not be – especially not if we view human societies as involving open rather than closed systems, as Bhaskar does. There are often exceptions to general rules, and people may have information about the cases they are concerned with that enables them to assess the application of a general principle more effectively than those who do not have that information. Furthermore, there is often room for reasonable disagreement about how the scope of a knowledge claim is to be defined, and how its constituent terms are to be formulated. This latter point is illustrated by an example that Bhaskar and Collier themselves use: the issue of whether Britain is now a classless society (Bhaskar and Collier 1997: 387). 'Class' is a concept that is open to a very wide range of interpretations, and these can generate different answers to that question (see Marshall et al. 1988; Saunders 1990 and 1995; Pakulski and Waters 1996). So, on these grounds too, scientific findings do not *automatically* imply criticism of people's beliefs or of institutional assumptions.

The problem becomes even more complex once we abandon the notion that belief is a matter of simple acceptance or rejection, and acknowledge that there can be *degrees* or *kinds* of belief. Here the effect of the publication of scientific findings that question P may simply be to reduce the degree of belief in P, or to change the kind of belief in it, rather than to eliminate belief completely; and with good reason. Much depends here upon the current standing of available alternatives. While scientists are able simply to remain agnostic about issues where there is no single, well-confirmed answer, practical actors are frequently not at liberty to do this. Indeed, they may sometimes feel, quite reasonably, that they must act on beliefs whose validity is uncertain or even doubtful.[10]

So, in the context of practical action, despite a reduction of confidence in its validity as a result of scientific findings, P might continue to be acted on because

---

[10] Lacey (1997: 217) usefully distinguishes between having and holding a belief; between beliefs informing an action or an activity and the actor reflectively endorsing those beliefs. Elsewhere, he distinguishes between adhering to a belief, accepting it, and provisionally entertaining it as a working hypothesis (Lacey 1999: 13). For an analysis of the interesting case of superstitions, see Campbell (1996: 157), who comments: 'This then is perhaps the most puzzling feature of modern superstition: it involves individuals engaging in practices in which they don't believe; that is to say, they are reluctant to admit that they do believe in them, even if they are sometimes also reluctant to say that they do not. In other words, they would appear to "half-believe" in the superstitions they practice.'

the action strategy in which it is involved still seems to be the best available. This points to the fact that what we treat as true, in the sense of what beliefs we choose to act on, is determined not just by our assessments of their cogency, but also by judgments about whether action informed by them seems to work in the relevant circumstances, whether there is a viable alternative that offers anything better, and so on. Indeed, it cannot be assumed that correcting a false assumption will always improve the performance of a practical activity; sometimes it may even damage it – for example, because it leaves us more uncertain about what to do (see Hammersley 2002a: ch. 2). Furthermore, the practical costs of different kinds of error will also need to be taken into account. Here, Pascal's 'wager' and James's 'will to believe' capture an important aspect of a practical orientation.[11]

There is a third problem too. This is that the sort of explanatory critique advocated by critical realists shares with some concepts of ideology the assumption that beliefs which are false are caused in a different way from, or at least by different factors than, beliefs that are true. The simplest formulation of this is that true beliefs are caused by reality whereas false beliefs are generated in other ways. However, I suggest that, if we wish to speak in this confusing manner, we must accept that all beliefs are caused by reality, and that it remains to be demonstrated whether there is a strong relationship between *how* they are caused and *whether or not they are true*. This is a difficult issue, but in my view whatever one thinks of the subsequent development of the social studies of science movement, its original insight – the principle of symmetry – was correct (see Barnes 1974; Bloor 1976). This principle held that we should not assume that true knowledge claims are generated in any *fundamentally* different way from those in which false knowledge claims are produced.

One argument that might be presented against the symmetry principle is that it undercuts social science itself: that it denies that there are ways of pursuing inquiry that are more likely than others to generate sound knowledge. However, this conclusion does not follow. What is denied is that there is any *strong*, systematic causal relationship between how inquiry is pursued and whether or not the conclusions reached are true: such as a scientific method that *guarantees* the validity of the findings produced. And much the same applies at the meta-level of determining whether any set of conclusions is true or false. This leaves it open for us to recognize that some methods – for example, those labelled by Peirce (1877) as the methods of tenacity, authority, and a priori argument – are unlikely to produce the truth, while those of science are more likely to do so. The key point is, though, that people adopting the first three methods may, nonetheless, reach true conclusions, while much rational inquiry has produced false findings. Furthermore, while we can argue that inquiry following a certain institutionalized pattern is desirable in

---

[11]For an illuminating discussion of James's position, see Mounce 1997. See also Hammersley 2011a: ch. 5.

minimizing the chances of error, compared to following some other method, what is involved here is not the adoption of an utterly distinctive form of behaviour but rather a specialized refinement of what is to be found in other contexts too. In addition, all manner of motivations may operate on the decision to engage in research in a scientific way, of the same kinds that motivate other, very different, forms of action.

There is a related point: it seems to be assumed by critical realists that false beliefs will function in negative ways in society, while true ones will function in positive ways. Along these lines, Collier (1994: 190) quotes Althusser: 'true ideas always serve the people; false ideas always serve the enemies of the people' (Althusser 1971: 24). Now, while this was an influential Enlightenment assumption, it is difficult to see why we should still believe it. Intrinsic to it is a highly rationalistic conception of the operation of societies, one which Marx inherited from Hegel – though, of course, a historical, dialectical relationship was assumed between the validity of a belief and its social functioning, rather than a simple logical one. Bhaskar does not defend this assumption, but it does need a defence. And any attempt to test it faces a practical problem. This derives, first, from the fallibility of any knowledge claim: as noted earlier, we can never know with absolute certainty what is true and what is false. For the same, and additional, reasons, we can never know for sure what is socially beneficial and what is not.[12] This makes establishing any fixed correlation between the two difficult, and probably impossible. And the problem is exacerbated by the fact that the unavailability of experimental method in the study of society makes the identification of causal relations more uncertain than it is in natural science (see Collier 1994: especially ch. 5 and 247–59; see also Lawson 1997).

In summary, I think there are particular practices that, other things being equal, will be likely to increase the chances of our coming to sound conclusions, compared to others: for example, those practices that are usually labelled scientific, compared, for instance, with those which seek to draw conclusions about the nature of the physical universe by explicating what is written in religious books. There are also structural processes that tend to generate outcomes that may involve certain sorts of bias. But just as scientific method does not guarantee the validity of our conclusions nor do these structural processes always produce error. The most fundamental point of all is that systematic causal relations may well tend to generate particular kinds of belief in particular sorts of circumstance, but truth/falsity is an evaluative categorization that does not have any intrinsic or internal relation to causality. And, finally, we should not assume that true beliefs always have good consequences, and false ones bad.

---

[12]The additional reasons are to do with the fact that there is always scope for different value perspectives on what is beneficial: see Hammersley 2011a: ch. 3; and Chapter 3 in this volume.

There is also a problem with the other component of the cognitive argument: about the role of institutions. The assumption seems to be that institutions either generate false beliefs or they generate true ones. However, even if we assume that institutions produce, or are constituted in terms of, specific sets of beliefs in some reasonably straightforward fashion that can be documented, and I am not sure this is true, we can expect that most institutions will generate *both* true and false beliefs. Given this, no evaluation or prescription would follow in the manner that critical realists wish it to do from the fact that an institution generates some false beliefs, unless we were to assume that we should try to change all institutions until they only generate entirely true beliefs. This would be futile, and, once again, it involves a form of intellectualism: the idea that other social activities should be evaluated in exactly the same manner as scientific inquiry – in terms of whether the beliefs that they produce are true. In my view, different sorts of activity require different kinds of rationality, depending upon their goals.

So, contrary to the claims made for it, the cognitive argument does not succeed in deriving value conclusions solely from factual evidence. As a result, it does not provide a secure basis for arguing that realism, or social science, can and should be 'critical'.

The non-cognitive argument

The second argument that critical realists have put forward to legitimate their 'critical' orientation appeals to the concept of need. To a large extent, this operates on the same basis as the first one: it claims that, just as showing a belief to be false implies that it should not be held or promoted, so the identification of a need implies that it must be met. Not surprisingly, then, this component suffers from many of the same problems as the first. It smuggles a value conclusion into scientific findings, this time through ambiguity in the meaning of 'need'. This term sometimes has a factual sense, as for example when it is stated that animals need food and water, meaning only that without these they die. Of course, very often when we say that there is a need for something, we *also* imply that the consequences of not meeting it are bad and should be avoided. This introduces a value premise. In the example mentioned, the premise is the idea that animal life is of value and should be preserved. Only on the basis of that value assumption does it follow that any animal in need of food and water ought to be provided with them.

So, this also fails as a purported *logical* derivation of value conclusions solely from factual evidence, because 'need' is itself a quasi-evaluative term: it concerns an actual or potential gap between what is and what ought to be (see Miller 1999: ch. 10). Any practical evaluation of this kind can and should be sharply distinguished from a factual statement to the effect that there is a difference between what exists and what *would be* judged desirable or necessary in terms of some evaluative standard. For instance, we must draw a line between the factual statement that some person does not have food and is likely to die as a result, and the evaluation that this is an undesirable situation. The implicit value assumption involved is: 'no human being should starve to death'.

Of course, as with the first critical realist argument, it can be suggested that even though, strictly speaking, there is a logical gap between factual evidence and value conclusion here, the implicit principle on which reliance is being placed is built into the very fabric of human life: that someone should not be allowed to starve to death is a fundamental ethical principle (see Elder-Vass 2008). This may be so, but the key point is that at least one value assumption is required to reach a value conclusion. Moreover, even in this case, there are situations where human beings do not apply this value principle, and may well be prepared to justify not doing so. After all, one of the strategies used in wars is to cut off supplies to the opposing armies, and we might feel few qualms about this if the people whom we were effectively condemning to starvation were responsible for the most terrible atrocities, and this was the only way of defending ourselves against them. Elder-Vass (2008: 16) argues that 'it is a rather minimal implication of valuing humans that we should support their staying alive', but adds 'assuming that they rationally wish to do so', a qualification that points to another situation where leaving someone to starve could be the right thing to do. This undercuts the argument from need.

Furthermore, while humans do have some basic needs, in the sense that there are things without which they could not physically survive, there are many other things whose absence might make them unhappy, and for which it might therefore be declared that they have a need. Here it is even more obvious that there is no absolute requirement that such 'needs' always be met. To take a trivial example, it might make me unhappy if boxing or motor racing were banned, since I enjoy watching them, and so do many other people. But the fact that we experience a need to watch them, for example because they take our minds off other concerns, does not, in itself, logically imply that they should not be banned, nor does it even provide very strong grounds for this. Indeed, there are cogent arguments in both cases as to why they *should* be banned.

A third problem is that each human being has multiple needs, and satisfying one is sometimes only possible at the expense of not satisfying others. Similarly, given scarcity of resources, satisfying some people's needs will usually be possible only at the expense of not satisfying other people's needs of the same or different kinds. More than this, some 'needs' are relational, in that their satisfaction on the part of one person depends directly on the extent to which they have been satisfied for others. This is true, for instance, of so-called 'positional' goods, where the relationship between satisfaction on the part of one person and another is inverse (Hirsch 1977). And the same problem also often arises where the concern is with equity, in the form of distributional justice: we could satisfy this principle by reducing everyone to the same miserable state.

Bhaskar's inclusion of an 'other things being equal' clause in this second argument, as in the first, indicates that he recognizes that there are circumstances where even basic needs ought not to be met. However, Collier (1994), Sayer (1997 and 2007), and Elder-Vass (2008) have pointed to problems associated with appeals to *ceteris paribus* in this context. The questions for me are: who should decide when relevant considerations are and are not 'equal', and on what grounds? More particularly, is the social scientist in a position to do this with any distinctive intellectual authority? Or, to put the point another way, can it be done entirely on the basis of factual evidence? My answer to the last of these questions is 'no', and this implies that social scientists have no distinctive expertise in making decisions about whether 'other things *are* equal' in any particular case. This argument, too, undercuts any direct inference from factual evidence to value conclusions within 'critical' social science.

The point is worth elaborating. What seems to be involved in drawing value conclusions is something like this:

> We have a description of a situation, along with some explanation of how it has come about, and perhaps also some prediction about what will result. Taking the range of value principles that are available, some of them (usually more than one) will be found relevant to this situation. Each of these values sets up a line of evaluative and/or prescriptive argument, or perhaps several. Given this, in evaluating the situation we must decide on the priority that ought to operate among these value principles, or how they should be combined, and we must determine what the implications of this are for how we evaluate the situation. Note that the value judgment that results here is unlikely to be the outcome of some fixed ranking of these value principles. Instead, what relative priority we give them on this occasion will depend upon our purposes, what we see as our responsibilities, our relation to the people involved, and so on (see Hammersley 2014).

If this is a fair characterization of the nature of the task, formulating what is involved as the application of a single value principle whose relevance derives from the facts of the case, and which must be applied 'other things being equal', is not helpful. At the very least, my account here makes clear that no conclusion about what is good or bad about the situation, or about what should or should not be done, can be logically derived solely from social science evidence about the matter. Rather, actors must adjudicate among and combine relevant value principles in ways they judge to be appropriate in the circumstances.

Furthermore, as already noted, many needs are more problematic than basic ones like hunger. Indeed, often, basic needs merge into more complex and controversial ones. For example, it could plausibly be argued that literacy and numeracy are basic needs in contemporary society. But how exactly are we to define 'literacy' and 'numeracy' here? For instance, should we limit their meaning to what is functional or ought we to be introducing students to the worlds of literature and pure mathematics? In this case, and others, there is considerable room for reasonable disagreement about what does and does not count as a need, as well as about whether or not a need should be met in any particular circumstance and what would count as meeting it. And these problems cannot be resolved entirely in terms of descriptive and explanatory evidence. Any resolution would require value argument, using devices like appeals to notions of what is a good life, rights, obligations, universalizability, or precedent; to other cases that are similar or different in key respects; to cases generated by counterfactual hypotheses; and so on. Moreover, there are likely to be multiple reasonable views in most instances. This partly reflects the fact that, while in the case of disagreement about well-formulated factual questions there is a single underlying correct answer, this is not the case with value questions (see Larmore 1987; Gray 1995: ch. 2; Habermas 2003; Hammersley 2011a: ch. 3; see also Chapter 3 in this volume).

So, once again, there is no direct or immediate route from factual research evidence to value conclusions. Rather, any such inference necessarily depends upon value assumptions, about both any particular need *and* whether there are other overriding values. Moreover, value pluralism, the fact that there are always multiple values that can be seen as relevant, means that there is frequently much scope for reasonable disagreement. Given this, there are no grounds to claim that social scientists can conclusively determine what counts as a need that should be met on any particular occasion. For them to make this claim would amount to a form of scientism: they would be exceeding the authority that can be claimed for scientific research. Yet this is precisely what 'critical' researchers do.

Of course, it might be argued that while research cannot legitimately claim to produce value judgments about particular situations, it can tell us what value principles ought to be taken into account in human social life. Two points need to be made here. First, this does not provide sufficient basis for the argument that social research should be 'critical' in the required sense, since the latter involves social scientists 'taking a stand' about what is wrong and what ought to be done in some particular socio-historical situation. Second, while biological and social science can show why particular value principles have tended to emerge within human communities at particular times, this does not *in itself* tell us that, as humans or even as members of a particular community, we should adopt those principles.[13]

---

[13]Elder-Vass (2008: 18) argues that, in conditions approximating to Habermas's ideal speech situation, ethical discussion could resolve conflicts of interest, and presumably also conflicts in priority given to different values. While this may sometimes be possible, I suspect that very often it will not be (Hammersley 2011a: ch. 3). Furthermore, there is no distinctive role in this for social scientists. For example, they do not have superior expertise in judging whether people are conducting ethical discussion honestly and sincerely, whether all who should participate are doing so, or whether the discussion is being distorted by power differences. These matters *also* involve value judgments.

It should be clear, then, that the first component of the non-cognitive argument is not defensible; and since the second one depends upon it, that fails too. Moreover, there are further problems with this second component. We can expect that any institution is likely to meet some needs but frustrate others, and so any assessment of it will have to take account of both aspects. There can also be disputes about *how* needs are or are not met. These are matters for practical value judgment, so here too social science cannot claim any distinctive authority.

Conclusion

I have argued that, in the context of critical social science today, critical realism is distinctive in putting forward a clear rationale for how evaluative conclusions can be derived directly from research evidence, such that social scientists can present evaluative and prescriptive conclusions as validated by their work. In other words, critical realism offers an explicit rationale for being 'critical', in a way that most other 'critical' approaches today do not. However, I have shown that neither of the two arguments making up this rationale is convincing. Of course, establishing this does not automatically undercut the project of 'critical' social science, but it weakens it considerably, as against the alternative prospect of a social science committed solely to producing value-relevant factual conclusions. Moreover, there are other reasons why we should reject the 'critical' project. One of the most important is that the attempt both to produce knowledge and to bring about social change of some kind (or, for that matter, to preserve the status quo) is liable considerably to increase the chances of error in the conclusions reached (Foster et al. 1996; Hammersley 2000).

Note that my commitment to the value-neutrality or objectivity of inquiry does not imply that value argument is unimportant, or that it is irrational. Indeed, such argument is essential to politics and government, for instance, so that the fact that it is currently of poor quality in much public discussion is a major concern. My point is simply that social scientists, whether realists or non-realists, have no distinctive authority to determine what is good or bad about the situations they seek to describe and explain; or what, if anything, should be done about them. They *do* have the authority to claim expertise in relation to factual matters, though even here not sole or absolute authority. In other words, because they are not able to validate any teleological meta-narrative or to derive value conclusions directly from factual evidence, their authority does not extend to drawing value conclusions: to producing evaluations and prescriptions as if these can be validated through the research process or on the basis of their expertise. While social scientists, like others, can engage in value argument, to which both factual evidence and value principles will be relevant, they must not suggest that the value conclusions they reach in doing this can be validated through their work, given that there is almost always scope for reasonable disagreement about which value principles are relevant and about the appropriate priority among them on any particular occasion. What is required to reach value conclusions is practical, situated argument: neither philosophy nor science can tell us, on its own, whether a situation is good or bad, or what we should do about it.

This is not to deny that academic social science has an important and distinctive role in relation to many forms of political practice. Its role is to establish relevant facts about social actions, events, and institutions. This contribution is essential, especially in a political culture of the kind in which we now live, where spurious debates based upon taken-for-granted assumptions of doubtful validity are common. But it is also important that the appropriate limits on what social research can offer are recognized by both researchers and their audiences. The claim made by critical realism that social science can and should move beyond these limits is not convincing, and is likely to have undesirable consequences.

FIVE

Can social science tell us whether a society is meritocratic? A Weberian critique

During the twentieth century, the study of social mobility was a major area of social science research, and it continues to be today.[1] It is a field where new methods of measurement (for example, Coxon et al. 1986; Coxon 1999) and new forms of analysis (for instance, Blau and Duncan 1967) have been developed or applied. It is also an area where there has been sophisticated conceptual and theoretical work that is closely tied to empirical investigation (for example, Stewart et al. 1980; Goldthorpe 1988). In Britain, one of the main issues addressed has been the degree to which meritocracy has been achieved, or the extent to which there was a shift in this direction over the course of the twentieth century. There has been a great deal of work on this topic.[2] Furthermore, more generally, much sociological research has focused upon ways in which structures, processes, and practices within education systems may discriminate against particular types of student and thereby generate inequalities in educational achievement and in occupation-based life chances.[3]

---

[1]For views on its state and future prospects, see Morgan et al. 2006.

[2]See, for example, Heath and Ridge 1983; Heath et al. 1992; Marshall and Swift 1993, 1996; Saunders 1994, 1995, 1996, 1997, 2002; Goldthorpe 1996a, 2003; Lampard 1996; Hellevik 1997; Marshall et al. 1997; Savage and Egerton 1997; Bond and Saunders 1999; Breen and Goldthorpe 1999, 2001, 2002; Bynner and Joshi 2002; Swift 2003; Cooper 2005; Ringen 2005; Cooper and Glaesser 2008; Gorard 2008.

[3]For a critical review of research on inequalities in educational processes, see Foster et al. 1996. While this book is nearly 20 years old, the criticisms put forward there continue to apply to most research in the field.

Different foci of social mobility research

It is of some importance to recognize that research in the field of social mobility has been designed to address several, rather different, questions. There is considerable variation among studies as to which of these is given priority, though also a tendency for studies to address more than one of them at once. All of these issues have sometimes been conceptualized through the notion of meritocracy, with the result that this term has come to have multiple, albeit partially overlapping, meanings.[4]

The three main issues that have been the focus for social mobility research are as follows:

1. A concern with the nature of governing elites and recruitment into them. Here, the empirical focus is on the extent to which a ruling elite (or set of elites) within some polity, or within some other sector of a society, draws recruits from outside itself; in other words, the issue is elite social composition.
2. A preoccupation with lower class formation, political representation, and/or revolutionary potential. Here, the focus is on the ease with which able and motivated people within the lowest classes can move into higher classes or status groups. So, the topic for investigation is the extent to which there is movement *out of* the lowest classes or status groups in a social hierarchy.
3. An interest in the extent to which social class origins or other ascribed characteristics play a role in determining occupational destinations or income levels. Here the empirical focus is on the factors determining levels of educational achievement and/or of occupational destination and income. This is often associated with debate about whether there has been a general trend towards greater mobility over the course of the development of Western industrial societies, or within a particular society.

Underpinning these three issues are somewhat different (though not necessarily incompatible) models of society, and specifically of social stratification.[5] As regards the first, where the concern is with *who rules*, the key social division is between elites and the hinterland populations which they govern.[6] The primary dimension of interest here is power, though of course economic and social differences will be relevant to this. The second issue focuses upon a different social division: between the lowest classes or status groups and higher level ones, the latter by no means restricted to governing elites. Moreover, here the stratification dimensions of interest may be differences in income, wealth, social status as well as in power. The third issue assumes a ranking of occupations, or of classes of occupations, graded

---

[4]Heath 1981 provides an excellent account of the history of social mobility research and of the main approaches within it, albeit one that is now somewhat out of date. One recent trend, for example, has been the influence of work on this topic by economists.

[5]For a classic discussion of different images of 'class structure', see Ossowski 1963.

[6]'Mass' is the complementary term that usually goes along with 'elite', but this carries so much theoretical and political baggage that it is perhaps best avoided in this context.

according to the rewards or powers available at each level and/or the social functions they perform. Once again the focus may be on differences in income, wealth,
social status, and/or power (this time viewed as distributed goods or as rewards), but
it may also be on other features, such as workplace autonomy, security of employment, or intrinsic job satisfaction. Furthermore, the primary interest here is in what
determines recruitment to positions within the whole occupational structure, and
especially into those positions towards the top of it.

It is also necessary to recognize that these three issues stem from at least partially
divergent practical or political perspectives, and are therefore anchored in rather
different sets of value concerns. The first is framed by a concern with good governance. This is often, though not always, thought to be facilitated by a meritocratic
openness of governing elites to all comers, from whatever social background. Here
the primary interest is in the extent to which those people who have the most relevant and best developed knowledge, skills, virtues, etc., become part of the ruling
elite. However, on the other side, it has sometimes been argued that openness must
be limited so as to ensure cultural continuity within a governing elite, and/or to
preserve a commitment to protecting the interests of the dominant families or those
members of society with most property. In other words, while there is a common
empirical focus here – the extent of movement into and out of governing elites –
and one that highlights a particular set of value concerns focused on governance,
different political attitudes can nevertheless be taken towards any findings. At the
same time, there are political positions that may well deny the importance of this
issue. These include anarchism, commitment to direct democracy, and other views
that challenge the need for or desirability of government by elites.

The second issue also allows for conflicting political orientations (see Heath
1981: 224). There could be concern about whether there is adequate representation of lower class interests in government. There may also be fear of, or desire
for, working-class revolt. Either way, relatively high mobility out of that class is
often viewed as relieving the pressure for change, for example through hinder-
ing the development of a class-for-itself. Mobility out of the lower classes may
also be regarded as undesirable because it deprives that class of political leader-
ship (Young 1958, 2001). Those who take this view fear that people leaving the
working class through gaining educational credentials will be changed by the
experience, no longer retaining their working-class commitments. Once again,
there are political perspectives from which this issue is likely to be of negligible importance, for example those that treat political rule as founded primarily upon coercion, terror, and propaganda, that regard political allegiances as
largely fixed by class origin and relatively impervious to change, or that see no
need for the political interests of the working class to be represented (see also
Heath 1981: 225–6).

My main focus in this chapter will be on the third issue: whether recruitment
to positions in the occupational structure is open equally to all, or more specifically whether social class origin is a determinant of attaining high positions

in that hierarchy.[7] In this context, 'meritocracy' refers to a situation in which ascriptive factors like social class origin have no systematic effect on eventual occupational destinations – in other words, the evaluative standard employed is usually 'perfect mobility'. In practice, research operating within this meritocratic paradigm is generally concerned with documenting how much deviation there is from the meritocratic ideal and with explaining it. Furthermore, given the key role that the education system is usually believed to play in meritocracy, there is particular interest in the degree to which there is equality of opportunity within that system.[8]

As with the other two foci for research on social mobility, there are conflicting value positions relevant to this research. These centre on varying interpretations of the notion of equality of opportunity, and different views about whether relative equality on the part of those from different social class backgrounds in statistical chances of, say, getting service-class jobs is more or less important than changes over time in the statistical chances that people from working-class origins have of getting such jobs.[9] There are also political views that would deny the importance of this whole issue, for example, those that are committed to the abolition of any occupational hierarchy involving differential rewards, as well as ethical and religious perspectives that downgrade the value of the sorts of virtue and/or reward that are central to this meritocratic ideal. I will elaborate on this later.

The focus of this chapter

My aim here is not to answer the question 'Is Britain a meritocracy?', or to explain why Britain, or any other society, may fall short of this ideal, but rather to address

---

[7]Of course, other kinds of inequality (in terms of gender, ethnicity, sexual orientation, or disability) have also been given attention, and would be relevant to any assessment of whether a society is a meritocracy. To simplify the discussion, I have limited my focus here to social class inequalities, but most of the points I make apply to the study of other types of inequality.

[8]Sometimes, in research on both social mobility and educational selection, control is exercised over other factors that (as judged from within the meritocratic paradigm) *ought* to affect outcomes, notably ability. However, there is debate about whether control of this and other variables is necessary. In social mobility research, especially, it is often assumed that ability is randomly allocated across children born into different social classes, or at least that their potential for developing ability is equal at birth.

[9]This is one of the central themes in the debate between Saunders and various other researchers in the field: Saunders 1994, 1995, 1996, 1997, 2002; Marshall and Swift 1996; Marshall et al. 1997; Breen and Goldthorpe 1999, 2002. It is also worth noting that, in one of the landmark contributions to research on social mobility in Britain, Goldthorpe (1980: 252–3) justifies his primary concern with the second issue, that of class formation, on the grounds that trends in the twentieth century suggest that significant reduction of class inequalities in occupational destination can only come about through working-class political action that changes the whole structure of British society.

the assumptions that frame much research concerned with exploring social class inequalities in educational achievement and occupational destination; assumptions which are often left implicit or vague (see Swift 2004: 1).[10] More clarity about these matters is important, and some authors have done a great deal to explore the range of value perspectives involved (notably, Marshall et al. 1997; Swift 2000, 2004).

A more fundamental issue is how social scientists should respond to variation in the value assumptions that can underpin an interest in meritocracy, as well as the value perspectives that challenge this interest. One response would be to argue that social science can adjudicate among these value positions.[11] However, I do not believe that social science can, or should try to, resolve value disputes, including those concerning which interpretation of the meritocratic ideal is the most convincing, or whether that ideal itself is desirable. It can supply factual knowledge that may lead to a reassessment of particular value positions, since these necessarily depend upon factual assumptions; but, generally speaking, it can neither offer strong support for nor disqualify particular value perspectives: 'the facts' are always compatible with a range of these. Another reaction might be to turn to philosophy for a decision about which value perspective ought to be adopted – and there are signs of this approach in the work of Marshall et al. (1997). However, I am not convinced that philosophy can resolve such disputes, though it can certainly explore the implications of different positions, point to gaps and inconsistencies in argument, and thereby contribute to more fruitful reflection. Rather, these are matters of practical value judgment and in my view no academic discipline can legitimately claim superior expertise in relation to them.

Given this, it seems to me that the task for social scientists is to focus their energies exclusively upon providing factual knowledge that is relevant to debates about meritocracy, and to restrain themselves from drawing value conclusions, or seeking to adjudicate between different value positions. This methodological stance is, of course, a broadly Weberian one (see Chapters 2 and 3). Weber argued that the topics investigated by social science are necessarily specified by means of value-relevance frameworks that allow for conflicting attitudes, a point that I tried to

---

[10]There is also sometimes a mismatch between the domain marked out by the value framework that seems to be adopted and the particular knowledge claims being put forward. This is at the core of the debate between Hellevik and Ringen, on the one hand, and Goldthorpe, Marshall, and Swift, on the other. Part of the former's argument is that if we are concerned with meritocracy, we must be interested in more than the relative chances that those from different social class backgrounds have of reaching a specified occupational level. Other considerations would include trends in the differences between occupations in the levels of various types of reward to which they provide access. For references to this debate, see Ringen 2005.

[11]Critical realism is one approach that offers an explicit rationale for inferences from factual premises alone to value conclusions, and could presumably be applied in this context, but see Chapter 4.

illustrate earlier in discussing the three main issues that social mobility research has addressed. And this involves recognizing that the particular value principles, and the priorities among them, upon which these frameworks depend, will not be universally shared or open to conclusive determination. However, it is important to emphasize that this reliance of research upon value-relevance frameworks does not require political commitment on the part of the researcher to the framework adopted, but rather simply use of it to identify phenomena that are worth investigation.[12] Research cannot establish the validity of one value perspective over another. And, within the adopted value framework, empirical inquiry must focus entirely upon discovering the truth about relevant factual matters, rather than drawing value conclusions in the form of practical evaluations or recommendations. In other words, the legitimate findings of social research are restricted to factual conclusions, albeit ones whose relevance is always relative to some set of values.[13]

In the sections that follow I will address the question of the limits that ought to operate, from this Weberian perspective, on research into educational inequalities and social mobility. In doing so, I will highlight some significant assumptions that underpin most research concerned with whether societies are meritocracies and why deviation from this ideal occurs. There are three sorts of limit I will discuss; and all of these are breached by much research in the field. One limit – already mentioned – stems directly from the Weberian notion of value-neutrality itself: conclusions should be restricted to factual matters.[14] A second arises from the particular value-relevance framework adopted by most research in this area. The final one relates to the task of explaining deviation from the meritocratic ideal.[15]

Commitment to value-neutrality

The first limit rules out the very possibility of social science being able to answer the question 'Is Britain (or any other country) a meritocracy?', *except under some*

---

[12]It is irrelevant, in principle, whether or not the researcher is personally committed to the value positions presupposed, though in practical terms this may be important for readers of research reports to know in order to assess the likelihood of bias in the relevant direction. The crucial point is that research is not to be pursued in such a way as to promote a particular value position.

[13]For further justification of this methodological position, see Hammersley 1995 and 2000. For a detailed account of Weber's views on these matters, see Bruun 2007, although, for me, more hangs on the validity of this methodological perspective than on whether or not it corresponds exactly to Weber's views.

[14]'Factual' here is intended to mean descriptive and/or explanatory knowledge claims, as opposed to evaluations or prescriptions.

[15]Elsewhere (Hammersley 2012d) I have discussed another kind of limit on this type of research, again frequently ignored, concerned with the problems surrounding inference from outcomes to opportunities.

particular value-relevant specification of what would count as a meritocracy, which should be treated as only one option among several conflicting but reasonable alternatives. This limit derives from Weber's concept of value-neutrality, which insists that as social scientists we cannot legitimately draw practical, that is evaluative or prescriptive, conclusions about the phenomena being studied. Our task is limited to the production of factual conclusions about them. This means that, in terms of commitments, social scientific work must seek to be neutral as regards practical values, though it is of course committed to *epistemic* values, notably truth and the value of knowledge (see Chapter 3). In other words, the only sort of non-epistemic evaluation or prescription that would be legitimate is that which is explicitly conditional, stating that *given certain value premises* the factual conclusions reached would imply a particular evaluation or recommendation for action.[16]

In these terms, 'Is Britain meritocratic?' is not the kind of question to which social science can give a definitive answer because the word 'merit' is clearly an evaluative one: any answer would involve making a practical judgment about what is meritorious and about whether merit, of relevant kinds, is rewarded appropriately in Britain. Furthermore, not only can sociologists not legitimately offer a single, conclusive answer to this question, but they should take precautions against their readers treating what they write as advocating such an answer. There is considerable danger of this because background value assumptions often lead people immediately to read what are intended to be factual statements as if these were evaluations or recommendations. Moreover, in this case, the danger is heightened because some of the key terms used in discussing social mobility and educational selection are ambiguous in their status. Words like 'inequality', 'discrimination', and 'bias' have both factual and evaluative meanings, and these are often conflated or confused (Foster et al. 2000). The result is that considerable effort may be necessary to remind readers that they are *not* being offered practical evaluations or recommendations, or that the latter do not follow *automatically* from the factual conclusions presented by research.

However, in fact, researchers in these fields frequently draw or imply value conclusions, and they hardly ever point out that diverse value conclusions can be reached on the basis of the findings they present. In other words, in research on social mobility and educational inequality, the distinction between adopting a value-relevant framework in order to produce factual knowledge and producing practical evaluations and recommendations is frequently overlooked, neglected, or in effect denied. One result of this is to increase the danger of epistemic bias, in the sense that what are thought to be desirable evaluations or recommendations can

---

[16]The relevance of any factual findings is also conditional in this sense. It is necessary to underline here that I am drawing a distinction between commitment or attachment to value perspectives and their adoption for working purposes.

come to drive the investigation, and lead to false conclusions.[17] Another problem is that this tendency amounts to a form of scientism: the authority of scientific findings is effectively being misused in the public sphere because particular evaluations and recommendations are treated as validated by research when they cannot be, and they may thereby acquire greater influence than they ought to have, other things being equal (see Hammersley 2008b; and see Chapter 3).

Limitations deriving from the value-relevance framework adopted

While, in itself, social science cannot tell us whether or not a society is a meritocracy, any more than it can tell us whether it *should be* a meritocracy, it *can* provide information that would be essential for reaching reasonable answers to both those reasonable questions. Yet there are some limitations operating even on what it can supply in this respect. These stem from the particular assumptions that are built into the value-relevance framework adopted. Because different frameworks are possible, the knowledge that any study produces will not usually be relevant to *all* of the arguments surrounding whether a society is or should be a meritocracy, and even less to all of the issues concerned with educational selection and occupational recruitment. Each sociological study of educational selection and/or social mobility will provide information that is only relevant to some public debates about these issues. As a result, there are audiences who will find the research irrelevant because in their view 'meritocracy' ought to be defined differently from the definition adopted for working purposes by the researcher, or because they are interested in the issues from a different angle. Indeed, some may regard the research as pointless because they reject the value assumptions on which all or most notions of meritocracy are based.[18]

As already noted, a requirement that follows from this is that the framework of value assumptions on which a study relies must be made explicit, as must the fact that this framework is only one among several that could reasonably be used to identify worthwhile research questions in the field. Above all, it must not itself be presented as a product of research, or as simply reflecting reality, or even as being validated through an appeal to current public consensus. Indeed, as indicated earlier, precautions need to be taken against the danger that readers will assume that the normative perspective implicit in any particular study, for example the particular

---

[17]For evidence that bias of this kind has operated in research on educational inequalities, see Foster et al. 1996.

[18]It is perhaps worth noting that if the concept of meritocracy being used by researchers is not clearly defined, then their work may well appear to be relevant to a wider audience than, in fact, it is.

interpretation of equality of opportunity adopted, is the only legitimate one: there will always be other views about what is meritorious, what should and should not be rewarded, and so on.[19]

To illustrate my argument here, I will briefly examine and comment upon some of the assumptions that typically underpin sociological research on inequalities in educational selection and occupational recruitment, those that make up what I referred to earlier as 'the meritocratic paradigm'. As I discuss each of these assumptions, I will point to what they exclude, since this is what provides the basis for alternative perspectives. Taking studies of social mobility first, these generally have the following characteristics:

- The focus is on certain sorts of benefit that are taken to be differentially associated with particular types of occupational position. These benefits usually include: varying levels of income, of social status, and of some aspects of employment and work conditions. It is important to note, however, that by no means all the things that people value are usually included, not even all rewards that derive from occupational work. For instance, people sometimes evaluate forms of work in terms of whether they feel these are worthwhile, the scope they provide for sociability, or even whether they involve indoor or outdoor tasks. We should also recognize that, within the meritocratic paradigm, there is no counterbalancing concern with the differential demands and costs of particular occupational positions, even though these are considerations that may often play a role in people's decisions about which jobs to aim at, which to apply for, which to accept, etc. For instance: 'I don't want the level of responsibility associated with that kind of job, it would be too stressful'.[20] Nor is occupation the central source of rewards in everyone's life. For many, this lies elsewhere, for instance, in family life, in leisure pursuits, charity work, etc., and occupations may be judged primarily in terms of how far they allow engagement in these.

- It is assumed that there is a consensus about how occupations are hierarchically ranked in terms of the level of benefits they offer. One difficulty here concerns whether people value equally the various sorts of occupational benefit included in the meritocratic paradigm. In fact, it seems likely that many people will weight these differently from one another. This makes it unlikely that possession of the various kinds of benefit by different occupational positions will co-vary positively in a linear fashion. There is also the question of how far the benefits of an occupational position are independent of the orientation and actions of incumbents. It is possible that different orientations towards doing a job can generate different amounts of some sorts of benefit, for example, psychological satisfaction or even workplace autonomy. Another problem is measuring differential amounts of each benefit, especially given that what is crucial here is

---

[19]With Weber and others (Berlin 1969, 1990; Larmore 1987; Hanson 2009), I am assuming a fundamental value pluralism. For a useful discussion of the different values that can operate in the field of social mobility, and in relation to equality of opportunity and social justice more generally, see Marshall et al. 1997: ch. 2 and 8; Miller 1999: ch. 9 and *passim*. Cavanagh 2002 offers a systematic critique of arguments for equality of opportunity in relation to occupational recruitment.

[20]I am not implying that occupational demands co-vary positively with the level of benefits provided.

how people perceive or experience benefits (including what they do and do not view as benefits). Even in the case of income, there are various forms of remuneration that may or may not be included: bonuses, goods in kind, expenses, share options, etc. There is also the question of whether we need to take account of variations in the marginal value of increases or decreases of income for different people. The other kinds of benefit involve even greater measurement problems, for example status evaluations of particular occupational positions may vary considerably across different groups of people, including social classes. The key point here is not about the technical problems of measurement, but rather the nature of the underlying dimensions to be measured.[21]

- There is the assumption that certain sorts of personal characteristics – those that facilitate upward mobility – are to be treated as meritorious. The focus within the meritocratic paradigm is on 'ability and effort', conceived very much in terms of cognitive capabilities relevant to high-level occupational positions, and the sorts of motivation necessary to achieve these. However, many other kinds of ability, and other sorts of virtue, can be regarded as meritorious. Indeed, from some points of view, what is treated as of value within this meritocratic framework could be regarded as undesirable. While a shift towards valuing what we might call meritocratic ability and effort is often portrayed as a feature of the transition from traditional to modern forms of society, even if this is true by no means everyone would regard it as progress; and, certainly, the fact that there has been such a shift, if there has, does not amount to moral validation of it.

As already noted, from the perspective of the meritocratic paradigm, the education system plays a key role in occupational recruitment, and there are some further assumptions that relate to this, that:

- The function of schools and colleges is to develop those forms of knowledge, skills, and virtues necessary for acquiring educational credentials that will facilitate occupational recruitment. It is not hard to see that there are many other conceptions of what the function of schooling should be, associated with diverse educational and other philosophies.[22] In large part, what will be involved here are different views about what children and young people need to be prepared for, as well as what it is they need in order to be so prepared. For example, education could be framed according to the goals of scholarship, political citizenship, ethical virtue, or religious ideals, rather than in terms of facilitating the acquisition of educational credentials or movement into higher-level occupations.
- Within the education system, specific sorts of merit are to be rewarded. These will relate not just to cognitive capacities of the kinds needed to achieve credentials (at various levels), but also to the sorts and degrees of motivation thought necessary to

---

[21]In practice, a great deal of research on social mobility does not directly measure variations in reward, these are assumed to be largely known. Some research has sought to measure variations in the prestige or status assigned to different occupations. See Coxon et al. 1986 for a discussion of the problems involved in this.

[22]A certain kind of naïve functionalism would, of course, treat the fact that schools increasingly function in this manner as proving that this is how they *ought to* operate and that these are the terms in which they should be evaluated. I am assuming here that there is no need to argue against this.

acquire these. As the first point indicates, these are not the only forms of ability or kinds of virtue that might be judged valuable from an educational point of view. For example, practical abilities of various kinds – whether in cookery, woodwork, or sport – could be judged of value irrespective of whether they are accompanied by the literacy and numeracy skills that are now essential for achieving educational credentials in these fields. Furthermore, various sorts of skill, for example some social skills, may not be credentialized, and (as already noted) the scope for valuing virtues that lie outside those associated with motivation-to-achieve-credentials is not hard to recognize.

- Specific kinds of reward are assumed to be the most important in an educational context: positive evaluations of work given by teachers, allocation to top bands and sets, and ultimately the award of credentials itself. There are, however, other sorts of reward that students may value (reasonably or unreasonably), for example those coming from their parents or from their peer groups, and these may be of a very different character from those emphasized by schools. Indeed, in some contexts, students invert the official values of the school (see Hargreaves 1967; Lacey 1970). There is also the possibility that a student may value praise and reward for one particular sort of activity included in the school curriculum, say music or swimming, but not in other areas.

The main point of listing these assumptions is to highlight what they exclude, thereby showing that the meritocratic paradigm, the framework underpinning most studies of social mobility and educational inequalities, is a partial one. There are other ways in which 'meritocracy' might be defined, as well as other ways of evaluating both schooling and work.

Equally important to note, however, is that these 'meritocratic' assumptions set up models of expected attitudes and behaviour on the part of actors that are used in the process of analysis. In short, the framework provides models of the 'meritocratic agent' as regards those engaged in educational selection and occupational recruitment *and* those subjected to these processes. For example, in relation to social mobility, it is assumed that people's central concern in life is to achieve the highest occupational position that is possible, in terms of the specified hierarchy, and that most of their attention and effort will be directed towards this goal. Similarly, in relation to education, it is assumed that students will be primarily concerned with maximizing their achievement of educational credentials. Moreover, it is expected that as part of this they will, above all else, value in themselves and in one another the sorts of ability and virtue that facilitate such achievement, and that they will value the rewards on offer from teachers to motivate them for this. What is not allowed for here is that reasonable judgments could be made about the balance between pursuing credentials and various other kinds of learning, between school work and other activities, including leisure, and so on. It is also assumed that students should aspire to and seek to achieve the *highest* possible level of educational achievement, whereas in fact they may aim lower, taking other considerations into account when, for example, they decide what educational institutions to attend, which subjects to take, and so on. Where they do not do this, it tends to be inferred that their aspirations have been distorted by external factors. In short, the meritocratic paradigm employs ideal types, involving particular assumptions about what is rational, as tools for analysing the actual attitudes and motivations of relevant agents.

The discussion above is designed to show that the meritocratic paradigm provides quite a narrow perspective as regards what might reasonably be judged to be of value in life, even in Western societies; in terms of what goals people ought to aim at, how they should be evaluated and rewarded, and so on. As a result, research operating within its confines does not tell us *all* that we might reasonably want to know, even about social mobility and educational inequality. Not only can it not tell us, on its own, whether or not a society is meritocratic, but the information it offers will only be relevant to *some* interpretations of meritocracy, and may well be completely irrelevant to other value perspectives. In short, it does not tell us as much as we are often led, or inclined, to believe.[23]

Limitations relating to the task of explanation

There is a third limit on what social science can provide in this area. This concerns the nature of the explanations that social scientists offer about why there is deviation from the meritocratic ideal, in other words, from the ideal types just outlined. An important implication of the Weberian perspective is that research findings must not be presented as simply capturing the intrinsic natures of the phenomena investigated. As indicated earlier, in this respect what is distinctive about Weber's position – as against those of Marx, Durkheim, and many other sociologists – is that he argues that it is not possible to produce explanations for particular social phenomena without relying upon value assumptions that not only identify these phenomena as important and worth explaining, but also frame how they are described and what sorts of explanation would be relevant. In these terms, all social scientific investigation is perspectival, in the specific sense that the *relevance*, though not the *validity*, of a study's findings is relative to the adopted value perspective within which it operates (see Chapter 2).

There are at least two main sites for explanations about why meritocracy has not been achieved in a particular society. The first concerns deviation from meritocratic norms of selection on the part of gatekeepers within the education and occupational systems. Clearly, if these gatekeepers do not select people on the basis of merit (defined in the relevant way), then it is unlikely that meritocracy will be achieved in aggregate terms. The other site for explanations concerns those who are subjected to selection processes. Here, the major focus is usually on factors that lower or deform their aspirations and levels of motivation, and the effects of

---

[23]Needless to say, I hope, this is certainly *not* to say that what it *can* tell us is of no value.

this on the development of their ability to compete successfully within the educational and occupational systems.

I will look in more detail at each of these two sites of explanation. There are various types of explanation for deviation from meritocratic norms on the part of gatekeepers. Some are straightforwardly intentional, appealing to some set of interests that leads gatekeepers to act in ways that are at odds with the meritocratic expectations implied by the model. For example, in the case of those charged with recruiting people for a particular job, social characteristics that are not directly relevant to the capacity to do the job may nevertheless be included in the operational recruitment criteria because these characteristics are valued by those currently involved in that work context, or because recruiting on this basis is seen as sustaining or improving the social status of the occupation or organization concerned. This would lead to deviation from the meritocratic ideal in terms of social class if there were a greater or lesser tendency for members of one social class to have these characteristics, or to be perceived to have them. We should note that this focus on an intentional process governed by other goals than those deemed relevant within the meritocratic paradigm may be combined with appeal to further factors which explain how such bias could have been allowed to operate (for instance, lax supervision or a lack of accountability) or why gatekeepers have this orientation (for example, because their occupation or organization is in a weak position in relation to competitors), and so on.[24]

In practice, the distinction between intentional explanations and other types of explanation is often blurred, because there is uncertainty about how consciously or deliberately gatekeepers have acted in this way. However, sometimes explanations involve an explicit denial that the gatekeepers intended the outcome or were even aware of it. Here, the main emphasis often falls on the functions that deviation from the meritocratic ideal allegedly serves for the occupation or organization concerned, or for a wider social system of which these are part. In these terms, it is often argued that ideological assumptions lead gatekeepers to act in the ways that they do without their being aware of what motivates them.

We find a similar range of types of explanation if we turn to the second explanatory site: that concerned with why people with *potential* access to particular educational routes or rewards, or to occupational positions, might deviate from the behaviour specified by the meritocratic model as required to achieve them. It may be argued, for instance, that children from lower social classes tend to have lower aspirations than those coming from higher social classes, and that this means that they tend not to work as hard in school, not to stay

---

[24]Of course, in some societies at some times, or within particular organizations, there may even be official rules barring some category of person from being recruited to particular types of post. However, in general, Western societies have moved away from this, although restrictions in terms of age, criminal record, and mental health status operate in some contexts.

on after compulsory schooling, not to apply for university, or not to apply to elite universities, and not to aim at or value high-level occupational positions. Here, intentional explanation, where it occurs, is almost always combined with an appeal to other factors that are held to shape aspirations or preferences, put obstacles in the way of pursuing educational or occupational success, etc. For example, the level or kind of aspirations displayed by those in lower social classes may be explained as an adaptation to the perceived reality of where 'people like us' typically end up. Or it may be argued that they have been taken in by the dominant ideology which portrays people of their kind as incapable or unworthy of high-level educational and occupational performance.[25]

There are some important points to be made about the modes of explanation employed in research framed by the meritocratic paradigm. A first one is that conformity to meritocratic norms, on the part of either gatekeepers or the people being selected or recruited, is treated as not in need of explanation, or at least the explanation for it is taken as given. In general terms, this follows from what I referred to earlier as the perspectival character of social scientific explanation. One of the functions of any value-relevance framework is precisely to determine what does and does not require explanation. This does not amount to epistemic bias, *so long as the value-relativity of judgments about what requires explanation is recognized and made explicit.* However, it is not uncommon for this relativity to be forgotten or denied so that, in effect, the meritocratic paradigm is inscribed into reality by the analyst, with conformity to meritocratic norms being treated as the product of natural or rational processes, whereas deviance is conceptualized as the result of irrationality, false motivation, or causal processes operating 'behind people's backs'.[26]

A clear illustration of this danger, albeit relating to gender rather than social class, is provided by Nussbaum's (2001a) discussion of 'adaptive preferences' on

---

[25]Here, there is often an oscillation between intentional explanations and those which appeal to unconscious processes or mechanisms that operate 'behind the backs' of those involved (see Gomm 2001). This may be generated by ethical objections both to 'blaming the victim' and to portraying people as passive victims of circumstance rather than being active agents. An interesting approach which puts forward an intentional explanation is Goldthorpe's (1996b) adaptation of Boudon's rational choice model. Goldthorpe argues that it may be rational for individuals starting from lower-class positions not to aspire to reach the highest educational or occupational levels, whereas it is rational for those born into higher social groups to aspire to retain their positions.

[26]The problem here is by no means restricted to rational choice theory, but it can be illustrated by this approach. For example, what Goldthorpe presents as rational adaptations to different starting points within the occupational system, and the differential benefits and costs of reaching various destinations, is rational on the basis of a rather economistic model that, while by no means implausible, should not be assumed to be universal, any more than should the conception of rationality inscribed in the meritocratic paradigm.

the part of women.[27] She addresses the question of whether we must simply accept people's preferences as given, and judge what is desirable in terms of how far there is equality in the degree to which those preferences are satisfied. She argues that while we should not ignore such preferences – or seek to replace them with objective judgments about what people *ought to* want, or would want if they were being rational – they must be appraised and in some cases treated as adaptations to unjust conditions, and therefore as in need of re-evaluation. Thus, in the course of her argument she discusses the factors that can 'deform' preferences (p. 71). These include: insufficient or false information, 'utterly unreasonable wants' (p. 72), non-ideal decision-making conditions, false setting of value priorities as a result of early experience, carelessness, distractions, fear, and a low sense of one's own worth and dignity.[28]

From the point of view of a concern with factual inquiry, there are two problems with Nussbaum's argument. First, the factors held to explain adaptation are described in evaluative terms: in other words, in ways that involve implicit comparison with some standard of adequacy or propriety. Thus, in relation to the availability of information, assumptions are made about what information is necessary and what would be sufficient, and what should be accepted as true or treated as false. As regards wants, there is judgment about what would and would not be reasonable. In the case of distractions, there is the issue of what is and is not an appropriate focus of attention. In relation to each of these factors, then, we need to be aware of the value judgments being made and the assumptions on which these rely. It seems to me that, from the point of view of social science, there is much to be said for formulating causal factors in ways that do not involve evaluations of this kind, not least because the chances of reaching agreement about them even within the research community are low. To avoid this problem, we could, for example, seek to determine how far the particular preference adopted followed from the information that was accessible to actors, and would have been different had other information been available, leaving on one side any judgment on our part about whether or not this was sufficient or true. Similarly, we could investigate how far the action stemmed from particular wants, and perhaps also seek to explain how people came to have these wants, without evaluating them as reasonable or unreasonable. And similarly for the other factors.

---

[27] I have focused on Nussbaum's article because it provides an explicit and philosophically sophisticated account. Few, if any, social scientists present a rationale for treating assumptions about social justice as factual matters. While Nussbaum departs from Aristotle's teleological view of nature, she adopts his method whereby value considerations are taken into account in making factual claims (see Nussbaum 2001b: 320–1). On the work of Nussbaum in this area, see Alexander 2008.

[28] She is spelling out Harsanyi's views here, but her concern is to expand his account of how preferences may be deformed. There is an interesting parallel with more recent arguments for 'libertarian paternalism' (Thaler and Sunstein 2009).

The second point to note about Nussbaum's approach to explaining adaptive preferences is that it strongly implies that the preferences she judges to be rational were *not* formed through operation of the factors she lists. Yet, a moment's thought will indicate that probably all of our preferences are developed in situations where we rely upon what can be judged insufficient or false information, where there are what can be seen as distractions, and so on. Similarly, our wants will be determined by prior experience, not freely chosen in an absolute sense. Nussbaum seems to assume that there are two sorts of preference-formation processes operating in the world: one that relies upon rational considerations, for example generating preferences in line with meritocracy; and another that is shaped by causes of various kinds that deform these natural preferences. Yet, there is no good reason to make this assumption. Rather, we should assume that the same kinds of social processes can generate both the preferences that we evaluate to be rational (in terms of some framework) and those that we judge to be irrational. And much the same applies to aspirations and actions.[29]

In short, there is a danger here of forgetting our reliance on a particular value-relevance framework, and thereby, in effect, reading it into the world. Yet, as I have stressed, there are always other frameworks that would lead us to treat somewhat different things as normal or rational, and thereby different things as needing to be explained. The effect of forgetting this is to assume that, and/or to allow it to appear as if, conformity to the meritocratic ideal is simply a product of commitment to that ideal and is otherwise uncaused. Even more dangerous is the obverse: a tendency to deny or overlook the possibility that deviance from the meritocratic model could have been a product of genuine commitment to ideals, and to assume instead that it must be explained in terms of self-interest or subjection to some causal process operating beyond the awareness of the actors concerned, for example as part of a systemic process of socio-cultural reproduction. Given the perspectival character of sociological explanation, it is essential to underline that people may be motivated by other conceptions of merit or reward, by different ideas about the nature and function of education, or by other concerns, including attachments to kin and peers, that they judge to be incompatible with pursuit of educational or occupational success (as defined by the meritocratic paradigm) or that in effect serve as obstacles to it.[30]

---

[29]My argument here is a version of what, in the sociology of scientific knowledge, came to be referred to as the principle of symmetry, see Barnes 1974 and Bloor 1976. A presentation of the same idea in a different context is Matza's notion of an 'appreciative stance', see Matza 1969. More fundamentally, this is one aspect of the ideal of value neutrality.

[30]I am adopting here what Swift refers to as a compatibilist conception of the relationship between evaluations of the reasonableness of action and causal explanation of that action (Marshall et al. 1997: 175).

As noted earlier, a problem with terms like 'bias', 'discrimination', 'prejudice', etc. is that they are often laden with both descriptive and evaluative meanings (see Foster et al. 2000). To show that there is bias from the meritocratic ideal on the part of some actor is not in itself to imply that her or his behaviour *deviated from an ideal that ought to have been adhered to*. In much the same way, to show that those involved in educational selection or occupational recruitment discriminate among candidates on grounds outside those specified by some particular meritocratic ideal *does not in itself imply that this is undesirable or unjustifiable*. These value conclusions only follow if we adopt the meritocratic ideal (as specified earlier) as the only appropriate standard of behaviour, and it is not legitimate for researchers to do this in their work. The point is that research cannot adjudicate among the reasons that people have for acting in one way rather than another; and so the value framework adopted for the purposes of investigation must not be treated as if it were the only rationally valid one.[31]

It is also important to recognize that social science cannot determine what is or is not, was or was not, within an actor's freedom of social action. Such judgments may well be reasonable, but they always rely upon value assumptions about what *ought and ought not* to be treated as a constraint, what *should be* reflected upon or deliberated about, which costs *ought or ought not to be* borne, which risks *should and should not be* anticipated and/or taken, and so on. The point is not simply that social science is incapable of authoritatively deciding on these matters, but also that *there is no need for it to do so*. Its task is to examine value-relevant factors that generated some outcome, and by what processes this occurred, not to determine whether or not the agents involved could or should have done otherwise. It is crucial in the task of explanation, then, to avoid implying that deviation from the meritocratic ideal was produced by self-interest or caused, whereas conformity with it was not. Similarly, any implication should be avoided that deviation is a culpable matter, whereas conformity is desirable. These are issues that are outside the scope of social science.

There is a further important way in which the value-relevance framework affects the process of explanation. This is that it properly frames the selection of explanatory factors. The task of explaining differences in educational achievement or occupational mobility does not amount to discovering the unique and exhaustive set of determinants of these phenomena, treated as making up a closed system (see Chapter 2). As with all social explanation, there is potentially an infinite number of operating causal factors, since any outcome is usually caused by more than one factor, each of which will have been shaped by several earlier causes, and so on, *ad*

---

[31]The point I am making here was highlighted many years ago by Murphy (1981, 1990). It might be argued that research can at least adjudicate regarding the factual assumptions built into value judgments. This is true to an extent, but even its capacity in this respect must not be overestimated: research is not the only source of sound factual knowledge, and very often cannot provide information about the local contexts in which decisions have to be made.

infinitum. In explaining anything, we necessarily select out from this infinite field those causes that are relevant to the value framework within which the research is being carried out. Selection here is likely to be further determined by notions, adopted for working purposes, of what is and is not likely to be open to change (for example, via policy), how the distribution of responsibilities across agents might be adjudged, and so on.

Of course, within the limits set by value relevance, we still have to develop and check the validity of causal hypotheses: the value-relevance framework does not tell us what actually causes what, only which candidate causes would have direct relevance for the point of view we have adopted. Moreover, while it is true that there is a potentially infinite number of causal factors operating, this does not mean that we can assume that they all have equal causal power, or that they all function in the same ways. Rather than simply identifying a list of value-relevant factors, we need to get a clearer sense of how they relate to one another and to other factors that do not have direct value relevance themselves but are implicated with those that do in the causal process. For example, we might identify the level of aspirations of applicants for university from lower social class origins as one of the factors that could explain why they enter elite universities less frequently. We need to determine, first, the likelihood that, if these aspirations were changed, more people from lower social classes would enter elite universities. The next step might be to try to discover how these aspirations are formed and what sustains them. There are some standard types of explanation here, most obviously explanations that appeal to early childhood socialization, point to the influence of peers, emphasize adaptations to circumstance, or stress the role of reference group comparisons.[32]

Summarizing this section, then, explanations must not be put forward as if they *exhaustively* captured the real causes operating, but instead as identifying significant causes from the point of view of the value-relevance framework adopted. However, this does not mean that the *validity* of the knowledge presented is relative to this framework, so that if we were to adopt a different framework a contradictory conclusion would be true. Epistemological relativism is not involved. If the explanation

---

[32]It must be emphasized that none of these explanations rules out rational deliberation on the part of the people concerned: what they point to are different contexts, in terms of which that deliberation takes place, as regards what is treated as given, who is taken to provide a worthwhile model, what would be a rational course of action, and so on. An associated issue concerns the completeness of any causal account provided. Given the infinity of causes that could, in principle, be selected, any account will be incomplete in absolute terms. However, any particular value framework will indicate a range of factors that *would be* relevant, and this initially defines what needs to be investigated. Thus, one criticism that can be made of a study is that it fails to take into account all of the factors that are relevant given the value framework adopted. An opposite criticism would be that it includes factors that are not relevant in terms of that framework, either directly or indirectly. It is also possible that a framework is inadequately specified, so that it is unclear what would and would not be relevant.

is true, the causes identified will be real, but they will not be the *only* causes that have been involved in producing the outcome. The key point is that *what* is taken to be in need of explanation, and *which* operating causal factors are identified, will be relative to the value framework adopted, so that other frameworks may quite legitimately pick out other factors, perhaps an overlapping set or a quite different one.

More fundamentally, it is crucial, above all, not to treat those aspirations, preferences, or actions that are in line with the meritocratic ideal as if they were rational or natural, while portraying deviance from this ideal as self-interested, irrational, or caused. Deviance from the meritocratic ideal may well have taken place for what the actors involved regarded as good reasons, and which from other value perspectives may well be good reasons. Actors may or may not accept the version of the meritocratic ideal assumed by a particular research study; and, even if they do, they may regard other considerations as more important in the circumstances. This does not alter the fact that deviation has occurred, but it does carry implications for how we explain it. There is a tendency built into the debunking tradition of sociology to appeal to self-interested or unconscious motivations in explaining such deviance. The point is not that these sorts of explanation have no bite; it is simply that conformity could be explained in the same terms. In the case of both conformity and deviance, the reasons given by actors should not be dismissed, but neither should they be immediately accepted as valid or as sufficient explanation. Moreover, we must expect that the same sorts of causal processes could be operating in relation to both. Most important of all, research is not capable of determining, on its own, what are and are not good reasons, or what could or could not have been done in the circumstances; nor is this part of its task.

Conclusion

In this chapter I began by noting that research on social mobility has been guided by at least three distinct sets of practical political concerns. Furthermore, as might be expected, these rely upon rather different value principles. In the context of this, I outlined a broadly Weberian perspective on the nature of sociological research in this field. In the remainder of the chapter I explored the implications of this, focusing on the task of investigating how far Britain, or any other society, deviates from being a meritocracy and of explaining this deviation. This Weberian methodological perspective generates a series of limits that properly operate on the contribution that social science can make to public discussion of social problems and policy issues in general, and of issues of social class inequality in educational selection and occupational destination in particular.[33]

---

[33]It might be noted that much research in this field has adopted a broadly Weberian stance in substantive terms, but has generally failed to recognize the implications of the methodological position that Weber adopted.

A first implication is that social science cannot, on its own, provide an answer to the question 'Is Britain (or any other society) a meritocracy?' This would require practical value judgments, notably regarding what counts as merit and whether it is appropriately rewarded, and such value judgments cannot be derived solely from the factual evidence generated by social scientific research. The latter can provide relevant factual knowledge but it cannot legitimate practical evaluations or recommendations. At most, it can only offer conditional judgments as regards what *would be* the evaluation or the recommendation *if one set of value assumptions, rather than another, were adopted*. To aim research at drawing evaluative or prescriptive practical conclusions both involves increasing the risk of systematic error in the findings and amounts to a form of scientism, in the sense of over-extending the distinctive authority of research. Given this, it is important that social scientists underline the limits to what they can offer in this respect, albeit while nevertheless stressing its value. The difficult task of re-educating audiences for social research may also be involved here.

A second type of limit derives from another tenet of Weberianism: the notion of value-relevance. This indicates that any factual investigation operates within a framework set by a particular complex of value principles through which social phenomena worth studying are identified. Given that many different frameworks can be adopted, it is necessary to spell out the value assumptions which provide the framework for any particular study. In the course of my discussion, I outlined some of the assumptions that seem to have guided much research on social mobility and educational selection, assumptions that are generally left implicit. I also indicated what these excluded in order to show that the factual information generated by social science within the meritocratic paradigm will be relevant only to *some* of the political and practical views that may be operating within this area, and could be regarded as irrelevant from other perspectives. In other words, the relevance, though not the validity, of the knowledge any study provides is dependent upon (relative to) the particular value assumptions on which it relies to identify its research focus (for example, about what would constitute meritocracy).

A third implication of a Weberian perspective is that great care must be taken in developing explanations for why there is deviation from the meritocratic ideal. These explanations too are necessarily framework-dependent, in the sense that relevance to particular values provides the basis not just for determining what is and is not in need of explanation, but also for selecting among the many factors that are involved in generating the outcome to be explained; in other words, deciding which ones are to be included in the explanation offered. I noted that, in research on meritocracy, there has sometimes been a tendency to assume that structures, processes, procedures and actions that are conducive to its achievement are the product of rationality or virtue, whereas those which seem to generate deviation are the result of irrationality, self-interested motives, or causes operating 'behind the backs' of the people involved. I argued that this assumption is false, that the same *sorts* of causal mechanism are likely to underpin both those social outcomes we judge to be desirable and those we deplore. The sort of asymmetrical approach to explanation I am rejecting here also sometimes goes along with a tendency to treat what are viewed as socially unjust inequalities as if they were simply factual matters, so that their inequitable nature is open to observation or would be recognized from any authentic value perspective. I argued that it is necessary to guard against any temptation to treat the explanations produced within the framework of the meritocratic paradigm as if they simply reflected reality; to avoid any tendency to forget the value-relevance assumptions on which they rely; and to counter any desire to move automatically from these to practical evaluations of, or recommendations about, the processes involved.

The limitations operating on studies of social mobility and educational inequalities I have identified here are quite severe ones, and are frequently breached by research in these fields. To the extent that my arguments are sound, this needs to be remedied. It is important to repeat, however, that identifying limits on what sociological research can achieve does not amount to dismissing it as worthless. What is required is that we are clear about what can and cannot be achieved; and that we avoid exaggerating the contribution that social science can make in addressing important issues such as whether or not Britain, or any other society, is a meritocracy.

SIX

We didn't predict a riot! On the public contribution of social science

> The question of prediction in economics [...] brings together most of the main questions [...]: [...] of what economists can or should try or claim to do, and what it is presumptuous, pretentious, or even dangerous and damaging, for them to try or claim to do. (Hutchison 1977: 8)

> The actual riots are rarely predicted; but when they happen, people with political opinions tend to immediately know why they happened – what *really* caused them. (Green 2011)

My specific focus in this chapter is the explanations put forward by social scientists for riots that occurred in London and other English cities in August 2011. I examine whether these explanations had distinctive features, as compared with those offered by non-social scientists, such as participants in the riots or politicians. More precisely, the empirical question I am addressing is: If social scientists have expertise about the nature and causes of the riots, does this expertise display itself in their public contributions? But the underlying concern is much broader than this: it relates to the nature of, and prospects for, social scientific knowledge, and its role in the public sphere.[1]

---

[1] Most, but by no means all, of the social scientists who commented on the riots were sociologists. I will use the terms 'sociologist' and 'social scientist' interchangeably, though I recognize that those from different disciplines can claim somewhat different forms of expertise. There were also commentaries from academics who are not social scientists, for example David Starkey, the historian (see www.guardian.co.uk/media/2011/aug/15/david-starkey-newsnight-race-remarks and www.youtube.com/watch?v=uFpzjaXYmfA), and also the epidemiologist Gary Slutkin, see www.guardian.co.uk/uk/2011/aug/14/rioting-disease-spread-from-person-to-person, as well as the psychiatrists Aiello and Pariante (2013). See also: www.kcl.ac.uk/iop/news/records/2012/August/London-riots.aspx

That social scientists have an obligation to participate in public discussion of problematic events, and in relation to policy issues more generally, has long been widely accepted, even though, of course, social scientists have varied in the degree of emphasis they have given to this sort of work and how they have conceived and practised it.[2] The most influential recent version of this position, Burawoy's (2005) argument for 'public sociology', identified complementary types of sociology and appeared to give them all equal status. However, the general effect of his writings on this topic has nevertheless been very much to suggest that there is a requirement for social scientists to 'publicly engage', and this call has been taken up by others, although there has also been criticism of various aspects of his position, and from a variety of directions (see, for example, Deflem 2005; Clawson et al. 2007; Holmwood 2007, 2011b; McLaughlin and Turcotte 2007; Nichols 2007; Goldberg and van den Berg 2009; Wacquant 2009).

Of course, in making public statements about current issues, social scientists join with many other kinds of commentator. These include people engaged in practical occupations that give them relevant experience and expertise, which in the case of riots would take in police officers, community activists, social workers, and probation officers; though, in fact, there seems to have been relatively little public commentary coming from these sources about the UK riots, apart from senior police officers. By contrast, there were, of course, many commentaries from journalists, politicians and academics. Furthermore, via the media, and some research (notably Lewis and Newburn 2011; and Morrell et al. 2011), some of the participants in the riots, or witnesses to these events, were also able to present explanations publicly. There was, in short, considerable competition in the public sphere to offer explanations for the riots, from several quarters.

It is against this background that the issue of what is distinctive about social scientists' contributions can be raised. Of course, there have long been questions about how social scientists can claim superior knowledge to that of others, especially in relation to those with direct and long-term experience of the phenomena being investigated.[3] Moreover, social scientists' claims to expertise in contributing to discussions of problems and policy in the public sphere have frequently been challenged. Here is a recent example, from within the academic community:

---

[2]For instance, there have been recurrent debates about whether or not social scientists, and academics more generally, should act as public intellectuals, and what form this should take (Hammersley 2000: ch. 1, and 2011a: ch. 2; Boudon 2001). There have also been recent complaints that social scientists have failed to offer public accounts of significant events; for example, the alleged failure of those outside economics not only to predict the financial crash of 2008, but even to contribute to discussions about its nature and consequences, and the solutions required: see Chakrabortty 2012 and the reply by Brewer 2012b.

[3]Similar questions also apply to journalists and politicians, and to academic commentators from outside social science.

> How much authority should we give to [social science] in our policy decisions?
> [...] Media reports often seem to assume that any result presented as 'scientific'
> has a claim to our serious attention. But this is hardly a reasonable view. [...]
> The core natural sciences [...] are so well established that we readily accept their
> best-supported conclusions as definitive. [...] Even the best-developed social sci-
> ences like economics have nothing like this status. [...] The [difference] lies in [...]
> predictive power [...]. (Gutting 2012)

This critique raises questions about the nature of the public contribution that social scientists can make, and about its intellectual authority. Moreover, it links to similar criticisms around the beginning of this century, in the wake of calls for evidence-based policymaking and practice (see Hammersley 2013: Introduction).[4]

Gutting seems to regard prediction as the most valuable contribution that social science can offer, or at least as the foundation on which any contribution could be made. And, of course, the desire for predictions is a felt practical need, one that is filled by various attempts at 'futurology' or 'scenario planning'. As part of this, social scientists do sometimes make predictions. So, too, do lay people: for instance, Lammy (2011: 11) claimed to have been predicting social unrest in the Tottenham area for a year before the riots began there in 2011.[5]

However, there are doubts about whether anyone can predict social events in a reliable way. Open-ended statements like 'I predict a riot' may well prove correct, on occasion, but their vagueness seriously detracts from their practical value. By contrast, accurate statements of a more specific kind – to the effect that riots will occur in specified locations at specified times – while of greater value are very difficult, if not impossible, to produce. Discussing the UK riots, Bauman (2011b) makes the point via an analogy: 'Minefields are areas filled with randomly scattered explosives: one can be pretty sure that some of them, some time, will explode – but one can't say with any degree of certainty which ones and when'. And, of course, there are many fields of physical science, notably seismology and vulcanology, where prediction is equally desired yet also uncertain. Given this, it seems to me that one important contribution that social scientists can make is to encourage caution about predictive claims.[6]

---

[4]There is also criticism of claims to social scientific knowledge from other directions, such as philosophy: for example, from those who challenge the claim that there can be any such thing as a social *science*: see Hutchinson et al. 2008.

[5]See also www.guardian.co.uk/uk/2011/aug/12/riot-predict-trouble-not-over

[6]Hutchison 1964: 89–102 provides an illuminating discussion of the problems of prediction in economics, noting variation in what 'prediction' means. That there are costs and dangers involved in publishing predictions is highlighted by the case of the Italian scientists imprisoned for failing to provide clear predictions about an earthquake: see www.guardian.co.uk/world/2012/oct/23/italian-scientist-earthquake-condemns-court and www.washingtonpost.com/blogs/worldviews/wp/2012/10/24/the-deeper-issues-behind-italys-conviction-of-earthquake-scientists/

Not surprisingly, perhaps, social scientists typically offer explanations, after-the-fact, rather than predictions, but these can nevertheless be very valuable, as regards policy discussion, formation, and implementation. Most discussion of the 2011 riots was concerned with presenting explanations for why they had occurred, or why they had the character that they did. As already noted, these explanations came from a range of sources. Moreover, those offered by social scientists themselves in the last five months of 2011, which is the period on which I will focus, took a variety of forms: from a few lengthy published reports of research into these riots to much briefer contributions, usually not based on specific research.[7] These were given at conferences on the topic and/or published in journals and newspapers, and were often reprinted in other places, on- and off-line, in full or in extract. Such contributions also varied, of course, according to how accessible they were to lay audiences and how likely they were to gain attention from those audiences. At one end of this spectrum is the work of Lewis and Newburn (2011), some of which was originally published in the pages of the *Guardian* newspaper, while at the other extreme are articles in academic journals that were not freely available to the public. However, I think it is clear that most of the accounts of the riots that were offered by social scientists were intended for public consumption, rather than being addressed solely to colleagues. Given this, I will not attempt to distinguish among them in terms of likely public accessibility.

Some sociologists' accounts were explicitly designed to highlight the distinctive contribution of the discipline. For example, in a letter in the *Guardian* newspaper, on behalf of the British Sociological Association (BSA), Brewer and Wollman (2011) wrote:

> One of the first things that disappears when considering disturbances such as these is perspective. One loses sight of the fact that nine out of 10 local residents aren't rioting, that nine out of 10 who are rioting aren't local to the area, and that nine out of 10 of these non-locals aren't doing it to commit crime. [...] Crime is a motive, but crowd behaviour is a more complex process, and it is sociology as a discipline that best understands crowd behaviour.

Here the authors are claiming that it is sociology that can provide 'perspective', and they are pointing to the fact that there is a considerable body of sociological work on 'collective behaviour', and specifically on the role of crowds in social unrest.[8] Brewer and Wollman's clear implication is that this sociological knowledge facilitates superior understanding of the riots.

---

[7]For examples of later contributions see Briggs 2012 and *Sociological Research Online* 18, 4, 2013.

[8]This can be traced back at least as far as the writings of Le Bon in the nineteenth century, see Le Bon 1895/2002; Turner and Killian 1987; Marx and McAdam 1993.

This emphasis on the expert understanding that social science can offer is also found in the introduction to a set of explanations for the riots presented in the British Sociological Association *Network* newsletter (No. 109 Winter 2011, p. 22).[9] Here it is stated that: 'Social scientists and other social researchers are beginning to dig behind the headlines that filled the front pages of the UK's newspapers during the August street disturbances'. And this introduction goes on to suggest that 'their conclusions about the causes paint a more nuanced picture than was found in most of the media'. So, here, there is an evaluative contrast between social scientific accounts and those of journalists and other media commentators.

Even where there was no explicit claim about the distinctive capabilities of social science to explain the riots, many social scientific explanations were presented as a direct challenge to those coming from other sources, notably from Conservative politicians, and especially the Prime Minister. Thus, the BSA newsletter presentation, just mentioned, was described as taking a look 'at some of the points [social scientists] have made in trying to explain what the Prime Minister said was "criminality, pure and simple"'. In effect, this statement projects a contrast between a concern with explanation and simple condemnation, and this is the nub of the sociological expertise claimed.[10]

In much the same way, the conference about the riots organized by the Academy of Social Sciences was specifically centred on the explanation offered by Cameron and some of his ministers: that Britain is 'broken' and that the rioters were 'just criminals' (Academy of the Social Sciences 2011). Finally, in one of the accounts reprinted in the BSA *Network* issue, and coming out of the Academy of the Social Sciences conference, Shildrick (2011) commented:

> When David Cameron posits that 'there are pockets of our society who are not just broken, but frankly sick' he perpetuates a moral smokescreen that obscures the real causes of the recent events and feeds pernicious myths about the causes of poverty and worklessness. The UK is deeply economically divided and severe and entrenched poverty exists [...]. Most poverty is not caused by [...] individual fecklessness, idleness or irresponsible consumption habits: [it] is primarily caused by low pay and inadequate benefits.

---

[9]Many of these had already appeared, in longer versions, elsewhere.

[10]In an oft-cited quote, on a visit to one of the areas affected in August 2011, Boris Johnson, Mayor of London, insisted: 'It's time we stopped hearing all this (you know) nonsense about how there are deep sociological justifications for wanton criminality and destruction of people's property. Whatever people's grievances may be, it does not justify smashing up someone's shop, wrecking their livelihood and kicking them out of a job.' This can be found at: www.reuters.com/article/video/idUSTRE7782LX20110809?videoId=218130029 (accessed 25.10.12). See also www.youtube.com/watch?v=gPotJHenTCI for more or less the same comment. Cameron's and Johnson's statements here raise an important issue about how closely explanations are linked to the assignment of responsibility. For a different view on this from the one I take here, see Louch 1966.

Here we have a very strong contrast set up between an ideological account that obscures the real causes of the riots and a true, social scientific one that identifies those real causes as socio-economic inequalities and structurally-generated poverty.[11]

In short, then, as might be expected, many social scientists claimed distinctive expertise in explaining, if not predicting, the riots. In the next sections I will examine some of the explanations for the riots provided by them, and by others, with a view to detecting differences that might relate to social scientific expertise.[12]

Diverse explanations

When we examine the explanations put forward for the riots we find that they refer to a wide range of causal factors. A useful starting point in exploring this range is one of the most widely referred to social scientific contributions, that of Zygmunt Bauman. This was originally published in the online journal *Social Europe*, but was quoted and commented on in many other places. In part, Bauman wrote:

> This was not a rebellion […] of famished and impoverished people or an oppressed ethnic or religious minority – but a mutiny of defective and disqualified consumers, people offended and humiliated by the display of riches to which they had been denied access. We have all been coerced and seduced to view shopping as the recipe for the good life and the principal solution of all life problems – but then a large part of the population has been prevented from using that recipe. (Bauman 2011a)

This is a sophisticated explanation, one that draws implicitly on well-established sociological ideas, notably Merton's (1968) theory of anomie, to which Bauman gives a distinctive twist in focusing on what Campbell (1987) has called 'the spirit of modern consumerism' (see also Moxon 2011; Treadwell et al. 2012).

Bauman's explanation was significantly different from that of many other social scientists. More representative, in the causal factors to which it appeals, was that of Solomos, and he specifically challenged Bauman's account:

---

[11]Of course, social scientists were not the only ones challenging the account of the riots that dominated much of the media and was to be found in the statements of Conservative politicians, depicting rioters as criminals without morals. Similar challenges were posed, for example, by some comedy writers (an entertaining example is Nathaniel Tapley's 'An Open Letter to David Cameron's Parents', available at: http://nathanieltapley.com/2011/08/10/an-open-letter-to-david-camerons-parents/ (accessed 25.10.12), and by centre-left and left-wing groups, including Ed Miliband, the leader of the Opposition (www.guardian.co.uk/uk/video/2011/dec/14/ed-miliband-riot-report-video).

[12]I will only be able to examine a small sample of explanations for the riots in this chapter, but I have endeavoured to ensure that they are broadly representative in key respects.

> Without wanting to say that Zygmunt Bauman's analysis is simplistic [...], one of the dangers of calling the riots consumer riots is that we bring an individualised notion into this discussion. [...] Many social issues that existed in the 1980s and 1990s have not disappeared – unemployment, inequality, policing. [Let's] not fall into the trap of saying that the riots of today are consumer riots and the riots of 1980s and 2001 were different in that kind of way. (Solomos 2011a, see also Solomos 2011b)

Here we find rather different factors being highlighted, indeed ones that Bauman specifically ruled out, though they were emphasized by other social scientists, including Shildrick (quoted earlier). Moreover, neither of these explanations mentions the role of crowd behaviour, emphasized by Brewer and Wollman (2011). My first point, then, is that social scientific expertise did not lead to a single explanation for the riots, but rather to different, and indeed apparently conflicting, explanations.

Equally important is that we find parallels between these social scientific accounts and lay ones. Thus, Bauman's explanation is prefigured or echoed in accounts provided by some of those involved in the riots, or who had witnessed them:

> There was a culture of 'wanting stuff', said an 18-year-old man [...] 'It's like, seen as if you're not wearing like, and you're poor, no one don't want to be your friend'. Some interviewees blamed corporations, advertising and the media for fuelling this acquisitional consumerism. [One said] 'That night those young people they had freedom, because they're pushed with certain things in their face all day [...] 'Buy phones, clothes, cars, jewellery'. (Lewis and Newburn 2011)[13]

What must be concluded from this is either that this sociological theory was developed out of more widely available commonsense explanations for social behaviour and/or that Bauman's account, or other versions of the same idea, have been influential upon lay people.

Of course, we can also find lay explanations that appeal to poverty, relative deprivation, and discrimination, along much the same lines as that of Solomos and most other sociological accounts. For example:

> 'If you're black or coloured skin, basically, you're at the bottom sort of thing,' said one interviewee in the capital. 'And then white people, they start off in the middle and then can get to the top. But black people always start from the bottom'. Another interviewee, an 18-year-old man of mixed race from Birmingham, directly linked those who took to the streets to people's concerns about inequality. 'If they give us, the black people, the opportunities like they give the white community, then that wouldn't have happened,' he said. 'If people had jobs on the line ... if people had college on the line ... if they had something to look forward to or getting a decent income, do they want to ruin it by going to the riots?' (Lewis and Newburn 2011)[14]

---

[13]This publication is an ebook and there is no page numbering.

[14]This sort of explanation was also employed by President Mahmoud Ahmedinajad of Iran, as Giddens points out: www.polity.co.uk/giddens6/blog/post.aspx?id=109

So, my point in this section has been to show that social scientists differed significantly among themselves in the explanations that they put forward, some appealing to the nature of crowd behaviour (Brewer and Wollman), others portraying the rioters as frustrated consumers (Bauman), and many pointing to the role of unemployment, poverty, and social division (for example, Shildrick and Solomos). Equally significant, the explanatory factors appealed to by social scientists were also often to be found in lay accounts, such as those provided by people who had participated in, or witnessed, the riots.[15]

In the next section I want to look at some of the explanations offered by politicians, including that of David Cameron, since, as we saw, these were often directly challenged by social scientific commentators.

Politicians' accounts

There is a fairly obvious difference between the explanatory factors identified by most social scientists and those picked out by some politicians, especially David Cameron. Here are extracts from one of the Prime Minister's speeches about the riots:

> It is all too clear that we have a big problem with gangs in our country. [...] [T]here are pockets of our society that are not just broken but frankly sick. [...] It is a complete lack of responsibility in parts of our society, people allowed to feel the world owes them something, that their rights outweigh their responsibilities and their actions do not have consequences. [...] We need to have a clearer code of standards and values that we expect people to live by and stronger penalties if they cross the line. (Cameron 2011)

What is offered here differs from the social scientific accounts I have looked at in at least two important respects. First, it involves negative evaluations of the rioters, in the sense either of blaming them or of pointing to a deficit on their part.[16] Secondly, it appeals to candidate causal factors that were not usually foregrounded, or even mentioned, in most social scientists' accounts: the role of gangs, of local cultures that emphasize 'rights' and downplay 'responsibilities', and of a code of standards and values that is not sufficiently clear and well enough enforced.

---

[15]Gorringe and Rosie's (2011) discussion reinforces this aspect of my argument here in an interesting way: they challenge the account put forward by Brewer and Wollman (2011), agreeing instead with that presented in the revised *Manual of Guidance on Keeping the Peace* produced by the Association of Chief Police Officers (ACPO 2010).

[16]It is arguable that Bauman's portrayal of the rioters also involves negative evaluation, in the sense that he presents them as having been gullible consumers of consumerist ideology. By contrast, we might argue that other sociological accounts tend to deflect accusations of responsibility and blame away from the rioters, if not actually evaluating their behaviour positively.

While these are significant differences, it is important not to rush to the conclusion that they signal a fundamental divergence in character between social scientists' accounts and those of Conservative politicians. The first point to make is that while Cameron focuses on the personal characteristics of the rioters in his explanation – that they lack a sense of responsibility and have an exaggerated view of their rights – he presents these characteristics as having been socially produced by 'parts of our society', which he labels as 'broken' or 'sick': these have 'allowed' or encouraged these young people to feel the way they do. Moreover, it is suggested that it is 'our' wider society that has failed to provide and enforce a clear enough 'code of standards and values'. Cameron also points to another, related, social factor: the prevalence and influence of gangs in some areas. So, while there are certainly significant differences here, we do not have a simple contrast between, on the one hand, social scientists pointing to social factors and, on the other, Conservative politicians appealing to individual responsibility or to psychological factors.

Moreover, the explanation that Cameron sketches here bears a close resemblance to one that has been influential in sociological studies of delinquency, and that is still accepted in some sections of the sociological community. This is what is sometimes referred to as 'control theory'. One of its main advocates, Hirschi (2002: 16), writes that 'control theories assume that delinquent acts result when an individual's bond to society is weak or broken'. And he points out how this theoretical approach draws on Durkheim's argument that: 'The more weakened the groups to which [the individual] belongs, the less he depends on them, the more he consequently depends only on himself and recognizes no other rules of conduct than what are founded on his private interests' (Durkheim 1951: 209; quoted in Hirschi 2002: 16). Moreover, it is also sometimes argued within this context that, where there is such a weakening of control, dysfunctional groups (such as gangs) may emerge to fill the gap. In broad terms, then, the kind of explanation offered by Cameron is close in character, though of course not in level of sophistication or origin, to Durkheim's interpretation of anomie; this interpretation differing from that of Merton, on which Bauman's explanation for the riots seems to have been based, as I noted earlier.[17]

---

[17]Social control theory is also close to the social disorganization theory that was influential in the Chicago School of the 1930s and 1940s: see Carey 1975. It is worth noting that it might be argued that Hirschi's appeal to Durkheim is misdirected. For example, Hilbert (1989) argues that Durkheim regarded the occurrence of crime as normal, and its punishment as healthy for society. By contrast, a situation of anomie makes the identification of crime impossible since it is a state of normlessness. This reading could, of course, lead to another, very different, sociological perspective on the riots, in which they are seen as functional rather than dysfunctional, since the societal response to them signals the boundaries of 'acceptable behaviour' (see Erikson 1966). On the history of how the meaning of 'anomie' changed across different contexts and over time, see Besnard 1993.

The difference between the accounts of the riots put forward by social scientists and that of the Prime Minister is not, then, that one side presented a *social scientific* explanation while the other did not; nor is it clear that we have a display of social scientific expertise versus one of lay ignorance (even if, personally, one is inclined to find the social scientists' accounts more convincing). Rather, it is that they employ *different* sociological theories. Moreover, while there may be considerable variation in awareness of the nature of the ideas being drawn upon, social scientists' accounts are often no more explicit about this than are those of politicians: for example, Bauman makes no mention of Merton.

A final point I want to make in this section is that, just as the explanations that social scientists put forward varied significantly, so too there was variation in the explanations presented by Conservative politicians. Indeed, accounts from the same politician differed significantly across occasions. Here, for example, is a comment provided by Boris Johnson, Mayor of London, which was produced the following year after the riots:

> There were people who joined in out of a sheer sense of collective intoxification – a kind of madness that gripped a lot of people. But there were people who feel that there is not enough in society for them and were just shockingly nihilistic. We need to know what is going on in these people's lives and why they can feel such a sense of exclusion. [...] I want to try to deal with these kids at an earlier age and try to crack illiteracy – that is at the heart of this. It is crucial that we invest in literacy. (Johnson 2012)

The explanation (or set of explanations) hinted at here seems different from that put forward by Cameron. In fact, there are similarities with the explanations presented by some social scientists. Like Brewer and Wollman (2011), Johnson highlights processes involved in crowd behaviour. In addition, he acknowledges that 'exclusion' has played a role, filling this out with a reference to inadequate educational provision. In doing this, he points to the potential causal role of one particular type of inequality in generating the riots.

Yet, as I noted earlier, Johnson had been widely quoted just after the riots as dismissing, as 'nonsense', 'deep sociological justifications for wanton criminality and destruction of people's property'.[18] This was in the context of his visiting areas damaged by the riots where the immediate audience, apart from the media, was people engaged in cleaning up. Murji and Neal (2011) suggest that there was a change in politicians' accounts over time, from simple to more complex explanations.[19] This may be true in general terms, however we should note that even a few days after his dismissal of 'sociological justifications', Johnson provided the following discussion in a newspaper:

---

[18]See note 10.

[19]Though they seem to step back from this claim in places: 'our point is not that the complexity viewpoint replaces or supersedes simplistic causal explanations, rather both elements are in play at the same time' (Murji and Neal 2011: 3).

I am afraid the explanations will turn out to be [...] complex and [...] various. Some – quite a few – were acting out of greed. Some seem to have been actuated by a feeling of power, a desire to be 'noticed'. Some, especially members of gangs, were perhaps doing it because other people were doing it in other parts of London, and they did not want to be left out. Some of them were doing it for 'fun', or excitement, or because they wanted to get one over on the 'feds'. Some of them were certainly relatively affluent, [...] but the overwhelming majority, of course, came from the lower socio-economic groups, from the ranks of those who have been left the furthest behind; and the most recent figures I have seen suggest that 69 per cent of those charged have previous convictions. It has been said of these young people – and they say it themselves – that the world holds nothing for them, that they have no jobs, no hope and no future. In so far as that is true, it is something we can try to tackle. We can invest, we can 'create' jobs, we can boost our apprenticeship programme, already standing at 30,000. But it is just not true to say that there are no jobs available. The London service economy is substantially dependent on migrant labour, much of it from eastern Europe, and employers confirm that these migrants have skillsets and a work ethic they cannot find in many native-born Londoners. Yes, these young people have been betrayed; but they have been betrayed by an educational system and family background that failed to give them discipline, or hope, or ambition, or a simple ability to tell right from wrong. We still have one in four London 11-year-olds functionally illiterate. No wonder they are angry and alienated. [...] We can change the law to allow the police to administer sjambok drubbings, or we adults can collectively take charge and recognise that it is up to us to give young people hope, boundaries and a moral framework. We can be less squeamish about police violence, or we can be less squeamish about the realities of young people's needs. Of course, we could do both – and I certainly believe that robust policing is essential – but I know which is the best long-term answer.

Here Johnson draws on a very wide range of factors, including ones highlighted by social scientists, acknowledging the complexity of the phenomenon, yet, in so far as there is an overall framework, it is one that is not very far from that adopted by Cameron.[20]

Discussion

I have shown that social scientific commentators presented their explanations for the 2011 riots as superior to the accounts coming from other sources; indeed,

---

[20]One implication of the discussion here is that we need to pay attention to how the contexts in which accounts are given shape them. There has, of course, been much sociological discussion of the occasioned nature of accounts, and of the difficulties of using them to read off stable beliefs, attitudes, etc.: see Hewitt and Hall 1973; Hewitt and Stokes 1975; Stokes and Hewitt 1976; Lyman and Scott 1989. Central here are the 'performative' functions that the provision of explanations may serve, which have been examined by discourse analysts: see, for example, Potter and Wetherell 1987; Potter 1996.

that they explicitly challenged some lay accounts, notably those of Conservative politicians. However, I argued that if we compare these various accounts, it is not obvious that those from social scientists display a distinctive form of expertise. This is because:

1. Social scientists put forward different explanations *from one another*; as do other commentators, including politicians.
2. At the same time, there is considerable *overlap* between the explanatory factors that social scientists and many lay people identified.
3. While there is more of a divide between social scientists' accounts and those of prominent Conservative politicians, especially Cameron, even the latter's explanations nevertheless approximate to a sociological theory, albeit not one on which the social scientific commentators drew.

So, whatever expertise social scientists possess did not lead them all to the same conclusions about the causes of the riots, nor did it result in their identifying a quite different set of explanatory factors from many non-social scientists. Moreover, even the explanation for the riots that many social scientists were particularly concerned to challenge can itself be justified through appeal to the sociological literature.

There are several reasons why this failure to display distinctive expertise could have arisen. One would be that, as Gutting (2012) implied, in fact social scientists do not have any such expertise. This might be because authoritative conclusions about the causes of the riots are not possible, in principle. Perhaps here we are just faced with conflicting ideological viewpoints, each of which only makes sense in its own, incommensurable, terms? Alternatively, it might be argued that social scientific knowledge identifying the causes of the riots *is* possible, but that social scientists have not yet succeeded in developing it sufficiently. A further, rather different, type of explanation would be that while social scientists *do* have expert knowledge, or the capacity for it, they have not managed to translate this into statements in the public sphere in a way that preserves its distinctiveness and evident authority. This may be because of the very nature of the public sphere, or because of how it currently operates: for example, because of the speed at which any account needs to be produced if it is to make a timely contribution to public debate, and/or because of constraints on the length and degree of complexity of effective public contributions.

It is worth exploring this issue a little more, and particularly the question of whether there can be social scientific knowledge explaining the riots, and if so what form this takes. We might ask, first, what sort of distinctive expertise social scientists are claiming, and whether they can make good on that claim. In their accounts, they sometimes emphasized the complexity of the riots and, by implication, perhaps of all social phenomena. For example, the headline on the front of the issue of the BSA *Network* newsletter, in which several sociological explanations for the riots were re-published, reads 'Simple to explain?' The message here is that the accounts offered by politicians and others are simplistic, whereas those of social scientists are more 'nuanced' (p. 22). Indeed, many social scientific accounts made an even stronger claim: to have identified *the* key causal factors. As I noted earlier, Shildrick (2011) declared that social scientists can identify 'the real causes', whereas the accounts coming from Cameron and other Conservative politicians amounted to 'pernicious myths'. Along much the same lines, Reicher and Stott's book has the subtitle 'Myths and realities of the 2011 riots'.

While Shildrick does not indicate explicitly *how* social scientists have gained knowledge of 'the real causes' of the riots, Reicher and Stott (2011: Preface) point in a direction that is probably in line with what most of the lay public would assume. Emphasizing the scope for diverse candidate explanations, these authors comment that:

> The riots were due to spending cuts, they were due to educational policies, they were due to rap music, black culture, single-parent families, lack of respect, liberal education ... and the list goes on. [But] how can one explain an event before we really know what that event was? One might as well suggest that the riots happened because of the place of Mars in relation to Venus or because a five-footed calf was born in June. Without evidence, any opinion is equally good or bad.

So, evidence is required to determine which of the many possible explanations put forward is the correct one. These authors elaborate on this as follows:

> We need a more systematic account of what went on rather than a selection of eye-catching events. We need a more thorough understanding of behaviour in riots in order to know what questions to ask. Only then can we begin to work toward a definitive conclusion as to what happened and why. Only then can we devise effective responses. To do so beforehand is to run the risk of advancing 'solutions' that are both irrelevant to the real problems that we face and which repeat the mistakes of the past.

And these authors believe that it is social scientists who can provide this evidence; indeed, that they have already produced much relevant evidence:

> As students of crowds and of riot behaviour over some thirty years, we also wondered why ['pundits and politicians'] don't learn from the lessons of the past? Back in the 1980s we heard almost identical explanations and responses to the riots – all of which are now accepted to be completely inadequate. Worse still, any advances in understanding crowds and riots that we have gained since then are being either ignored or actively rubbished. What chance do we have of getting things right if we go against the weight of experience?

We should note that, in seeking to explain the riots, social scientists could, in principle, appeal to evidence of several kinds, arising from:

1. Specific research into the 2011 riots;
2. The application of findings from studies of other riots;
3. The application of theories previously developed to explain this, and related, types of event;
4. The application of general theories (Marxism, Rational Choice, Anomie theory, Frustration/Aggression theory, etc.).

Yet, in fact, most social scientists' commentaries on the riots did not appeal explicitly to *any* of these types of evidence. They simply presented conclusions about the riots' causes, without much indication of how these had been reached. Moreover, evidence specifically about the 2011 riots was largely confined to the studies produced by Reicher and Stott (2011), Lewis and Newburn (2011), and Morrell et al. (2011). And even these studies involved rapid, and therefore necessarily rather superficial, investigations.

Of course, this reflects, in large part, the fact that all these social scientific accounts were specifically designed to contribute to public discussion of the riots *quite soon after these events had occurred*, recognizing that public interest in them would rapidly wane given the press of other concerns. Thus, Reicher and Stott (2011: Acknowledgments) report that 'over three weeks, we worked day and night to complete this book in time (we hope) to be of use'. Here, as with 'rapid response' sections of journals, for example in *Sociological Research Online*, there was an attempt to bridge the very different chronologies of research and of public concern with social issues (see Pels 2003).

So, the appeal to evidence was rather limited and problematic in many social scientific accounts. Equally important to note is that some lay accounts *did* cite evidence. This is most obviously true of the book by the Labour politician, MP for Tottenham, David Lammy (2011): he draws on his own contacts with people in Tottenham before and at the time of the riots, as well as on media reports, official statistics, and some academic research. Of course, there is scope for discriminating between systematic and less systematic (or more and less rigorous) uses of data, but it is not clear that there is any significant overall difference in this respect between the three books produced by social scientists and that of Lammy. Moreover, as already noted, many of the explanations offered by social scientists did not draw explicitly on evidence anyway.

As I indicated, the need for social science was promoted on the grounds that understanding the riots is a complex and difficult task. Indeed, arguably, it is more challenging even than Reicher and Stott and other social scientist commentators seem to acknowledge. Certainly, this is a conclusion that could be drawn from reading the methodological literature in sociology, which displays little consensus as regards what is required if we are to establish the validity of causal explanations of the kind required here (see, for instance, McKim and Turner 1997; Ragin 2008; Byrne and Ragin 2009; Cooper et al. 2012; and see Chapter 1). Moreover, showing the effects of *remote, structural* causes of the sort to which most social scientific explanations for the riots appealed is especially demanding; though these problems also arise where appeal is made to an alleged breakdown in moral restraints within particular communities. It is normally much easier to show connections between particular actions and features of the immediate situation which the agent faced (for example, the response to a killing, to an opportunity to loot, to an absence of police, etc.) or between actions and particular motives (these perhaps being expressed in interviews, or shown in what action was taken – for instance, attacking police stations rather than robbing stores). There are those who would raise questions about whether social scientists currently have the means for producing cogent social structural explanations for riots, or for anything else.

Beyond this, though, I want to question whether it would ever be possible to produce a single explanation that identifies 'the real causes' of the riots. There are considerable resources available within the literature of social science to throw doubt on this claim. Some of these arise from various forms of sceptical constructionism: are there not simply different accounts of the world, different narratives, founded upon distinct ontological and epistemological assumptions? Or discrepant accounts occasioned by different contexts or sets of interests?

Even putting these constructionist arguments aside, there are still some reasons for doubting the availability of a single correct explanation. The first is that there is not just one thing to be explained here, but rather various features of the riots that might be the focus for explanation: why they occurred *when* they did; why they occurred *where* they did; why particular types of people were involved; why the riots took one predominant form rather than another (looting, arson, etc.); why some buildings, vehicles, and people were targeted and others were not; why the police response took the forms that it did at various stages and the consequences of this; and so on. The sorts of explanatory factor appealed to are likely to vary considerably depending upon which aspects of the riots are treated as the main concern – in other words, as being most in need of explanation.

Another reason for doubting that there is a single correct explanation is that, as some social scientist commentators pointed out, the riots were not a single event, with participants all being the same throughout as regards the nature of their involvement and their motivation. Thus, Reicher and Stott (2011) note that there is great danger in the way in which many media accounts treated a single image as representing what was done by the rioters and its consequences. Like some other authors, they trace the changing character of the riots as these 'moved' from Tottenham to other areas (see also Morrell et al. 2011: 4). Given this heterogeneity, multiple factors will have played a part, opening up the need for different explanations for the behaviour of different groups of rioters at *different places* and *times*, or even for the actions of different individuals in the *same* place at the *same* time (see Morrell et al. 2011: 25).

Even more fundamentally, we might question whether any aspect of any part of the riots is explainable in terms of a single causal mechanism. Instead, it might be argued that in each case there are always a very large number of factors involved. Not only is there usually a range of factors that have an immediate effect on people's actions (in the case of the riots, perhaps a felt need for revenge, desire for particular kinds of consumer good, imitation of others, opportunity provided by the absence of the police, etc.), but each of these factors is, in turn, itself the product of one or more other factors (peer pressure in particular directions, police stop-and-search policies, the advertising strategies of shops and other companies, and so on), and the same is true of each of this second set of more remote factors, *and so on*. This means that all explanations are necessarily selective in what factors they include and exclude, and in the priority they give to some factors rather than others, *over and above any assessments of the distinctive causal contribution of each of these factors* (see Chapter 2). Thus, any notion of a complete explanation, in absolute terms, is meaningless. And there is no incompatibility as regards factual matters between explanations for the riots in terms of response to perceived injustice and those appealing to a weakening of norms in particular communities. Assuming that the factors identified within both frameworks play a significant causal role, and they may well do, arguments about which perspective is appropriate are primarily about what is the proper framework for understanding the riots. And this is, in part, a value issue, relating to such matters as: who should be held responsible for what type of outcome, what might be a remedy for the problems involved, and so on. Also implicated here are assumptions about what could and could not have been different in the situation, what can and cannot be changed, and also what *should* and *should not* be changed.

It might seem from this that the difference in the explanatory factors appealed to by social scientists and by Conservative politicians does indeed simply reflect a reliance upon different value perspectives, rather than a differential reliance upon empirical evidence. If so, once again, this could imply that there is no scope for any claim to social scientific expertise.

It is certainly possible to formulate what is involved here as a conflict in value perspectives. At one end of the political spectrum, for David Cameron and some of his colleagues the proper explanation lies in a low sense of personal responsibility on the part of the rioters, their actions being portrayed as patently lacking any justification and having no excuse. Moreover, this derives from a background picture of a society in which there are broadly equal opportunities for everyone to get paid employment and to achieve high economic rewards and social status. The main barriers to this are seen as policies that operate as dis-incentives to such aspirations, plus families and communities that develop cultures which dissuade or do not support those aspirations, or even offer instead a model of dependence on the state or of engagement in criminal activity.[21]

---

[21]It may be tempting to assume that the background picture here is simply a factual matter, and that it is false. However, it is not purely factual: it relies upon assumptions

Meanwhile, at the other end of the political spectrum is the following sort of value-perspective:

> the horrors imposed on the world economy by the IMF, neo-liberalism, the crimes of the international bankers and support for criminal wars against civilian populations, [mean that] what passes for rule of law in the 21st century commands [...] little respect.[22]

Here it is implied that the rioting can be justified, or at least excused, on the grounds that social inequalities in wealth and income mean that many young people do not have access to the products that the adverts continually tell them they need and deserve ('you're worth it'). Furthermore, this is a society in which the rule of law has been debased by its selective application: those committing relatively minor offences are punished, and even those stereotypically *suspected* of offences are repeatedly stopped and searched, while those responsible for illegal policies that cause death on a major scale or those who engage in reckless financial speculation with other people's money avoid any penalty, indeed they accrue massive economic and social rewards. I suggest that something like this value-perspective lies behind many social scientists' accounts of the riots.[23]

This implies that the conflict between social scientists' and Conservative politicians' perspectives concerns what are seen as the most important social problems in contemporary society, and what is and is not justifiable or excusable in light of this. Moreover, it could be argued that, even in a situation approximating to Habermas's (2001) 'ideal speech situation', dialogue would be difficult between representatives of these two ideological positions: they have different starting points and priorities among felt commitments, and there is no absolute bedrock

---

about what counts as equal opportunity, how close an approximation to equality of opportunity is justifiable given other considerations, etc. Furthermore, some of Boris Johnson's comments indicate recognition that there are barriers to equality of opportunity beyond those just mentioned that need tackling in the UK, and David Cameron might well agree. However, for them, these are subordinated to other considerations in relative importance. It is also necessary to recognize that their emphasis on individual responsibility is by no means alien to some parts of the sociological tradition, notably those that place more emphasis on 'agency' than 'structure'.

[22]This was published under the heading 'Smash and grab on a global scale', by follow the money, available at: http://letters.mobile.salon.com/opinion/greenwald/2011/08/10/victor_davis_hanson/view/index3.html (accessed 25.10.12).

[23]It is important to recognize that the range of political perspectives is more complex than this spectrum suggests. This is illustrated by Žižek's (2011) account. He argues that 'it is difficult to conceive of the UK rioters in Marxist terms, as an instance of the emergence of the revolutionary subject; they fit much better the Hegelian notion of the "rabble", those outside organised social space, who can express their discontent only through "irrational" outbursts of destructive violence – what Hegel called "abstract negativity".'

of common assumptions to which they could appeal in trying to resolve specific areas of disagreement, even if there were commitment to trying to do this.[24] In any case, the public sphere, at present and for the foreseeable future, is a long way from the 'ideal speech situation' (Hammersley 2006: Epilogue). And, even if it approximated to this, it is hard to see how social scientists could claim expertise in resolving such ideological disputes, except in one specific respect – where the differences relate primarily to factual matters. And it is easy to overestimate the extent to which ideologies are sensitive to variation in factual assumptions. Equally important, it might be argued that ideological differences underlie some of the fundamental theoretical and methodological disagreements to be found *within* social science.[25]

It is worth adding that Shildrick's (2011) contrast between social scientists' accounts and those of Cameron and other Conservative politicians does not just claim a difference in epistemic status, the first being true and the second false, but also hints at a difference in orientation between the two parties: to promote a 'pernicious' account, to put up a 'moral smokescreen', is to be primarily concerned with the performative effect of the account on audiences, whereas to present an explanation that identifies the 'real factors' suggests a pre-eminent concern with the truth. Of course, it would not be surprising if politicians were mainly concerned with diverting blame away from their own policies, and/or laying it on others, using the riots as a way of highlighting issues that they already have a commitment to prioritizing, reinforcing political messages designed to bolster support for their own party, and/or seeking to undercut support for the opposition, and so on. But we must ask: are social scientists exempt from this kind of motivation? Their critics, including Conservative politicians, would no doubt argue that many of them have fixed theoretical or even political agendas, and that these will have determined the sorts of account *they* provided of the riots. Indeed, social scientists are in any case often quick to attribute precisely such motives to colleagues with whom they disagree (see Hammersley 1995: ch. 4 and 2000: ch. 5). Beyond this, many social scientists today claim that research is necessarily political, that it inevitably reflects the political commitments and purposes of the researcher, and/or of those who sponsor their work. In addition, there are social scientific approaches that portray all accounts as necessarily reflecting the adoption of particular 'vocabularies of motive' (Mills 1940) or discursive strategies

---

[24]This is not to say that any value framework is as good as any other: frameworks can be judged in terms of how comprehensive they are in taking account of all that might be deemed relevant, and in whether they give appropriate priority to particular values, and make reasonable judgments about the degree to which various features of the situation are and are not acceptable, how internally consistent they are, and so on. But often there will be disagreement about these matters.

[25]This has long been argued, from Gouldner 1970 onwards.

(Potter 1996), that are partial and indeed constitutive of the social world rather than simply representing it (Clifford and Marcus 1986). Given this, how can the contrast that Shildrick employs, and on which many other sociological commentators rely, be justified?

While the social scientists who offered explanations for the riots hardly ever explicitly declared a political commitment, there were signs that some were concerned to push public discussion in a particular direction, over and above simply documenting the facts. As we saw, many were concerned to challenge and discredit the accounts presented by Conservative politicians and by influential parts of the news media. In more specific terms, Reicher and Stott (2011: online publication) write:

> As long as [readers] feel, after reading what we have to say, that perhaps the riots were not all about criminality, that they were not entirely mindless and meaningless eruptions, and that policing our streets with baton rounds and water cannons will not provide an answer, then we will have achieved what we set out to do.

This makes clear that they, like some others, and like the politicians as well, were concerned not just with establishing what happened and why, but also with drawing and/or promoting political lessons from the riots.

Given this, we seem to be faced with the conclusion that the conflict between social scientists' accounts and those of Conservative politicians is indeed largely a clash of political perspectives, rather than a contrast between a concern with finding the truth through examining evidence versus producing an ideological account designed to serve particular political purposes. In this respect, once again, the grounds for claims to expertise seem to have been undercut.

However, in my view, these lines of argument are too pessimistic. Social scientists do have access to greater factual knowledge and resources for understanding riots, and other social phenomena, as compared with most lay people; even if the difference is only a matter of degree. And it *is* possible to focus primarily on building this knowledge, rather than upon constructing an account that serves particular political purposes. Moreover, while it is not possible to identify some single set of 'real causes', it *is* feasible to eliminate some factors as not making any, or at least only a very small, contribution. In addition, social scientists can successfully document the operation of some of the key factors that play a role in producing outcomes like riots.

But I suggest that doing this requires that they recognize that there are important limits on what they can legitimately claim to produce. At most, social science can only claim to provide authoritative accounts of the operation of the causal factors deemed relevant from within a particular value perspective, rather than determining a single set of 'real causes'. And, given this, they must not present practical evaluations or recommendations as validated by their research, since it cannot do this on its own. This is because social scientists cannot claim any distinctive expertise in relation to value issues, for example in determining which social problems are more and less important, who should be held responsible, or blamed, for what, and so on.[26] As I noted, assumptions about these matters necessarily shape the selection of causal factors and their combination into explanations. Given this, it is necessary not only for social scientists to present cogent evidence in support of their knowledge claims, but also to make explicit the value-framework within which their research has been carried out, and to recognize that this is not the only one that could have been adopted. Some recognition of the difficulties and dangers involved in producing descriptions and explanations for social phenomena would also be desirable.

The position being adopted here is, of course, a broadly Weberian one. It preserves the idea that, while all accounts or explanations are necessarily partial, there should be a significant difference in orientation between social scientists, and particularly academic researchers, and others: the aim of any inquiry in social science should be to provide true answers to factual questions that have value-relevance.[27] And it is only on this basis that social scientists, whose sole occupational goal should be to produce knowledge, can claim distinctive expertise. Indeed, it seems to me that any claim to social scientific expertise hinges precisely on this difference in orientation. If it is absent, then no expertise can be claimed.

On the basis of this discussion, then, social scientists' expertise lies in the capacity to pursue answers to factual questions more effectively than others. And, to the extent that they have adopted this orientation, social scientists will hopefully have built up a body of knowledge and understanding that allows them to generate factual explanations of events like riots that are more likely to be true than those offered by others – even though they cannot claim to provide a single conclusive explanation.

Conclusion

There is, then, scope for social scientific expertise about what actually happened in the riots, about some of the causal processes that were operating and how they were related to one another, about the extent to which (under a particular definition of equality of opportunity) there are inequalities between young people from different social backgrounds, or between young people and older generations, and

---

[26]See Chapter 3. Of course, in their role as citizens, social scientists do have a right to put forward diagnoses and recommendations.

[27]Of course, it is not that non-social scientists have no concern with the truth of accounts; this is sometimes a priority for them too. However, they will almost always have to take into account other considerations, and sometimes these will override epistemic concerns.

about what role these played in generating the riots. At the same time, the scope of this expertise is limited in significant ways. Any social scientific account must operate within an explicit value framework that picks out some features of the riots as important, and some causal factors as significant; and social scientists cannot claim any expertise in determining which value framework is most appropriate, and should not pretend to do so. And, given *this*, they must not present value conclusions – practical evaluations or recommendations – as if these could be validated by research, implicitly or explicitly. Moreover, they are obliged to present their arguments clearly, along with the evidence relevant to them, and to address potential and actual criticisms in the spirit of discovering the truth about the factual matters concerned, even if this threatens their own political, social, or economic commitments (Hammersley 2011a).

Most of the contributions made by social scientists in explaining the 2011 riots, and indeed much other social scientific work today, transgresses the limits I have outlined here. And most versions of public sociology or civic sociology *seem to demand this*, requiring social scientists to put forward evaluations and recommendations, and to do so in 'rapid response' mode. Appeal may be made, of course, to various sociological traditions which suggest that the sociologist's role is to diagnose the ills of society and propose remedies. The belief that social science has distinctive expertise in doing this is to be found both within the positivist tradition, notably in Comte and Durkheim, and in the 'critical' tradition, deriving from Marx. However, the grounds for this claim to expertise have been systematically demolished over the past 50 years. As post-Enlightenment thinkers of many hues have pointed out, from Nietzsche onwards, even the values that seem to be characteristic of Western societies today conflict sharply with one another – social order versus freedom, freedom versus equality, equality versus excellence, and so on – without there being any general mode of reconciliation available. One aspect of that diverse body of thought often given the label of postmodernism in Anglo-American academic circles precisely focuses on the dangers of totalizing attempts at reconciling values or presenting a single, comprehensive, theoretical viewpoint.

My conclusion, then, is that social scientific expertise in explaining events like riots is available, in principle, even if it is not actually displayed very clearly in social scientists' accounts of the UK riots of 2011. But it is more limited in character than often supposed. It is not hard to see that the neo-Weberian orientation I have adopted here is significantly different from that of most social scientific commentators on the riots, and the expertise it recognizes is much more limited than what is assumed by most concepts of public sociology. But if this position is not adopted, it is hard to see how social scientists contributing to public discussion about the riots, or about anything else, can legitimately claim any distinctive expertise.

My point here is not to suggest that the explanations offered by social scientists for the riots are false, or that they are not better than those offered by politicians. It is rather to insist that we need to be much clearer about the sort of expertise we are claiming, and the grounds for claiming it. And that some currently influential conceptions of what the role of the sociologist should be – associated with their being 'public intellectuals' – make it very difficult to understand what distinctive expertise could legitimately be claimed. This is an ironic conclusion since, of course, the potential for social scientists to engage in public debates, *as social scientists*, hinges precisely upon the assumption that they have intellectual authority, and can offer superior accounts to those of lay people.

Epilogue

In this book I have addressed some perennial but nevertheless pressing issues about the character and function of social science: how it should be pursued, what it can produce, and what its relationship is to many of the expectations and demands that are laid upon it. More specifically, I have examined whether its focus can and should be on causal analysis, and if so what this requires; whether its goal ought to be the production of theories that can be applied to many different situations, *or* whether the primary task is generating explanations for particular events, processes or trends in particular contexts (whether micro or macro, individual or aggregate). Finally, I considered what role values ought to play within the process of inquiry, whether research reports should contain practical evaluations and recommendations, and how social science necessarily relies upon value-relevance frameworks, and the consequences of this. My main message has been the need for sober reflection on what social science can, and cannot, produce: on its limits. In particular, I have argued that it cannot answer many of the questions that it is often expected to answer, and cannot offer what some social scientists today claim to supply, whether in the context of defending social science against cuts in funding, or in their work addressing particular topics, such as the study of social mobility and educational inequalities or of riots and social unrest.

I will briefly summarize the arguments supporting these conclusions, before going on to consider the implications.

Summary of the argument

Causation

Most of the findings presented by social science have the character of explanations rather than descriptions: they are concerned with *why* something happened, or with the *consequences* of actions or events. This is frequently true even when social scientists claim to be offering descriptions, for example 'thick descriptions' of social processes.[1] Furthermore, I argued that explanations, of the kind with which social science is typically concerned, involve claims about causal relationships.

---

[1]On the concept of thick description, see Hammersley 2008a: ch. 3.

Establishing the character and operation of a causal relationship is not a simple or easy matter (see, for instance, Mackie 1974; Mohr 1996); and certainly not when this is to be done at the superior level of reliability that people would normally expect from a *science*. Most of the sorts of causal relationship in which social scientists are interested are not open to observation. Rather, their character and likely validity must be inferred on the basis of theoretical resources and empirical data; with the latter consisting of patterns, both sequential and correlational, within and across cases. And what have to be employed here are not processes of strict logical inference, but rather ampliative inference that necessarily draws upon theoretical ideas, imaginative reconstruction, and metaphors.

Moreover, what is required is both abduction, generating productive hypotheses about causal processes, *and* the testing of these hypotheses as regards their likely validity. Both these aspects of inquiry need to be carried out systematically and explicitly. However, this is by no means always done in social science today, so that judgments of the cogency of causal conclusions, as against the plausibility of alternative interpretations, are often weak. It is easier to be misled in these matters than generally seems to be recognized. In my view, much social science, both quantitative and qualitative, significantly underestimates this risk, and does not use the full range of resources that are available for causal analysis, or does not deploy them in a systematic way. As a result, very often, the conclusions reached are premature, at best.[2]

Theorizing and explaining

A second theme, developed in Chapter 2, concerns whether theories are a viable product of social research. The term 'theory' is used in a variety of ways within social science, for example it may refer to normative principles, to explanatory frameworks, or even to explanations for singular events (Hammersley 2012c). I use the term here to refer to models of recurrent causal processes by which some *type* of event, action, etc. always produces, or generally tends to produce, some *type* of outcome. Theories have often been seen as the main, or the most important, product of social science, as well as a resource on which it draws. For example, the pursuit of theories has been held to distinguish it from historical work or from mere ethnographic description.

On occasion, the theories put forward have had the character of universal laws. One of the few explicit examples of this is Lindesmith's (1947) claim that opiate addiction is caused by a set of necessary and jointly sufficient conditions: taking opiates, experiencing the symptoms of withdrawal, recognizing the cause of

---

[2]Chapters 6 and 7 provide some evidence for this. Further evidence can be found in Foster et al. 1996 and Cooper et al. 2012: ch. 1–4. I am not suggesting, however, that the effective deployment of these resources is easy, far from it.

these symptoms, and then taking more opiates in order to eliminate the symptoms (for discussion see Cooper et al. 2012: ch. 5). However, more usually, the causal theories social scientists offer relate to historically specific types of social process or forms of society. For example, it may be claimed that capitalism tends to generate overproduction crises (Marx 1894/1991: ch. 15), that industrialization increases the level of social mobility in a society (see, for example, Torche and Ribeiro 2010), or, to take a more micro-level example, that academic and behavioural differentiation of students in schools generates a polarization in their attitudes between those at the top and those at the bottom of the hierarchy (Hargreaves 1967; Lacey 1970; see Hammersley 1985). It is intrinsic to all theories, however, whether universal or historically specific, that the causal relations identified apply, given certain conditions, to all instances of the specified types (all forms of capitalism or of some particular type of capitalism, all industrial societies, differentiation within any school, etc.). In this respect, theories are distinct from causal explanations for particular events, actions, or outcomes occurring in particular times and places, even though theories may be drawn upon as resources in producing such explanations.

In Chapter 2, I raised questions about how successful social science has been, and can be, in producing social theories, defined in this way. Doubts arise because these theories presuppose at least semi-closed systems of causes, in terms of which a small number of variables largely control some type of outcome. It is not clear that there are any naturally occurring systems of this kind in the social realm (Lindesmith's theory relies primarily on a biological rather than a social causal process). Indeed, it seems likely that the nature of social causation is more contingent than that which characterizes most physical or biological fields.[3] Furthermore, for the most part it is not possible to carry out experiments in which all relevant social variables are controlled, thereby enabling the detection of such systems operating beneath surface appearances, even if they exist.

Following on from this, if we look at the general principles on which social scientists typically rely in producing explanations for particular events, actions or outcomes, most of these are *not* systematically developed and tested theories. Instead, they are usually explanatory principles that are closer in character to rational models (what Weber referred to as 'ideal types'), for instance specifying plausible intentions and motives relating to what particular types of people are likely to do in particular types of circumstance.[4]

---

[3]See Mohr's (1996: 49) denial that causal laws are possible at the social level. Interestingly, Mill (1843–72) made much the same claim.

[4]Along these lines, an influential interpretation of 'economic laws' is that they assume a form of rational action based upon mundane and indisputable empirical facts about human beings: see, for instance, Robbins 1935.

Against this background, I drew on Weber's account of causal explanation in the social sciences, which focuses upon identifying causal relations in particular situations rather than on the production of theories. He provides a sophisticated account of what is involved, employing the concepts of objective possibility and adequate causation. It is important to recognize that such explanation does not apply solely to single cases at the micro level, but also to aggregates and to macro-level phenomena. Furthermore, while the ideas drawn on in producing explanations cannot be, and do not need to be, empirically tested, except as regards whether they apply in particular cases, they *do* require conceptual clarification and development in order to improve their effectiveness in generating sound explanations.

The role of values

The third main argument in the book concerns the role of values. I argued that, here too, Weber's position is broadly correct. He insisted that the sole task of research is to produce factual knowledge (descriptions and explanations): that seeking to answer value questions both increases the danger of bias in determining the facts, and exceeds the legitimate intellectual authority of scientific research. In both respects, I would add that this amounts to a breach of research ethics (Hammersley and Traianou 2012). From this perspective, a key epistemic virtue for researchers is objectivity, in the sense of only taking into account what is relevant to the task in hand; this task being to find cogent answers to factual questions, and to provide evidence allowing assessment of the likely validity of these answers (see Hammersley 2011b).

For Weber, the integrity of a researcher rests upon dedication to epistemic goals and virtues, and a partial suspension of other values in carrying out factual inquiry. However, whereas in the past at least lip-service was paid to this concern with objectivity, today it is widely assumed and stated that social science can and should produce value conclusions – indeed, that any commitment to value-neutrality is spurious.

Yet it should be obvious that expanding the goal of research to include producing value conclusions increases the danger of bias. As Stevenson (1944: 5) pointed out long ago, and it was hardly news then, our value-commitments can encourage us to indulge in wishful thinking as regards factual matters, and lead us to limit how far we check our interpretations, because we prefer to accept information that is friendly to our attitudes and to avoid unwelcome information. So, if factual inquiry is not motivationally and institutionally separated from the pursuit and promotion of value conclusions, there is a greater risk that our answers to factual questions will be distorted by our value commitments. This view is quite compatible with recognizing that value inquiry can be rational, and that it is important. The point is simply that, given the challenging nature of factual inquiry, there is much to be gained from restricting social science to this task, and much to be lost by not doing so.[5]

The second reason for a commitment to 'value-neutrality' in social research is that this is required in order to recognize and abide by the limits operating on what scientific research can legitimately claim distinctive authority to produce. As I argued in Chapter 3, while there are grounds for believing that it can generate more reliable answers to some sorts of factual question, there is little justification for any claim to intellectual authority in answering value questions. This is because value judgments frequently require us to deal with conflicting principles and always rely upon situational judgments.

Equally important, however, is Weber's recognition that social inquiry always operates within a value-relevance framework. Some such framework is necessarily built into research questions – this is what makes those questions worth addressing – but it also frames what would count as relevant answers to them. And Weber emphasizes the need for the particular value-framework employed in a study to be made explicit, and for it to be recognized as only one among several competing ones that could have been adopted. Yet this is rarely done in social science today.

In the final two chapters of the book I explored how these issues arise in two important areas of social scientific inquiry: investigation of educational inequalities and social mobility; and the study of riots, and of social unrest more generally. My point, here and elsewhere, is not to suggest that what social science has produced to date is of no value, but rather to insist on the need for a careful assessment by social scientists of their achievements, and for them to recognize what claims they can, and cannot, reasonably make about the sorts of knowledge they are able to produce.

It should be clear that my position here stands against notions of 'critical' and normative social science, as well as running counter to many proposals for public social science. These approaches encourage a very common tendency to underestimate the difficulties faced in producing causal knowledge, and to claim to supply scientifically well-established theories and value conclusions when this is not possible. In my view, a more realistic assessment of our achievements, and of what are the limits to what we can produce, is an essential precondition for building social science knowledge more effectively.

Conclusion

My conclusions have radical implications both for where social scientists should concentrate their energies, *and* for what they can legitimately claim to offer in

---

[5]Of course, the result may often be that the conclusions of social scientific research are less closely related to practical concerns than would be the case without this institutional separation (Hammersley 2002a). But this is a cost that has to be borne.

the public sphere. However, it may be necessary to reiterate that there is no implication that what I am excluding from social science is unimportant: political,
economic and social commentary; evaluation of systems, policies and practices;
policy recommendations; political advocacy; and the practical reasoning involved
in decision-making. To the contrary, I regard these as indispensable not just at
the level of government, but also in relation to everyday forms of action, and I
believe that they can be rational in form. Nor am I suggesting that researchers
cannot engage in these activities. My point is simply that they should not claim
to do this *as researchers* – in other words, claiming the authority of social science
for the views they put forward, or for the practices in which they engage, in these
other roles. Research can provide extremely valuable knowledge that can be used
in public discussions of policy and practice, and in decision-making, but it cannot provide the whole justification for decisions made within these activities, and
there should be no pretence that it can do so (Hammersley 2002a, 2013).

While my account of social science is clearly deflationary in the current context,
particularly as regards its public role, I believe that the knowledge research can
produce has considerable potential value for policymaking and practice of various kinds, and for public discussion more generally. Research can supply factual
knowledge relevant to practical projects, and this can be of great significance. It
may usefully raise questions about and/or correct the factual assumptions on the
basis of which people make decisions, and on some occasions it may also interrupt
their natural and understandable tendency to move rapidly from supposed facts to
conclusions about what is wrong and what should be done.

Here, the contribution of social science lies primarily in the sort of 'realism'
upon which Max Weber placed great emphasis (see Chapter 3). This entails insisting that practical proposals should take adequate account of the circumstances
and conditions in which action must take place, and of the likely consequences,
unintended as well as intended, that will result. Interestingly, this stands in stark
contrast to a common emphasis today on the value that social science has in
showing that what is widely taken to be normal, natural and fixed is, in fact, a
socio-historical product, is culturally variable, and is therefore (so the argument
goes) open to change. While this, too, can be a useful effect of social science, it is
no more its task to suggest that change is possible than to argue that it is not, or
that it is undesirable. Social science simply provides knowledge that is relevant to
making such judgments. Moreover, there is no guarantee that the 'impact' of the
knowledge social science produces will be desirable, from any particular value perspective. Not only will evaluations of its worth vary, but the effects of presenting
particular conclusions are always likely to be contingent on circumstances.

Providing knowledge and raising questions about common assumptions are peren-
nially important functions that social science can perform. Practical decision-making,
of whatever kind, will always be framed by a variety of assumptions that are not only
taken for granted, but also psychologically and socially 'defended' – in other words,

there will often be considerable resistance to revising them. Yet, there are occasions when these fixed assumptions will need to be reconsidered if practical action is to have desirable results, or if undesirable consequences are to be avoided. Moreover, I suggest that, currently, wise and careful deliberation about what is wrong, about what policies would be desirable, and about how best to implement them, is rarer than it should be among practical actors in many social and political realms; as, too, is recognition of the limits operating on what can be done effectively through policies and practices.

We might reasonably hope that social science would facilitate and assist such cautious deliberation. This function is perhaps particularly necessary in a climate in which ideologies of various kinds have great influence, and indeed function as coercive requirements, so that questioning them is (ironically) taken as a sign of being 'out of touch with reality' or, conversely, of being 'taken in' by false appearances or ideas. Whether the topic is economic austerity or child abuse, the problem of low social mobility or the causes of street riots, there is an important role for social science not just in providing relevant factual knowledge, but also in highlighting the assumptions involved in existing policies and practices, and in proposals for moderate or radical change, *in whatever direction*.

Of course, the deflationary account of social science presented here may not be well-received by external audiences, particularly at a time when it is demanded that social science demonstrate a substantial return on public investment. Nor will it be welcomed by many social scientists, many of whom see their main task as bringing about significant changes in policy, practice, or socio-political arrangements. Indeed, my arguments perhaps imply a level of public contribution that is below the threshold that would allow some social scientists to feel that research is worthwhile – for instance, those who hold 'great expectations' about the political and social impact of social science (Commission on the Social Sciences 2003; see also Gulbenkian Commission 1996). Even aside from this, my position certainly exacerbates the increasingly fraught problem of seeking and securing public funds for social science, given that governmental funding regimes have now generally shifted from a state patronage to an investment model, where the necessary 'returns' are conceived as 'impact' or practical payoff (Hammersley 2013: Introduction).

In Chapter 3, I noted that an instrumentalist cultural climate currently prevails which denies that knowledge can have value in itself, for example in allowing us to make sense of various aspects of our world more adequately – which even Comte regarded as science's highest calling (Thompson 1976: 51). Instead, what is demanded – externally and indeed by many social scientists themselves – is that the knowledge produced by social science be 'actionable': that it carries clear implications about what is wrong and what should be done in order to tackle some problem effectively or bring about 'change'. Indeed, it is sometimes argued that it is the responsibility of the researcher to try to ensure that the knowledge produced is acted on to guide the action that results (Gewirtz and Cribb 2006;

Hammersley 2008b). As I have tried to make clear, these are not reasonable expectations of social science in its current state – or, for the most part, in any conceivable future state. So I believe it is very important, as far as possible, to resist this instrumentalist pressure, even while recognizing that social scientific knowledge can have practical value.

Moreover, the dangers of continuing in the current manner must be recognized: of frequently failing to meet the minimal requirements for producing sound findings, in terms of systematic development and testing of explanations and the cumulation of knowledge; of over-claiming as regards what has been achieved; and of presenting conclusions that exceed the limits of what science, of any kind, can legitimately supply. In a very competitive market, there will always be others – think tanks, pressure groups of various sorts, commercial organizations, etc. – who will be even less restrained in making extravagant claims to knowledge. The only hope for social science is to preserve its epistemic integrity. My aim in this book has been to outline what this entails at the present time.

References

Abrams, P. (1982) *Historical Sociology*. Shepton Mallet: Open Books.

Academy of the Social Sciences (2011) Report on the riots of 2011 – social science perspectives conference. Available at: www.acss.org.uk/docs/Riots%20conference%20 Oct2011/webpages/Riotsevent.htm (accessed 2.10.12).

ACPO (2010) *Manual of Guidance on Keeping the Peace*. Specialist Operations Centre, Wyboston: On behalf of the Association of Chief Police Officers and ACPO in Scotland by the National Policing Improvement Agency.

Adorno, T., Albert, H., Dahrendorf, R., Habermas, J., Pilot, H. and Popper, K. (1976) *The Positivist Dispute in German Sociology*. London: Heinemann. (First published in German in 1969.)

Agevall, O. (1999) A science of unique events: Max Weber's methodology of the cultural sciences. Unpublished doctoral dissertation, Uppsala University, Sweden.

Aiello, G. and Pariante, C. (2013) 'Citizen, interrupted: the 2011 English riots from a psychosocial perspective', *Epidemiology and Psychiatric Sciences*, 22(1), pp. 75–9.

Alexander, J.M. (2008) *Capabilities and Social Justice: The Political Philosophy of Amartya Sen and Martha Nussbaum*. Aldershot: Ashgate.

Althusser, L. (1971) *Lenin and Philosophy*. London: New Left Books.

Anscombe, E. (1957) *Intention*. Oxford: Blackwell.

Archer, M., Bhaskar, R., Collier, A., Lawson, T. and Norrie, A. (eds) (1997) *Critical Realism: Essential Readings*. London: Routledge.

Atkinson, R. (1998) *The Life Story Interview*. Thousand Oaks, CA: Sage.

Baehr, P. and Wells, G. (2002) Introduction, in M. Weber, *The Protestant Ethic and the Spirit of Capitalism*. London: Penguin.

Baert, P. (1998) *Social Theory in the Twentieth Century*. Cambridge: Polity Press.

Ball, S. and Gewirtz, S. (1997) 'Is research possible? A rejoinder to Tooley's "On School Choice and Social Class"', *British Journal of Sociology of Education*, 18(4), pp. 575–86.

Baring, E. (2011) *The Young Derrida and French Philosophy: 1945–1968*. Oxford: Oxford University Press.

Barnes, B. (1974) *Scientific Knowledge and Sociological Theory*. London: Routledge and Kegan Paul.

Bauman, Z. (2011a) in 'The riots: not so "pure and simple" to explain', *Network* (the newsletter of the British Sociological Association), 109(Winter), p. 22.

Bauman, Z. (2011b) 'The London Riots – on consumerism coming home to roost', *Social Europe Journal*. Available at: www.social-europe.eu/2011/08/the-london-riots-on-consumerism-coming-home-to-roost/ (accessed 21.01.14).

Beauchamp, T. (1974) *Philosophical Problems of Causation*. Belmont CA: Dickenson.

Beauchamp, T. (2003) 'Methods and principles in biomedical ethics', *Journal of Medical Ethics*, 29(5), pp. 269–74.

Becker, H. (1967) 'Whose side are we on?', *Social Problems*, 14, pp. 239–47.

Becker, H.S. (1994) '"Foi por acaso": conceptualising coincidence', *Sociological Quarterly*, 35(2), pp. 183–94.

Becker, H.S. (1998) *Tricks of the Trade*. Chicago, IL: University of Chicago Press.

Beebee, H. (2006) *Hume on Causation*. London: Routledge.

Beebee, H., Hitchcock, C. and Menzies, P. (eds) (2009) *The Oxford Handbook of Causation*. Oxford: Oxford University Press.

Bellah, R. (1973) Introduction, in R. Bellah (ed.), *Emile Durkheim on Morality and Society*. Chicago, IL: University of Chicago Press.

Bellah, R., Madsen, R., Sullivan, W., Swidler, A. and Tipton, S. (1985) *Habits of the Heart: Individualism and Commitment in American Life*. Berkeley, CA: University of California Press.

Bendix, R. (1960) *Max Weber: An Intellectual Portrait*. London: Heinemann.

Bennett, A. and Elman, C. (2006) 'Qualitative research: recent developments in case study methods', *Annual Review of Political Science*, 9, pp. 455–76.

Berger, J., Zelditch, M. and Anderson, B. (eds) (1972) *Sociological Theories in Progress*. Boston, MA: Houghton Mifflin.

Berlin, I. (1969) *Four Essays on Liberty*. Oxford: Oxford University Press.

Berlin, I. (1981) *Against the Current*. Oxford: Oxford University Press.

Berlin, I. (1990) *The Crooked Timber of Humanity*. London: John Murray.

Bertaux, D. (ed.) (1981) *Biography and Society*. Beverly Hills, CA: Sage.

Besnard, P. (1993) 'Anomie and fatalism in Durkheim's theory of regulation', in S.P. Turner (ed.), *Emile Durkheim: Sociologist and Moralist*. London: Routledge.

Bevir, M. and Blakely, J. (2011) 'Analytic ethics in the central period', *History of European Ideas*, 37, pp. 249–56.

Bhaskar, R. (1978) *A Realist Theory of Science*. Brighton: Harvester.

Bhaskar, R. (1979) *The Possibility of Naturalism: A Philosophical Critique of the Contemporary Human Sciences*. Brighton: Harvester, pp. 56–103.

Bhaskar, R. (1986) *Scientific Realism and Human Emancipation*. London: Verso.

Bhaskar, R. (1991) *Philosophy and the Idea of Freedom*. Oxford: Blackwell.

Bhaskar, R. and Collier, A. (1997) 'Introduction (to Part III)', in M. Archer, R. Bhaskar, A. Collier, T. Lawson and A. Norrie (eds), *Critical Realism: Essential Readings*. London: Routledge.

Blackburn, S. (1993) *Essays in Quasi-Realism*. Oxford: Oxford University Press.

Blaikie, N. (2000) *Designing Social Research*. Cambridge: Polity.

Blau, P.M. and Duncan, O.D. (1967) *The American Occupational Structure*. New York: Wiley.

Blaug, M. (1992) *The Methodology of Economics, Or How Economists Explain* (Second edition). Cambridge: Cambridge University Press.

Bloor, D. (1976) *Knowledge and Social Imagery*. London: Routledge and Kegan Paul.

Blum, A. and McHugh, P. (1971) 'The social ascription of motives', *American Sociological Review*, 36, pp. 98–109.

Blumenberg, H. (1986) *The Legitimacy of the Modern Age*. Cambridge, MA: MIT Press. (First edition published in German in 1966.)

Blumer, H. (1969) *Symbolic Interactionism: Perspective and Method*. Englewood Cliffs, NJ: Prentice-Hall.

Bond, R. and Saunders, P. (1999) 'Routes to success: influences on the occupational attainment of young British males', *British Journal of Sociology*, 50(2), pp. 217–49.

Bornat, J. (2008) 'Biographical methods', in P. Alasuutari, L. Bickman and J. Brannen (eds), *The Sage Handbook of Social Research Methods*. London: Sage, pp. 344–56. Available at: http//:oro.open.ac.uk/12333/1/ (accessed 6.4.13).

Boudon, R. (2001) 'Sociology that really matters', *European Sociological Review*, 18(3), pp. 371–8.

Brand, M. (ed.) (1976) *The Nature of Causation*. Urbana, IL: University of Illinois Press.

Brecht, A. (1959) *Political Theory*. Princeton, NJ: Princeton University Press.

Breen, R. and Goldthorpe, J.H. (1999) 'Class inequality and meritocracy: a critique of Saunders and an alternative analysis', *British Journal of Sociology*, 50(2), pp. 217–50.

Breen, R. and Goldthorpe, J.H. (2001) 'Class, mobility and merit: the experience of two British birth cohorts', *European Sociological Review*, 17(2), pp. 81–101.

Breen, R. and Goldthorpe, J.H. (2002) 'Merit, mobility and method: another reply to Saunders', *British Journal of Sociology*, 53(4), pp. 575–82.

Brewer, J. (2012a) 'The new public university', BSA Sociology and the Cuts Blog, available at: http//:sociologyandthecuts.wordpress.com/2011/01/19/the-new-public-university-by-john-brewer/ (accessed 7.7.12).

Brewer, J. (2012b) 'Sociologists don't debate quibbles. We are tackling the financial crisis head-on', *The Guardian*, 5 June.

Brewer, J. (2013) *The Public Value of Social Science*. London: Bloomsbury.

Brewer, J. and Wollman, H. (2011) 'Sociologists' offer to unravel the riots', Letter to *The Guardian*, 11 August. Available at: www.guardian.co.uk/uk/2011/aug/11/social scientistsoffer-unravel-riots (accessed 9.9.11).

Briggs, D. (ed.) (2012) *The English Riots of 2011*. Hook: Waterside Press.

British Sociological Association (2011) 'Not so "pure and simple" to explain', *Network* (the newsletter of the British Sociological Association Network, 109(Winter), p. 22.

Bruce, S. and Wallis, R. (1983) 'Rescuing motives', *British Journal of Sociology*, 34(1), pp. 61–71.

Bruce, S. and Wallis, R. (1985) '"Rescuing Motives" rescued: a reply to Sharrock and Watson', *British Journal of Sociology*, 36(3), pp. 467–70.

Bruun, H.H. (2007) *Science, Values and Politics in Max Weber's Methodology* (Second edition). Aldershot: Ashgate.

Bruun, H.H. and Whimster, S. (eds) (2012) *Max Weber: Collected Methodological Writings*. London: Routledge.

Buchanan, A.E. (1982) *Marx and Justice*. London: Methuen.

Bulmer, M. (1982) *The Uses of Social Research*. London: Allen and Unwin.

Burawoy, M. (2005) 'For public sociology', *American Sociological Review*, 70, pp. 2–28.

Burch, R. (2010) Charles Sanders Peirce, *Stanford Encyclopedia of Philosophy*. Available at: http//:plato.stanford.edu/entries/peirce/#anti (accessed 8.8.13).

Burger, T. (1987) *Max Weber's Theory of Concept Formation: History, Laws and Ideal-types* (Second edition). Durham, NC: Duke University Press.

Burrow, J. (2000) *The Crisis of Reason: European Thought, 1848–1914*. New Haven, CT: Yale University Press.

Buss, A. (1999) 'The concept of adequate causation and Weber's comparative sociology of religion', *British Journal of Sociology*, 50(2), pp. 317–29.

Button, G. (ed.) (1991) *Ethnomethodology and the Human Sciences*. Cambridge: Cambridge University Press.

Bynner, J. and Joshi, H. (2002) 'Equality and opportunity in education: evidence from the 1958 and 1970 birth cohort studies', *Oxford Review of Education*, 28(4), pp. 405–25.

Byrne, D. (1998) *Complexity and the Social Sciences*. London: Routledge.

Byrne, D. (2009) 'Introduction', in D. Byrne and C. Ragin (eds), *The Sage Handbook of Case-based Methods*. London: Sage.

Byrne, D. and Ragin, C. (eds) (2009) *The Sage Handbook of Case-based Methods*. London: Sage.

Cameron, D. (2011) 'UK riots: David Cameron's statement in full', *The Daily Telegraph*, 10 August. Available at: www.telegraph.co.uk/news/uknews/crime/8693134/UK-riots-David-Camerons-statement-in-full.html (accessed 20.6.12).

Campaign for Social Science, see: www.campaignforsocialscience.org.uk/ (accessed 24.1.14).

Campbell, C. (1987) *The Romantic Ethic and the Spirit of Modern Consumerism*. Oxford: Blackwell.

Campbell, C. (1996) 'Half-belief and the paradox of ritual instrumental activism', *British Journal of Sociology*, 47(1), pp. 151–66.

Cannella, G. and Lincoln, Y. (2004) 'Epilogue: Claiming a critical public social science – reconceptualising and redeploying research', *Qualitative Inquiry*, 10(2), pp. 298–309.

Carey, J. (1975) *Sociology and Public Affairs: The Chicago School*. Beverly Hills, CA: Sage.

Carr, W. and Kemmis, S. (1986) *Becoming Critical: Education Knowledge and Action Research*. London: Routledge.

Cartwright, N. (2002) 'From causation to explanation and back'. Available at: http://www.lse.ac.uk/CPNSS/pdf/DP_withCover_Causality/CTR09–03-C.pdf (accessed 21.1.14).

Cartwright, N. (2007) *Hunting Causes and Using Them*. Cambridge: Cambridge University Press.

Cavanagh, M. (2002) *Against Equality of Opportunity*. Oxford: Oxford University Press.

Chakrabortty, A. (2012) 'The academics show their anger but they can't answer my criticism that there's too little analysis of our current crisis', *The Guardian*, 8 May.

Challenger, D. (1994) *Durkheim through the Lens of Aristotle: Durkheimian, Postmodernist, and Communitarian Responses to the Enlightenment*. Lanham, MD: Rowman and Littlefield.

Christensen, P. and James, A. (eds) (2008) *Research with Children: Perspectives and Practices* (Second edition). London: Routledge.

Ciaffa, J. (1998) *Max Weber and the Problems of Value-Free Social Science*. Lewisburg, PA: Bucknell University Press.

Clark, M. (1990) *Nietzsche on Truth and Philosophy*. Cambridge: Cambridge University Press.

Clawson, D., Zussman, R., Mistra, J., Gerstel, N., Stokes, R., Anderton, D. and Burawoy, M. (eds) (2007) *Public Sociology*. Berkeley, CA: University of California Press.

Clifford, J. and Marcus, G. (eds) (1986) *Writing Culture: The Poetics and Politics of Ethnography*. Berkeley, CA: University of California Press.

Code, L. (1987) *Epistemic Responsibility*. Hanover, NH: University of New England Press.

Coffey, A. and Atkinson, P. (1996) *Making Sense of Qualitative Data*. London: Sage.

Collier, A. (1994) *Critical Realism: An Introduction to Roy Bhaskar's Philosophy*. London: Verso.

Collingwood, R.G. (1940) *An Essay in Metaphysics*. Oxford: Oxford University Press.

Commission on the Social Sciences (2003) *Great Expectations: The Social Sciences in Britain*. London: Academy of Social Sciences.

Connolly, P. (1998) '"Dancing to the wrong tune": ethnography, generalization, and research on racism in schools', in P. Connolly and B. Troyna (eds), *Researching Racism in Education*. Buckingham: Open University Press.

Cooper, B. (2005) 'Applying Ragin's crisp and fuzzy set QCA to large datasets: social class and educational achievement in the National Child Development Study', *Sociological Research Online*, 10(2). Available at: www.socresonline.org.uk/10/2/cooper.html (accessed 2.12.08).

Cooper, B. and Glaesser, J. (2008) 'How has educational expansion changed the necessary and sufficient conditions for achieving professional, managerial and technical class positions in Britain? A configurational analysis', *Sociological Research Online*, 13(3), pp. 1–22. Available at: www.socresonline.org.uk/13/3/2. html (accessed 2.12.08).

Cooper, B., Glaesser, J., Gomm, R. and Hammersley, M. (eds) (2012) *Challenging the Qualitative–Quantitative Divide: Explorations in Case-focused Causal Analysis*. London: Continuum/Bloomsbury.

Coxon, A.P.M. (1999) *Sorting Data*. Thousand Oaks, CA: Sage.

Coxon, A.P.M., Davies, P.M. with Jones, C.L. (1986) *Images of Social Stratification: Occupational Structures and Class*. London: Sage.

Cressey, D. (1953) *Other People's Money*. Glencoe, IL: Free Press.

Crouch, C. (2012) *The Strange Non-death of Neo-liberalism*. Cambridge: Polity Press.

Dahrendorf, R. (1968) 'Values and social science', in *Essays in the Theory of Society*. London: Routledge and Kegan Paul.

Deflem, M. (2005) 'Public sociology, hot dogs, apple pie, and Chevrolet', *The Journal of Professional and Public Sociology*, 1(1), Article 4. Available at: http//:digitalcommons.kennesaw.edu/jpps/vol1/iss1/4/ (accessed 13.11.12).

Demeritt, D. (2000) 'The new social contract for science: accountability, relevance and value in US and UK science and research policy', *Antipode*, 32(3), pp. 308–29.

Dennett, D.C. (2003) *Freedom Evolves*. London: Allen Lane.

D'Entrèves, A.P. (1951) *Natural Law: An Introduction to Legal Philosophy*. London: Hutchinson.

Denzin, N. and Lincoln, Y. (eds) (2011) *Sage Handbook of Qualitative Research*. Thousand Oaks, CA: Sage.

Derman, J. (2012) *Max Weber in Politics and Social Thought*. Cambridge: Cambridge University Press.

Dibble, V. (1975) *The Legacy of Albion Small*. Chicago, IL: University of Chicago Press.

Diesing, P. (1972) *Patterns of Discovery in the Social Sciences*. London: Routledge and Kegan Paul.

Dreijmanis, J. (ed.) (2008) *Max Weber's Complete Writings on Academic and Political Vocations*. New York: Algora.

Durkheim, E. (1951) *Suicide*. London: Routledge.

Edwards, D. (1997) *Discourse and Cognition*. London: Paul Chapman/Sage.

Eisner, E. (1992) 'Objectivity in educational research', *Curriculum Inquiry*, 22(1), pp. 9–15.

Elder-Vass, D. (2008) 'Realist critique without ethical naturalism and moral realism', unpublished paper.

Eliaeson, S. (2000) 'Max Weber's methodology: an ideal type', *Journal of the History of the Behavioral Sciences*, 36(3), pp. 241–63.

Eliaeson, S. (2002) *Max Weber's Methodologies*. Cambridge: Polity Press.

Ellis, B. (2008) 'Essentialism and natural kinds', in S. Psillos and M. Curd (eds), *The Routledge Companion to Philosophy of Science*. London: Routledge.

Ellis, B. (2009) *The Metaphysics of Scientific Realism*. Durham: Acumen.

Engeström, Y., Miettinen, R. and Punamäki, R-L. (1999) *Perspectives on Activity Theory*. Cambridge: Cambridge University Press.

Erikson, K. (1966) *Wayward Puritans*. New York: Wiley.

Fann, K. (1970) *Peirce's Theory of Abduction*. The Hague: Martinus Nijhoff.

Fay, B. (1975) *Social Theory and Political Practice*. London: Allen and Unwin.

Fish, S. (1995) *Professional Correctness: Literary Studies and Political Change*. Oxford: Oxford University Press.

Fish, S. (2008) *Save the World on Your Own Time*. Oxford: Oxford University Press.

Fisher, A. and Kirchin, S. (eds) (2006) *Arguing about Metaethics*. London: Routledge.

Flyvbjerg, B. (2001) *Making Social Science Matter*. Cambridge: Cambridge University Press.

Foster, P., Gomm, R. and Hammersley, M. (1996) *Constructing Educational Inequality*. London: Falmer.

Foster, P., Gomm, R. and Hammersley, M. (2000) 'Case studies as spurious evaluations: the example of research on educational inequalities', *British Journal of Educational Studies*, 48(3), pp. 215–30.

Fox, C., Porter, R. and Wokler, R. (eds) (1995) *Inventing Human Science*. Berkeley, CA: University of California Press.

Fraser, I. (1998) *Hegel and Marx: The Concept of Need*. Edinburgh: Edinburgh University Press.

Freeden, M. (1986) *The New Liberalism*. Oxford: Oxford University Press.

Friedman, M. (2000) *A Parting of the Ways: Carnap, Cassirer, and Heidegger*. Chicago, IL: Open Court.

Gadamer, H-G. (1984) 'The hermeneutics of suspicion', *Man and World*, 17(3–4), pp. 313–23.

Gane, N. (2002) *Max Weber and Postmodern Theory*. Basingstoke: Palgrave.

Garfinkel, A. (1990 *Forms of Explanation*, 2nd edn. New Haven, CT: Yale University Press.

Garrett, D. (2009) 'Hume', in H. Beebee, C. Hitchcock and P. Menzies (eds), *The Oxford Handbook of Causation*. Oxford: Oxford University Press.

George, A. and Bennett, A. (2005) *Case Studies and Theory Development in the Social Sciences*. Cambridge, MA: MIT Press.

Gerring, J. (2006) *Case Study Research: Principles and Practices*. Cambridge: Cambridge University Press.

Gewirtz, S. and Cribb, A. (2006) 'What to do about values in social research: the case for ethical reflexivity in the sociology of education', *British Journal of Sociology of Education*, 27(2), pp. 141–55.

Gibbons, M. (1999) 'Science's new social contract with society', *Nature*, 402(C81), pp. 11–17.

Goertz, G. and Mahoney, J. (2012) *A Tale of Two Cultures: Qualitative and Quantitative Research in the Social Sciences.* Princeton, NJ: Princeton University Press.

Goldberg, A. and van den Berg, A. (2009) 'What do public sociologists do? A critique of Burawoy', *Canadian Journal of Sociology*, 34(3), pp. 765–802. Available at: http//:ejournals.library.ualberta.ca/index.php/CJS/article/view/6312/5577 (accessed 13.11.12).

Goldthorpe, J.H. (1980) *Social Mobility and Class Structure in Modern Britain* (First edition). Oxford: Oxford University Press.

Goldthorpe, J.H. (1988) *Social Mobility and Class Structure in Modern Britain* (Second edition). Oxford: Oxford University Press.

Goldthorpe, J.H. (1996a) 'Problems of "meritocracy"', in R. Erikson and J.O. Jonsson (eds), *Can Education be Equalized? The Swedish Case in Comparative Perspective.* Boulder, CO: Westview Press.

Goldthorpe, J.H. (1996b) 'Class analysis and the reorientation of class theory: the case of persisting differentials in educational attainment', *British Journal of Sociology*, 47(3), pp. 481–505.

Goldthorpe, J.H. (2003) 'The myth of education-based meritocracy: why the theory isn't working', *New Economy*, 10(4), pp. 234–9.

Goldthorpe, J.H. (2007) *On Sociology* (Vol. 1, Second edition). Stanford, CA: Stanford University Press.

Gomm, R. (2001) 'Unblaming victims and creating heroes: reputational management in sociological writing', *Discourse: Studies in the Cultural Politics of Education*, 22(2), pp. 227–47.

Gorard, S. (2008) 'A re-consideration of rates of "social mobility" in Britain: or why research impact is not always a good thing', *British Journal of Sociology of Education*, 29(3), pp. 317–24.

Gordon, P. (2010) *Continental Divide: Heidegger, Cassirer, Davos.* Cambridge, MA: Harvard University Press.

Gorringe, H. and Rosie, M. (2011) 'King Mob: perceptions, prescriptions and presumptions about the policing of England's riots', *Sociological Research Online*, 16(4), www.socresonline.org.uk/16/4/17.html (accessed 15.04.14).

Gouldner, A. (1962) 'Anti-minotaur: the myth of a value-free sociology', *Social Problems*, 9, pp. 199–213.

Gouldner, A. (1970) *The Coming Crisis of Western Sociology.* New York: Basic Books.

Gouldner, A. (1973) *For Sociology.* Harmondsworth: Penguin.

Gray, J. (1995) *Berlin.* London: Fontana.

Green, D. (2011) 'Predicting a riot', *The Jack of Kent Blog.* Available at: http//:jackofkent.blogspot.co.uk/2011/08/predicting-riot.html (accessed 29.3.13).

Gulbenkian Commission (1996) *Open the Social Sciences: Report of the Gulbenkian Commission on the Restructuring of the Social Sciences.* Stanford, CA: Stanford University Press.

Gurney, J. (2007) *Brave Community: The Digger Movement in the English Revolution.* Manchester: Manchester University Press.

Gutting, G. (2001) *French Philosophy in the Twentieth Century.* Cambridge: Cambridge University Press.

Gutting, G. (2012) 'How reliable are the social sciences?', *New York Times,* 17 May. Available at: http://opinionator.blogs.nytimes.com/2012/05/17/how-reliable-are-the-social-sciences/?_php=true&_type=blogs&_r=0 (accessed 24.1.14).

Haack, S. (2009) *Evidence and Inquiry: A Pragmatist Reconstruction* (Second edition). New York: Prometheus Books.

Haack, S. (2013) *Putting Philosophy to Work* (Second edition). New York: Prometheus Books.

Habermas, J. (1988) *Theory and Practice.* Cambridge: Polity Press. (First published in German, 1971.)

Habermas, J. (2001) *On the Pragmatics of Social Interaction.* Cambridge, MA: MIT Press.

Habermas, J. (2003) *Truth and Justification.* Cambridge, MA: MIT Press.

Hage, J. and Meeker, B. (1988) *Social Causality.* London: Unwin Hyman.

Hammersley, M. (1985) 'From ethnography to theory: a programme and paradigm for case study research in the sociology of education', *Sociology,* 19(2), pp. 244–59.

Hammersley, M. (1989) *The Dilemma of Qualitative Method: Herbert Blumer and Chicago Sociology.* London: Routledge.

Hammersley, M. (1992) *What's Wrong with Ethnography?* London: Routledge.

Hammersley, M. (1995) *The Politics of Social Research.* London: Sage.

Hammersley, M. (2000) *Taking Sides in Research: Essays on Bias and Partisanship.* London: Routledge.

Hammersley, M. (2002a) *Educational Research, Policymaking and Practice.* London: Paul Chapman/Sage.

Hammersley, M. (2002b) 'Research as emancipatory: the case of Bhaskar's critical realism', *Journal of Critical Realism,* 1(1), pp. 33–48.

Hammersley, M. (2004a) 'Reflexivity', in M. Lewis-Beck, A. Bryman and T. Liao (eds), *Encyclopedia of Social Science Research Methods.* Thousand Oaks, CA: Sage.

Hammersley, M. (2004b) 'Action research: a contradiction in terms?', *Oxford Review of Education,* 30(2), pp. 165–81.

Hammersley, M. (2006) *Media Bias in Reporting Social Research?* London: Routledge.

Hammersley, M. (2008a) *Questioning Qualitative Inquiry.* London: Sage.

Hammersley, M. (2008b) 'Reflexivity for what? A response to Gewirtz and Cribb on the role of values in the sociology of education', *British Journal of Sociology of Education,* 29(5), pp. 549–58.

Hammersley, M. (2008c) 'Causality as conundrum: the case of qualitative inquiry', *Methodological Innovations Online* [Online], 2(3). Available at: http://www.pbs.plym.ac.uk/mi/pdf/Volume%202%20Issue%203/1.%20Hammersley%20-%20 1–5.pdf (accessed 24.1.14).

Hammersley, M. (2011a) *Methodology, Who Needs It?* London: Sage.

Hammersley, M. (2011b) 'Objectivity: a reconceptualisation', in M. Williams and P. Vogt (eds), *The Sage Handbook of Methodological Innovation*. London: Sage.

Hammersley, M. (2012a) 'What's wrong with quantitative research?', in B. Cooper, J. Glaesser, R. Gomm and M. Hammersley (eds), *Challenging the Qualitative–Quantitative Divide: Explorations in Case-focused Causal Analysis*. London: Continuum/Bloomsbury.

Hammersley, M. (2012b) 'Qualitative causal analysis: grounded theorising and the qualitative survey', in B. Cooper, J. Glaesser, R. Gomm and M. Hammersley (eds), *Challenging the Qualitative–Quantitative Divide: Explorations in Case-focused Causal Analysis*. London: Continuum/Bloomsbury.

Hammersley, M. (2012c) 'Troubling theory in case study research', *Higher Education Research and Development*, 31(3), pp. 393–405.

Hammersley, M. (2012d) 'Quantitative research on meritocracy: the problem of inference from outcomes to opportunities', in B. Cooper, J. Glaesser, R. Gomm and M. Hammersley (eds), *Challenging the Qualitative–Quantitative Divide: Explorations in Case-focused Causal Analysis*. London: Continuum/Bloomsbury.

Hammersley, M. (2013) *The Myth of Research-based Policymaking and Practice*. London: Sage.

Hammersley, M. (2014) 'On ethical principles in research ethics', unpublished paper.

Hammersley, M. and Cooper, B. (2012) 'Analytic induction versus qualitative comparative analysis: similarities and differences', in B. Cooper, J. Glaesser, R. Gomm and M. Hammersley (eds), *Challenging the Qualitative–Quantitative Divide: Explorations in Case-focused Causal Analysis*. London: Continuum/Bloomsbury.

Hammersley, M., Gomm, R. and Foster, P. (2000) 'Case study and theory', in R. Gomm, M. Hammersley and P. Foster (eds), *Case Study Method: Key Texts, Key Issues*. London: Sage.

Hammersley, M. and Traianou, A. (2012) *Ethics in Qualitative Research: Controversies and Contexts*. London: Sage.

Hammersley, M. and Treseder, P. (2007) 'Identity as an analytic problem: who's who in "pro-ana" websites?', *Qualitative Research*, 7(3), pp. 283–300.

Hanson, S. (2009) *Moral Aquaintances and Moral Decisions: Resolving Moral Conflicts in Medical Ethics*. Dordrecht: Springer.

Hare, P. (ed.) (1976) *Handbook of Small Group Research* (Second edition). New York: Free Press.

Hargreaves, D. (1967) *Social Relations in a Secondary School*. London: Routledge, Kegan and Paul.

Hart, H. and Honoré, A. (1985) *Causation in the Law* (Second edition). Oxford: Oxford University Press.

Hartwig, M. (ed.) (2007) *Dictionary of Critical Realism*. London: Routledge.

Haskell, T. (2000) *The Emergence of Professional Social Science*. Second edition. Baltimore MD: Johns Hopkins University Press.

Hawthorn, G. (1976) *Enlightenment and Despair*. Cambridge: Cambridge University Press.

Heath, A. (1981) *Social Mobility*. London: Fontana.

Heath, A., Mills, C. and Roberts, J. (1992) 'Towards meritocracy? Recent evidence on an old problem', in C. Crouch and A. Heath (eds), *Social Research and Social Reform: Essays in Honour of A.H. Halsey*. Oxford: Oxford University Press.

Heath, A. and Ridge, J.M. (1983) 'Schools, examinations, and occupational attainment', in J. Purvis and M. Hales (eds), *Achievement and Inequality in Education*. London: Routledge and Kegan Paul.

Hedström, P. and Swedberg, R. (1998) *Social Mechanisms*. Cambridge: Cambridge University Press.

Heidelberger, M. (2010) 'From Mill via von Kries to Max Weber: causality, explanation and understanding', in U. Feest (ed.), *Historical Perspectives on Erklären and Verstehen*, Dordrecht: Springer, pp. 241–65.

Heilbron, J. (2003) 'Social thought and natural science', in T. Porter and D. Ross (eds), *The Cambridge History of Science*. Vol. 7: *The Modern Social Sciences*. Cambridge: Cambridge University Press.

Hellevik, O. (1997) 'Class inequality and egalitarian reform', *Acta Sociologica*, 40, pp. 377–97.

Hellevik, O. (1984) *Introduction to Causal Analysis*. London: Allen and Unwin.

Henderson, D. (1993) *Interpretation and Explanation in the Human Sciences*. Albany, NY: State University of New York Press.

Henderson, D. (2002) 'Norms, normative principles, and explanation: on not getting is from ought', *Philosophy of the Social Sciences*, 32(3), pp. 329–64.

Henig, R. (1989) *The Origins of the First World War* (Third edition). London: Routledge.

Hennis, W. (1988) *Max Weber: Essays in Reconstruction*. London: Allen and Unwin.

Hennis, W. (2000a) *Max Weber's Central Question* (Second edition). Newbury: Threshold Press.

Hennis, W. (2000b) *Max Weber's Science of Man*. Newbury: Threshold Press.

Herbst, J. (1965) *The German Historical School in American Scholarship: A Study in the Transfer of Culture*. Ithaca, NY: Cornell University Press.

Hewitt, J. and Hall, P. (1973) 'Social problems, problematic situations, and quasi-theories', *American Sociological Review*, 38, pp. 367–74.

Hewitt, J. and Stokes, R. (1975) 'Disclaimers', *American Sociological Review*, 40(1), pp. 1–11.

Hilbert, R. (1989) 'Durkheim and Merton on anomie: an unexplored contrast and its derivatives', *Social Problems*, 36(3), pp. 242–50.

Hill, C. (1992) *The World Turned Upside Down* (Revised edition). London: Penguin.

Hill, D. (2011a) 'Boris Johnson says London riots "are not a simple issue"', *The Guardian*, 12 August. Available at: www.guardian.co.uk/politics/davehillblog/2011/aug/12/boris-johnson-says-london-riots-not-a-simple-issue (accessed 19.8.12).

Hirsch, F. (1977) *Social Limits to Growth*. London: Routledge and Kegan Paul.

Hirschi, T. (2002) *Causes of Delinquency*. New Brunswick, NJ: Transaction.

Hollinger, D.A. (1997) 'James, Clifford and the scientific conscience', in R.A. Putnam (ed.), *The Cambridge Companion to William James*. Cambridge: Cambridge University Press.

Holmwood, J. (2007) 'Sociology as public discourse and professional practice: a critique of Michael Burawoy', *Sociological Theory*, 25(1), pp. 46–66.

Holmwood, J. (2011a) 'Viewpoint – the impact of "impact" on UK social science', *Methodological Innovations Online*, 6(1), pp. 13–17.

Holmwood, J. (ed.) (2011b) *A Manifesto for the Public University*. London: Bloomsbury Academic.

Homans, G.C. (1967) *The Nature of Social Science*. New York: Harcourt, Brace and World.

Hoover, K. (2004) 'Lost causes', *Journal of the History of Economic Thought*, 26(2), pp. 149–64.

Housley, W. and Fitzgerald, R. (2008) 'Motives and social organization: sociological amnesia, psychological description and the analysis of accounts', *Qualitative Research*, 8(2), pp. 237–56.

Hughes, E.C. (1958) *Men and Their Work*. New York: Free Press.

Hughes, H.S. (1958) *Consciousness and Society: The Reorientation of European Social Thought*. Cambridge, MA: Harvard University Press.

Hume, D. (1888) *A Treatise of Human Nature*. Oxford: Clarendon Press.

Hutchinson, P., Read, R. and Sharrock, W. (2008) *There is No Such Thing as a Social Science: In Defence of Peter Winch*. Aldershot: Ashgate.

Hutchison, T. (1964) *Positive Economics and Policy Objectives*. London: Allen and Unwin.

Hutchison, T. (1977) *Knowledge and Ignorance in Economics*. Oxford: Basil Blackwell.

James, L., Mulaik, S. and Brett, J. (1982) *Causal Analysis: Assumptions, Models, and Data*. Beverly Hills, CA: Sage.

James, W. (1909) *The Will to Believe and Other Essays in Popular Philosophy*. London: Longmans, Green.

Johnson, B. (2011b) 'London riots: this is no time to be squeamish', *The Sunday Telegraph*, 14 August. Available at: www.telegraph.co.uk/comment/columnists/borisjohnson/8701432/London-riots-this-is-no-time-to-be-squeamish.html (accessed 22.10.12).

Johnson, B. (2012) 'Boris Johnson says poor schools helped cause riots', *The Guardian*, 23 March. Available at: www.guardian.co.uk/politics/2012/mar/23/boris-johnson-bad-schools-london-riots (accessed 20.6.12).

Keat, R. (1981) *The Politics of Social Theory*. Oxford: Blackwell.

Khalifa, K. (2004) 'Erotetic contextualism, data-generating procedures, and sociological explanations of social mobility', *Philosophy of the Social Sciences*, 34(1), pp. 38–54.

Köhnke, K. (1991) *The Rise of Neo-Kantianism.* Cambridge: Cambridge University Press.

Kurki, M. (2008) *Causation in International Relations: Reclaiming Causal Analysis.* Cambridge: Cambridge University Press.

Lacey, C. (1970) *Hightown Grammar.* Manchester: Manchester University Press.

Lacey, H. (1997) 'Neutrality in the social sciences: on Bhaskar's argument for an essential emancipatory impulse in social science', *Journal for the Theory of Social Behaviour,* 27(2/3), pp. 213–41.

Lacey, H. (1999) *Is Science Value Free?* London: Routledge.

Lacey, H. (2007) 'Explanatory critique', in M. Hartwig (ed.), *Dictionary of Critical Realism.* London: Routledge.

Lachman, L. (1970) *The Legacy of Max Weber.* London: Heinemann.

Laffey, M. and Weldes, J. (1997) 'Beyond belief: ideas and symbolic technologies in the study of international relations', *European Journal of International Relations,* 3(2), pp. 193–237.

Lammy, D. (2011) *Out of the Ashes.* London: Guardian Books.

Lampard, R. (1996) 'Might Britain be a meritocracy? A comment on Saunders', *Sociology,* 30(2), pp. 387–93.

Larmore, C. (1987) *Patterns of Moral Complexity.* Cambridge: Cambridge University Press.

Laslett, P. (1971) *The World We Have Lost.* London: Methuen.

Lasswell, H. (1971) *A Pre-View of Policy Sciences.* New York: American Elsevier.

Law, J. and Hassard, J. (eds) (1999) *Actor–Network Theory and After.* Oxford: Blackwell.

Lawson, T. (1997) *Economics and Reality.* London: Routledge.

Le Bon, G. (1895/2002) *The Crowd: A Study of the Popular Mind.* Mineola, NY: Dover Publications.

Lerner, D. and Lasswell, H. (eds) (1951) *The Policy Sciences: Recent Developments in Scope and Method.* Stanford, CA: Stanford University Press.

Levine, J. and Moreland, R. (1990) 'Progress in small group research', *Annual Review of Psychology,* 41, pp. 585–634.

Levy, D. (1978) 'Adam Smith's "Natural Law" and Contractual Society', *Journal of the History of Ideas,* 39(4), pp. 665–74.

Lewis, P. and Newburn, T. (2011) *Reading the Riots: Investigating England's Summer of Disorder.* London: Guardian Books.

Lincoln, Y. and Guba, E. (1985) *Naturalistic Inquiry.* Beverly Hills, CA: Sage.

Lindesmith, A. (1947) *Opiate Addiction.* Evanston, IL: Principia Press.

Lindesmith, A. (1981) 'Symbolic interactionism and causality', *Symbolic Interaction,* 4(1), pp. 87–96.

Lipset, S. and Bendix, R. (1959) *Social Mobility in Industrial Society.* Berkeley, CA: University of California Press.

Lipton, P. (2004) *Inference to the Best Explanation* (Second edition). London: Routledge.

Little, I.M.D. (2002) *A Critique of Welfare Economics* (Third edition). Oxford: Oxford University Press.

Loader, C. and Kettler, D. (2002) *Karl Mannheim's Sociology as Political Education*. New Brunswick, NJ: Transaction.

Lobkowicz, N. (1972) 'Interest and objectivity', *Philosophy of the Social Sciences*, 2, pp. 193–210.

Louch, A. (1966) *Explanation and Human Action*. Oxford: Blackwell.

Löwith, K. (1949) *Meaning in History*. Chicago, IL: University of Chicago Press.

Löwith, K. (1965) *From Hegel to Nietzsche: The Revolution in Nineteenth-century Thought*. London: Constable.

Lukes, S. (1973) *Emile Durkheim*. Harmondsworth: Penguin.

Lukes, S. (1985) *Marxism and Morality*. Oxford: Oxford University Press.

Lundberg, G. (1929) *Social Research: A Study in Methods of Gathering Data*. New York: Longmans, Green.

Lundberg, G. (1947) *Can Science Save Us?* New York: Longmans, Green and Co.

Lyman, S.M. and Scott, M.B. (1970/1989) *A Sociology of the Absurd*. New York: Appleton-Century-Crofts. (Second edition, Dix Hills, NY: General Hall, 1989.)

Lyotard, J-F. (1988) *The Differend: Phrases in Dispute*. Manchester: Manchester University Press. (First published in French in 1981.)

Macfarlane, B. (2008) *Researching with Integrity: The Ethics of Academic Inquiry*. London: Routledge.

MacIntyre, A. (1971) *Against the Self-Images of the Age*. London: Duckworth.

MacIver, R. (1940) 'The imputation of motives', *American Journal of Sociology*, 46(1), pp. 1–12.

MacIver, R. (1942) *Social Causation*. New York: Ginn and Co. (Second edition, New York: Harper and Row, 1964.)

Mackie, J.L. (1974) *The Cement of the Universe: A Study of Causation*. Oxford: Oxford University Press.

Maclean, A. (1993) *The Elimination of Morality: Reflections on Utilitarianism and Bioethics*. London: Routledge.

Mahoney, J. and Goertz, G. (2006) 'A tale of two cultures: contrasting quantitative and qualitative research', *Political Analysis*, 14(3), pp. 227–49.

Marshall, G., Rose, D., Newby, H. and Vogler, C. (1988) *Social Class in Modern Britain*. London: Hutchinson.

Marshall, G. and Swift, A. (1993) 'Social class and social justice', *British Journal of Sociology*, 44(2), pp. 187–211.

Marshall, G. and Swift, A. (1996) 'Merit and mobility: a reply to Peter Saunders', *Sociology*, 30(2), pp. 375–86.

Marshall, G., Swift, A. and Roberts, S. (1997) *Against the Odds? Social Class and Social Justice in Industrial Societies*. Oxford: Oxford University Press.

Martin, M. (2000) *Verstehen: The Uses of Understanding in Social Science*. New Brunswick, NJ: Transaction.

Marx, G. and McAdam, D. (1993) *Collective Behavior and Social Movements: Process and Structure*. Englewood Cliffs, NJ: Prentice-Hall.

Marx, K. (1873/1970) 'Afterword to the second German edition', in *Capital* (Vol. I). London: Lawrence and Wishart.

Marx, K. (1894/1991) *Capital* (Vol. III). Harmondsworth: Penguin.

Matza, D. (1964) *Delinquency and Drift*. New York: Wiley.

Matza, D. (1969) *Becoming Deviant*. Englewood Cliffs, NJ: Prentice-Hall.

Maxwell, J. (2004a) 'Causal explanation, qualitative research, and scientific inquiry in education', *Educational Researcher*, 33(2), pp. 3–11.

Maxwell, J. (2004b) 'Using qualitative methods for causal explanation', *Field Methods*, 16(3), pp. 243–64.

Maxwell, J. (2012) *A Realist Approach for Qualitative Research*. Thousand Oaks, CA: Sage.

Mazlish, B. (1998) *The Uncertain Sciences*. New Haven, CT: Yale University Press.

McKim, V. and Turner, S. (eds) (1997) *Causality in Crisis? Statistical Methods and the Search for Causal Knowledge in the Social Sciences*. Notre Dame, IN: University of Notre Dame Press.

McLaughlin, N. and Turcotte, K. (2007) 'The trouble with Burawoy: an analytic, synthetic alternative', *Sociology*, 41(5), pp. 813–28.

Melden, A. (1961) *Free Action*. London: Routledge and Kegan Paul.

Menger, C. (1985) *Investigations in the Method of the Social Sciences (with special reference to economics)*. New York: New York University Press.

Merton, R. (1968) *Social Theory and Social Structure* (Second edition). New York: Free Press.

Mies, M. (1983) 'Toward a methodology for feminist research', in G. Bowles and R. Duelli-Klein (eds), *Theories of Women's Studies*. London: Routledge and Kegan Paul.

Mill, J.S. (1843–72) *A System of Logic Ratiocinative and Inductive* (Edition used: Vol. VIII, *Collected Works of John Stuart Mill*. Toronto: University of Toronto Press, 1974).

Mill, J.S. (1869) *On Liberty*. London: Longman, Roberts and Green.

Mill, J.S. (1874) *Essays on Some Unsettled Questions of Political Economy* (Second edition). London: Longmans, Green, Reader, and Dyer.

Miller, D. (1999) *The Principles of Social Justice*. Cambridge, MA: Harvard University Press.

Mills, C. Wright (1940) 'Situated actions and vocabularies of motive', *American Sociological Review*, 5(6), pp. 904–13.

Mills, C. Wright (1959) *The Sociological Imagination*. New York: Oxford University Press.

Mitchell, J.C. (1983) 'Case and situation analysis', *Sociological Review*, 31(2), pp. 187–211.

Mohr, L. (1996) *The Causes of Human Behavior*. Ann Arbor, MI: University of Michigan Press.

Mommsen, W. (1989) *The Political and Social Theory of Max Weber*. Cambridge: Polity Press.

Mommsen, W. and Osterhammel, J. (eds) (1989) *Max Weber and His Contemporaries*. London: Unwin Hyman.

Monroe, K. (2005) *Perestroika! The Raucous Rebellion in Political Science*. New Haven, CT: Yale University Press.

Montefiore, A. (ed.) (1975) *Neutrality and Impartiality: The University and Political Commitment*. Cambridge: Cambridge University Press.

Morgan, S.L., Grusky, D.B. and Fields, G.S. (eds) (2006) *Mobility and Inequality: Frontiers of Research in Sociology and Economics*. Stanford, CA: Stanford University Press.

Morrell, G., Scott, S., McNeish, D. and Webster, S. (2011) *The August Riots in England: Understanding the Involvement of Young People*. Prepared for the Cabinet Office, UK Government. London: NatCen.

Mounce, H.O. (1997) *The Two Pragmatisms: From Peirce to Rorty*. London: Routledge.

Moxon, D. (2011) 'Consumer culture and the 2011 "riots"', *Sociological Research Online*, 16(4), www.socresonline.org.uk/16/4/19.html (accessed 15.04.14).

Murji, K. and Neal, S. (2011) 'Riot: race and politics in the 2011 disorders', *Sociological Research Online*, 16(4), www.socresonline.org.uk/16/4/24.html (accessed 24.1.14).

Murphy, J. (1981) 'Class inequality in education: two justifications, one evaluation, but no hard evidence', *British Journal of Sociology*, 32, pp. 182–201.

Murphy, J. (1990) 'A most respectable prejudice: inequality in educational research and policy', *British Journal of Sociology*, 41(1), pp. 29–54.

Murphy, M. (2011) 'The natural law tradition in ethics', in Edward N. Zalta (ed.), *The Stanford Encyclopedia of Philosophy*. Stanford, CA: Stanford University Press. Available at: http://plato.stanford.edu/entries/natural-law-ethics/ (accessed 24.1.14).

Nagel, E. (1961) *The Structure of Science: Problems in the Logic of Scientific Explanation*. London: Routledge and Kegan Paul.

Nagel, T. (1986) *The View from Nowhere*. New York: Oxford University Press.

Nichols, L. (ed.) (2007) *Public Sociology: The Contemporary Debate*. New Brunswick, NJ: Transaction.

Nietzsche, F. (1886/1972) *Beyond Good and Evil*. Trans. R.J. Hollingdale. Harmondsworth: Penguin.

Nowotny, H., Gibbons, M. and Scott, P. (2001) *Re-thinking Science, Knowledge and the Public in an Age of Uncertainty*. Cambridge: Polity Press.

Nussbaum, M.C. (2001a) 'Symposium on Amartya Sen's philosophy: five adaptive preferences and women's options', *Economics and Philosophy*, 17, pp. 67–88.

Nussbaum, M.C. (2001b) *The Fragility of Goodness: Luck and Ethics in Greek Tragedy and Philosophy* (Second edition). Cambridge: Cambridge University Press.

Oakes, G. (1988) *Weber and Rickert: Concept Formation in the Cultural Sciences*. Cambridge, MA: MIT Press.

Oakley, A. (2000) *Experiments in Knowing: Gender and Method in the Social Sciences*. Cambridge: Polity Press.

Osler, A. (nd) '10 reasons why you need social science'. Available at: www.campaign forsocialscience.org.uk/sites/default/files/audrey_osler_10_reasons.pdf (accessed 18.2.13).

Ossowski, S. (1963) *Class Structure in the Social Consciousness*. London: Routledge and Kegan Paul.

Overington, M. (1977) 'Kenneth Burke and the Method of Dramatism', *Theory and Society*, 4, pp. 131–156. Available at: http//:uclinks.org/twiki/pub/SolanaBeach/PdfWeek5/Overington_BurkeArticle.pdf (accessed 19.4.13).

Owen, D. (1994) *Maturity and Modernity: Nietzsche, Weber, Foucault and the Ambivalence of Reason*. London: Routledge.

Owen, D. (1999) *Hume's Reason*. Oxford: Oxford University Press.

Owen, D. and Strong, T. (2004) 'Introduction', in Weber 2004.

Pakulski, J. and Waters, M. (1996) *The Death of Class*. London: Sage.

Pearl, J. (2000) *Causality: Models, Reasoning and Inference*. Cambridge: Cambridge University Press.

Pearson, K. (1900) *The Grammar of Science* (Second edition). London: Adam and Charles Black.

Pearson, K. (1911) *The Grammar of Science* (Third edition). London: Adam and Charles Black.

Peirce, C.S. (1877) 'The fixation of belief', *Popular Science Monthly*, 12, pp. 1–15.

Pels, D. (2003) *Unhastening Science: Autonomy and Reflexivity in the Social Theory of Knowledge*. Liverpool: Liverpool University Press.

Peters, R. (1958) *The Concept of Motivation*. London: Routledge and Kegan Paul.

Portis, E. (1986) *Max Weber and Political Commitment*. Philadelphia, PA: Temple University Press.

Potter, J. (1996) *Representing Reality: Discourse, Rhetoric and Social Construction*. London: Sage.

Potter, J. and Wetherell, M. (1987) *Discourse and Social Psychology*. London: Sage.

Principe, L. (2011) *The Scientific Revolution*. Oxford: Oxford University Press.

Purcell, E. (1973) *The Crisis of Democratic Theory: Scientific Naturalism and the Problem of Value*. Lexington, KY: University of Kentucky Press.

Putnam, H. (2002) *The Collapse of the Fact/Value Dichotomy*. Cambridge, MA: Harvard University Press.

Putnam, H. and Walsh, V. (eds) (2012) *The End of Value-Free Economics*. London: Routledge.

Quine, W. and Ullian, J. (1978) *The Web of Belief* (Second edition). New York: Random House.

Radkau, J. (2009) *Max Weber: A Biography*. Cambridge: Polity Press.

Ragin, C. (1987) *The Comparative Method: Moving Beyond Qualitative and Quantitative Strategies*. Berkeley, CA: University of California Press.

Ragin, C. (2008) *Redesigning Social Inquiry*. Chicago, IL: University of Chicago Press.

Ragin, C. and Sonnett, J. (2004) 'Between complexity and diversity: limited diversity, counterfactual cases, and comparative analysis', in S. Kropp and M. Minkenberg (eds), *Vergleichen in der Politikwissenschaft*. Wiesbaden: VS Verlag für Sozialwissenschaften. Available at: www.sscnet.ucla.edu/soc/soc237/papers/ragin.pdf (accessed 8.4.2013).

Ravetz, J. (1971) *Scientific Knowledge and its Social Problems*. Harmondsworth: Penguin.

Read, R. and Richman, K. (eds) (2007) *The New Hume Debate* (Second edition). London: Routledge.

Reason, P. and Bradbury, H. (eds) (2001) *Handbook of Action Research: Participative Inquiry and Practice*. London: Sage.

Reicher, S. and Stott, C. (2011) *Mad Mobs and Englishmen? Myths and Realities of the 2011 Riots*. London: Constable and Robinson.

Richardson, R. (1977) *The Debate on the English Revolution*. London: Methuen.

Rienstra, B. and Hook, D. (2006) 'Weakening Habermas: the undoing of communicative rationality', *Politikon: South African Journal of Political Studies*, 33(3), pp. 313–39.

Rihoux, B. and Ragin, C. (eds) (2009) *Configurational Comparative Methods*. Los Angeles, CA: Sage.

Ringen, S. (2005) 'The truth about class inequality'. Available at: http//:users.ox.ac.uk/~gree0074/en/en-publications.htm (accessed 5.2.09).

Ringer, F. (1997) *Max Weber's Methodology*. Cambridge, MA: Harvard University Press.

Risjord, M. (2000) *Woodcutters and Witchcraft: Rationality and Interpretive Change in the Social Sciences*. Albany, NY: State University of New York Press.

Robbins, L. (1935) *An Essay on the Nature and Significance of Economic Science* (Second edition). London: Macmillan.

Roberts, B. (2001) *Biographical Research*. Maidenhead: Open University Press.

Roberts, C. (1996) *The Logic of Historical Explanation*. Pennsylvania, PA: Pennyslvania State University Press.

Rogers, R. (1969) *Max Weber's Ideal Type Theory*. New York: Philosophical Library.

Root, M. (1993) *Philosophy of Social Science*. Oxford: Blackwell.

Ruben, D-H. (1979) *Marxism and Materialism* (Second edition). Brighton: Harvester Press.

Rule, J. (1997) *Theory and Progress in Social Science*. Cambridge: Cambridge University Press.

Runciman, W. (1972) *Critique of Max Weber's Philosophy of Social Science*. Cambridge: Cambridge University Press.

Russell, B. (1913) 'On the notion of cause', *Proceedings of the Aristotelian Society*, 13, pp. 1–26. Reprinted in *Mysticism and Logic* (George Allen and Unwin: London, 1917).

Russell, C. (1990) *The Causes of the English Civil War*. Oxford: Oxford University Press.

Saunders, P. (1990) *Social Class and Stratification*. London: Routledge.

Saunders, P. (1994) 'Is Britain a meritocracy?', in R.M. Blackburn (ed.), *Social Inequality in a Changing World*. Cambridge: Sociological Research Group, Faculty of Social and Political Sciences.

Saunders, P. (1995) 'Might Britain be a meritocracy?', *Sociology*, 29(1), pp. 23–41.

Saunders, P. (1996) *Unequal but Fair? A Study of Class Barriers in Britain*. London: Institute of Economic Affairs.

Saunders, P. (1997) 'Social mobility in Britain: an empirical evaluation of two competing theories', *Sociology*, 31(1), pp. 261–88.

Saunders, P. (2002) 'Reflections on the meritocracy debate in Britain: a response to Richard Breen and John Goldthorpe', *British Journal of Sociology*, 53(4), pp. 559–74.

Savage, M. and Egerton, M. (1997) 'Social mobility, individual ability and the inheritance of class inequality', *Sociology*, 31(4), pp. 645–72.

Sayer, A. (1997) 'Critical realism and the limits to critical social science', *Journal for the Theory of Social Behaviour*, 27(4), pp. 473–88.

Sayer, A. (2007) 'Understanding lay normativity', unpublished paper.

Sayer, A. (2011) *Why Things Matter to People: Social Science, Values and Ethical Life*. Cambridge: Cambridge University Press.

Schluchter, W. (1981) *The Rise of Western Rationalism: Max Weber's Developmental History*. Berkeley, CA: University of California Press.

Schofield, J. (1989) 'Increasing the generalizability of qualitative research', in E. Eisner and A. Peshkin (eds), *Qualitative Inquiry in Education*. New York: Teachers College Press.

Schram, S. and Caterino, B. (eds) (2006) *Making Political Science Matter*. New York: New York University Press.

Scott, M.B. and Lyman, S.M. (1968) 'Accounts', *American Sociological Review*, 30, pp. 46–62.

Shapin, S. (1996) *The Scientific Revolution*. Chicago, IL: University of Chicago Press.

Sharrock, W. and Watson, D. (1984) 'What's the point of "rescuing motives"?', *British Journal of Sociology*, 35(3), pp. 435–51.

Shildrick, T. (2011) 'The riots: poverty cannot be ignored', British Sociological Association blog, http://sociologyandthecuts.wordpress.com/2011/08/23/the-riots-poverty-cannot-be-ignored-by-tracy-shildrick/ (accessed 24.1.14). Partially reprinted in *Network* (the newsletter of the British Sociological Association), 109(Winter), 2011, p. 22.

Showalter, D. (2006) 'The Great War and its historiography', *Historian*, 68(4), pp. 713–21.

Sigmund, P. (1971) *Natural Law in Political Thought*. Cambridge, MA: Winthrop.

Solomos, J. (2011a) in *Network* (the newsletter of the British Sociological Association), 109(Winter), p. 22.

Solomos, J. (2011b) 'Race, rumours and riots: past, present and future', *Sociological Research Online*, 16(4), www.socresonline.org.uk/16/4/20.html (accessed 15.04.14).

Sorensen, R. (1992) *Thought Experiments*. Oxford: Oxford University Press.

Stevenson, C. (1944) *Ethics and Language*. New Haven, CT: Yale University Press.

Stewart, A., Prandy, K. and Blackburn, R.M. (1980) *Social Stratification and Occupations*. London: Macmillan.

Stokes, R. and Hewitt, J. (1976) 'Aligning actions', *American Sociological Review*, 41(5), pp. 838–49.

Storing, H. (ed.) (1962) *Essays on the Scientific Study of Politics*. New York: Holt, Rinehart and Winston.

Strawson, P. (1959) *Individuals: An Essay in Descriptive Metaphysics*. London: Methuen.

Strawson, P. (1985) 'Causation and explanation', in B. Vermazen and M. Hintikka (eds), *Essays on Davidson: Actions and Events*. Oxford: Oxford University Press.

Strong, P. (1979) 'Sociological imperialism and the profession of medicine: a critical examination of the thesis of medical imperialism', *Social Science and Medicine*, 13A, pp. 199–215.

Strong, T. (2002) 'Love, passion and maturity: Nietzsche and Weber on morality and politics', in J. McCormick (ed.), *Confronting Mass Democracy and Industrial Technology*. Durham, NC: University of Toronto Press (pp. 15–41).

Suarez, M. (ed.) (2009) *Fictions in Science: Philosophical Essays on Modelling and Idealization*. London: Routledge.

Swift, A. (2000) 'Class analysis from a normative perspective', *British Journal of Sociology*, 51(4), pp. 663–79.

Swift, A. (2003) 'Seizing the opportunity: the influences of preferences and aspirations on social immobility', *New Economy*, 10(4), pp. 208–13.

Swift, A. (2004) 'Would perfect mobility be perfect?', *European Sociological Review*, 20(1), pp. 1–11.

Sykes, G. and Matza, D. (1957) 'Techniques of neutralization: a theory of delinquency', *American Sociological Review*, 22(6), pp. 664–70.

Thaler, R. and Sunstein, C. (2009) *Nudge: Improving Decisions about Health, Wealth and Happiness*. London: Penguin.

Thompson, K. (1976) *Auguste Comte: The Foundation of Sociology*. London: Nelson.

Tooley, J. (1997) 'On school choice and social class: a response to Ball, Bowe and Gewirtz', *British Journal of Sociology of Education* 18(2), pp. 217–30.

Tooley, M. (1987) *Causation: A Realist Approach*. Oxford: Oxford University Press.

Torche, F. and Ribeiro, C. (2010) 'Pathways of change in social mobility: industrialization, education and growing fluidity in Brazil', *Research in Social Stratification and Mobility*, 28(3), pp. 291–307.

Treadwell, J., Briggs, D., Winlow, S. and Hall, S. (2013) 'Shopocalypse Now: consumer culture and the English riots of 2011', *British Journal of Criminology*, 53(1), pp. 1–17. (First published online, 8 October 2012.)

Truzzi, M. (1973) *Verstehen*. Reading, MA: Addison-Wesley.

Tuck, R. (1994) 'Rights and pluralism', in J. Tully (ed.), *Philosophy in an Age of Pluralism: The Philosophy of Charles Taylor in Question*. Cambridge: Cambridge University Press.

Turner, R. (1948) 'Statistical logic in sociology,' *Sociology and Social Research*, 32, pp. 697–704.

Turner, R. and Killian, L. (1987) *Collective Behavior*. Englewood Cliffs, NJ: Prentice-Hall.

Turner, S. (1995) 'Durkheim's "The Rules of Sociological Method": is it a classic?', *Sociological Perspectives*, 38(1), pp. 1–13.

Turner, S. (2003) 'Cause, teleology and method', in T. Porter and D. Ross (eds), *The Cambridge History of Science*. Vol. 7: *The Modern Social Sciences*. Cambridge: Cambridge University Press.

Turner, S. (2009) 'Many approaches, but few arrivals: Merton and the Columbia model of theory construction', *Philosophy of the Social Sciences*, 39(2), pp. 174–211.

Turner, S. and Factor, R. (1984) *Max Weber and the Dispute over Reason and Value*. London: Routledge and Kegan Paul.

Turner, S.P. and Factor, R.A. (1994) *Max Weber: The Lawyer as Social Thinker*. London: Routledge.

Vaihinger, H. (1923) *The Philosophy of 'As If'*. London: Kegan Paul.

van Fraassen, B. (1980) *The Scientific Image*. Oxford: Oxford University Press.

Velkley, R. (1989) *Freedom and the End of Reason: On the Moral Foundations of Kant's Critical Philosophy*. Chicago, IL: University of Chicago Press.

Vickers, D. (1997) *Economics and Ethics*. Westport, CT: Praeger.

Wacquant, L. (2009) *Prisons of Poverty*. Minneapolis, MN: University of Minnesota Press.

Waddington, C. (1977) *Tools for Thought*. London: Jonathan Cape.

Weber, M. (1919/2012) 'Science as a profession and a vocation', in H. Bruun and S. Whimster (eds), *Max Weber: Collected Methodological Writings*. London: Routledge.

Weber, M. (1948) 'The social psychology of world religions', in H. Gerth and C.W. Mills (eds), *From Max Weber: Essays in Sociology*. London: Routledge.

Weber, M. (1949) *The Methodology of the Social Sciences*. New York: Free Press.

Weber, M. (2004) *The Vocation Lectures*. Indianapolis IND: Hackett

Weiss, J. (2005) 'Werturteilsstreit [Value judgment dispute]', in G. Ritzer (ed.), *Encyclopedia of Social Theory*. Thousand Oaks, CA: Sage.

Wernick, A. (2001) *Auguste Comte and the Religion of Humanity*. Cambridge: Cambridge University Press.

Wetherell, M. (2008) 'Subjectivity or psycho-discursive practices? Investigating complex intersectional identities', *Subjectivity*, 22, pp. 73–81.

Whimster, S. (2007) *Understanding Weber*. London: Routledge.

Willey, T. (1978) *Back to Kant*. Detroit, MI: Wayne State University.

Williams, B. (1978) *Descartes*. Harmondsworth: Penguin.

Williams, B. (2002) *Truth and Truthfulness: An Essay in Genealogy*. Princeton, NJ: Princeton University Press.

Williams, M. (2001) *Problems of Knowledge*. Oxford: Oxford University Press.

Williams, R. (1976) 'Symbolic interactionism: fusion of theory and research', in D. Thorns (ed.), *New Directions in Sociology*. London: David and Charles.

Wittgenstein, L. (1953) *Philosophical Investigations*. Oxford: Blackwell.

Wittgenstein, L. (1969) *On Certainty*. Oxford: Blackwell.

Wood, A. (1981) *Karl Marx*. London: Routledge and Kegan Paul.

Wood, A. (1990) *Hegel's Ethical Thought*. Cambridge: Cambridge University Press.

Wood, A. (1993) 'Hegel's ethics', in F.C. Beiser (ed.), *The Cambridge Companion to Hegel*. Cambridge: Cambridge University Press.

Woodward, J. (1984) 'A theory of singular causal explanation', *Erkenntnis*, 21, pp. 231–62.

Wootton, B. (1950) *Testament for Social Science*. London: Allen and Unwin.

Worden, B. (2002) *Roundhead Reputations: The English Civil War and the Passions of Posterity*. London: Penguin.

Worden, B. (2009) *The English Civil Wars*. London: Phoenix.

Yin, R. (2002) *Case Study Research* (Third edition). Thousand Oaks, CA: Sage.

Young, J. (2008) 'Law and economics in the Protestant natural law tradition', *Journal of the History of Economic Thought*, 30(3), pp. 283–96.

Young, M. (1958) *The Rise of the Meritocracy*. London: Thames and Hudson.

Young, M. (2001) 'Down with meritocracy', *The Guardian*, Friday 29 June. Available at: www.guardian.co.uk/politics/2001/jun/29/comment (accessed 21.10.08).

Žižek, S. (2011) 'Shoplifters of the World Unite', *London Review of Books*, 19 August. Available at: www.lrb.co.uk/2011/08/19/slavoj-zizek/shoplifters-of-the-world-unite (accessed 23.5.13).

Znaniecki, F. (1928) 'Social research in criminology', *Sociology and Social Research*, 12, pp. 307–22.

Znaniecki, F. (1934) *The Method of Sociology*. New York: Farrer and Rinehart.

Name index

Subject index